# I LOVE YOUS
## ARE FOR
# WHITE PEOPLE

# I LOVE YOUS ARE FOR WHITE PEOPLE

a memoir

## LAC SU

HARPER PERENNIAL

NEW YORK • LONDON • TORONTO • SYDNEY • NEW DELHI • AUCKLAND

HARPER PERENNIAL

P.S.™ is a trademark of HarperCollins Publishers.

HarperCollins books may be purchased for educational, business, or sales promotional use. For information, please e-mail the Special Markets Department at SPsales@harpercollins.com.

FIRST EDITION

*Design by Laura Kaeppel*

Library of Congress Cataloging-in-Publication Data is available upon request.

ISBN 978-0-06-154366-1

17 18 19   OV/RRD   15 14 13 12 11

## To Pa,

I remember everything you've said to me, everything you've
never said to me, everything you've done to me,
and everything you've done for me.

# THE WRONG WAY HOME

My family shortly before we escaped Vietnam. That's me in the sailor suit.

My father's grip around my wrist is so tight that it burns me. I grit my teeth and continue running silently behind him. My fingers start to tingle before my whole hand goes mercifully numb. I've run faster and farther this afternoon with Pa than I ever have before.

It's amazing what you can do when you have no other choice. Pa pulls harder on my outstretched arm. We need to be moving faster. I can tell we're headed toward the bay. No one has told me where we're going, or why we need to move this fast, but I

don't really care. I have spent so little time with Pa these last few months that I welcome this frantic journey.

Monsoon season has started, and the air is moist and thick. The last sweet scents of summer emanate from the jungle behind us. The spots of morning sun have long since given up their fight against the swirling gray clouds, which now bide their time before unleashing the ritual afternoon downpour.

Pa is charging up the hill so fast that I stumble and fall on the clumpy grass as we near the crest. Pa releases my hand and spins around to survey the valley behind us. He sighs deeply. My mother and sister have just emerged from the tangled jungle below. I squint to make out the fear on Quy's face. Not yet three years old, she's terrified by our frantic pace. As Ma approaches the base of the hill, Quy stops running. Ma leans forward and continues up the slope, dragging Quy behind her like a rag doll. Pa stumbles and slides down the hillside to help them. A loud crack of thunder startles me.

Pa has helped Quy onto Ma's back, and I walk behind them as they struggle to reach the summit of the hill. Once we all reach the top, my parents seem to breathe a collective sigh of relief. I turn to Pa and Ma, who are staring at the ocean. I'm completely confused. Maybe we're going fishing.

Pa throws a silent look at Ma, and she nods. We start running down toward the water, but the violent thunder cracks nearby, sending us cowering to the ground. Ma, her face white and eyes wide with fear, crouches over Quy. I've never seen her look this way. Pa storms over and shouts at me.

"Get on my back!"

I don't want to, but I do as I am told. I've never had a problem keeping up with Pa until today.

Most evenings, when Pa came home from work, he'd clean up a bit and take me into town. We'd stroll the busy downtown strip of Da Nang.

Nothing was more satisfying for me than sucking on a frozen mango laced with chili powder and salt as I watched the rush-hour melee. I'd see adulterous men rendezvousing with mistresses at the local café, mothers catching their sons drinking and smoking, and corrupted officers blackmailing naïve citizens. The street was my cinema, and I had free admission.

I also had an embarrassingly proud father. I was his eldest child and only son, which virtually guaranteed that the street vendors would baby me—ruffle my hair, pinch my nose, feed me what they were selling—as they shouted the latest gossip to Pa over the bedlam of mopeds, rickshaws, and street officers blowing their whistles to direct traffic.

My father was well known and respected on the streets of Da Nang. The support of the community was the only thing that had kept him out of the hands of the Communists in the three years since they had taken over. During the war, Pa had dodged the Communists' draft and served as a commander fighting the North alongside U.S. troops. When the war ended, most of the Vietnamese who supported or fought for the South were tortured, killed, or sent to "reeducation" camps. The hard times were growing harder, so being well known also meant that a snitch looking for a quick buck might turn him in.

Not yet five years old, I hated it when Pa would bump into someone he hadn't seen for a while. This meant a halt to our walk so that he and his pal could catch up over a cup of coffee. I'd stand idly by while Pa and his friend chain-smoked and chatted about the latest activities of the country's new Communist government. I'd shuffle my feet, tap on his knees, but my signs of impatience always fell on deaf ears. I learned to wait quietly until he stood and grabbed my hand, signaling it was time to move along.

Today's journey had also started with a yank of my arm. Quy and I were playing in the garden when Pa came home unexpectedly

from work. I didn't pay him much attention. I thought he must have forgotten something. A moment later, Pa came running out of the house with Ma, and they grabbed Quy and me as we were playing beneath the mangosteen tree.

We haven't stopped running since.

Now we've made it all the way to the last hill overlooking the bay, and I realize that we need to get down it—fast. Pa, with me on his back, begins to scramble down the bumpy slope. We're bouncing so wildly that the landscape turns to a blurry mix of blues, greens, and grays. This reminds me of riding a horse.

I'm not accustomed to him acting so silly, and I can't help but giggle.

"Silence!" he spits.

I bite down hard on my lower lip to squelch my laughter and feel stupid for being so mindless. I spend the next several minutes bouncing in silence, save for the sounds of Pa's heavy breathing and the pounding of his footsteps.

And then I hear it again—thunder. It's much closer this time. Pa cuts to the right, like a soccer player after a loose ball. A split second later, I hear another boom, but this time the thunder is so close to us that the explosion knocks us to the ground. It's not thunder; it's the dull thud of something exploding against the ground. I pull my face out of the sand and can see that we're near the docks. Thick smoke hovers around me and chokes my throat shut. The ringing in my ears is so shrill that I at first can't hear Pa and Ma's speaking.

"Up!" Pa bellows. His command infuses some strength back into my shaking limbs, and I pull myself up by his shirt. Ma presses Quy tightly against her breast. My sister's screams are so piercing that I can hear them clearly over the ringing.

"Don't stop until you get to that boat!" Pa orders as he points to the middle of three dilapidated fishing boats moored to the docks on the edge of the harbor.

I'm too scared to run, so I squeeze my arms tightly around

Pa's leg. I can feel the sweat soaking through his shirt. "Run, son!" Pa pushes me away and darts toward the docks.

We run for our lives toward the boat. The sand is soft and clumsy, and I can hear the sound of bullets whizzing by from the soldiers' machine guns. I pass Ma, who is slowed by Quy's weight, and Quy's cries fade behind me in the distance.

When I reach the boat, Pa is at the railing, waiting to pull me aboard. I land hard on the splintered wood of the deck.

"Lie here and don't move. They're shooting!"

I watch as Pa runs into the cabin and emerges with a machete. He joins two other men who are hacking at the ropes that bind our boat to the dock. Bullets thud into the wooden railing above me. Light shines through the holes the bullets leave behind.

Strangers come hurdling over the railings onto the deck. I scurry up and down the boat on my hands and knees to search for Ma and Quy. When I don't see them, I stand up and peer over the railing to look. I see Ma running toward us as she drags Quy, who is now covered in sand and still screaming bloody murder.

The boat's engines begin to rumble, sending bubbles that reek of diesel through the muddy water. I can feel the tension on the last ropes remaining as the captain throttles the engines. Seconds before the last mooring is severed, Ma and Quy finally make it to the boat, and Pa pulls them over the railing. A grenade explodes on the dock as our boat pulls away, showering our deck with salty water and shards of wood.

As our boat chugs out into the deep water of the harbor, I sob with Quy in Ma's arms. It isn't long before the bullets stop whizzing overhead and we're allowed to stand. I can still see the Communist soldiers standing on the shoreline. As they shrink into the distance, they look less fearsome and more like the little green plastic army men I would play with in our garden. Our boat sputters along between two other boats, each packed with people who crowd at the railing for a glimpse of their homeland. Together we navigate the narrow mouth of the

harbor and make our way out into the open ocean. I don't know what lies ahead.

Ma looks relieved. She nuzzles the top of my head and then whispers in my ear, "Don't cry, Lac. It's nothing. Don't be scared. We're going away from all this now."

But I can't stop sobbing. "Where are we going, Ma?"

"There is no longer a place for us here. Vietnam belongs to the yellow star of the red Communist North." Ma sees the terror in my face. She kneels beside me and pushes her fingers through my hair in long, even strokes. "We'll make a new home somewhere else. You'll see . . . We'll be happy there, too."

"But can't we ever go back?"

"Never." Ma's voice grows stern. "We will never return to Vietnam."

Ma puts her face close to mine, sniffs my cheeks, and her voice softens. "I knew you were going to miss our garden, so I brought something for you to enjoy one last time. Give me your hands."

Ma reaches into her coat pocket and pulls out three bright red tomatoes from our garden. She places them in my outstretched hands. "Don't eat them all at once, Lac," she says with a cautious smile. "It will be a while before you have fresh fruit to eat again."

I sit motionless for a while, staring at the tomatoes cradled in my trembling hands. One of them is covered in juice and seeds— it's split at the seams, oozing pulp. The other two look perfect; they're ripe, shiny, and still joined at the vine. I wonder how they made it all this way in Ma's pocket without bursting.

I devour the wounded tomato, licking the juice and seeds from my fingers with great care. It's been so long since I've indulged in their sweet tang. They bring me back to thoughts of Vu.

That summer was particularly lonely for me. My sister and I had gotten along as well as siblings can, but playing with Quy just wasn't the same as it was with Vu, my neighbor and lifelong best

friend. He was a year older than I, and we spent every free moment together. Each morning I would slide out of bed, hop into my slippers, and run straight over to Vu's house—sneaking in the back door and up to his room to wake him up.

One breezy day on the brink of that summer, Vu and I picked tomatoes all morning in his mother's garden. She had more than fifty mature plants growing in neat rows, each dotted with the bulging red-ripe orbs. We filled our wide pockets so full of the fresh fruit that the weight nearly pulled our pants off our hips. When Vu and I couldn't stuff any more in our pockets, we cradled another bundle in our arms and waddled into his house.

We lined the tomatoes up on the kitchen counter for his mother, careful to leave our favorites in our pockets for later. We sprinted back out into the garden and hid between the swaying rows of plants to eat our bounty. Our bellies were soon full and our mouths dripping with seeds and juice. Swarms of dragonflies hovered over the garden. We ran about the yard, catching them in homemade nets we had fashioned the evening before by attaching sheet corners to bamboo sticks. Our game was to see who could capture the largest and most colorful of the bunch.

Vu's makeshift net was bursting with dragonflies. We peered into the opening to see them bumping spastically into each other inside the white sheet. My net was anemic in comparison. Only a couple of bugs knocked around, but when I looked inside, what I saw pleased me to no end. Among the dozen or so dragonflies in my sack, there was a rare one. It was smaller—maybe two inches in length—but its veiny wings were a strange hue of aqua-blue that cast a small colorful shadow on my shirt as I held the bug up toward the sun.

Vu dropped his sack and rushed over. "I'll give you three tomatoes for that dragonfly!" he said.

"No, it's mine." I stuttered slightly as I spoke. My mouth watered at the thought of the bright-red, juicy tomatoes we had left on his mother's counter. My family had a much smaller garden,

and a day when Ma had an extra ripe tomato for me was the exception.

I freed the other dragonflies and put my prized winged creature back in my sack for safekeeping.

"I'll give you five tomatoes for it," Vu persisted. "My ma will give me the tomatoes when she sees I want that bug. We can go inside now, and I'll give them to you." Vu's ma always did what he said. If he didn't get what he wanted on the first try, he would just cry until he got his way.

This was a difficult offer to turn down. A ripe tomato was better than candy, and five tomatoes were more than I would get from my ma in a week.

"Okay. Take it." I reached into my bag and handed him the prized dragonfly. Vu took the bug, stuffed it into his left pocket, and stood there with his head down. His shoulders began to shake, and he let out a quick series of small gasps for air. Was he crying already? Five is a lot of tomatoes, but his ma hadn't even said no yet.

Vu looked up at me and smiled broadly. Now I was really confused. My friend was laughing. "I'm not going to give you those tomatoes," he squealed. "And I'm keeping your dragonfly!"

Just like that, Vu bolted from the garden toward the house. It was a dirty hustle. Even at my young age, Pa had taught me to never let someone take me for a fool, so I ran after Vu with all my might. If I could catch him this time, he would know better than to trick me.

Vu circled the house, with me behind, and darted inside through the back door. We raced through the kitchen, past the foyer, toward the stairs. As Vu raced up them, I knew what was coming next: he'd lock himself in his room until I grew tired and went away. With my dragonfly to play with, he'd be entertained, and I'd be stuck. Game, set, match.

I leapt forward from the bottom stair, but my fingers only swiped his ankles. When Vu reached the top of the stairs, he

glanced over his shoulder to see if I was following and lost his bearings. He stumbled into the thin wooden railing bordering the second floor and crashed through it, falling headfirst onto the concrete floor below.

From where I lay at the bottom of the stairs, I didn't see much of his fall. I heard the sound of the railing snapping. I heard cries of agony from his mother, as well as her screaming at me. I don't remember much else.

Later, my parents tried to explain how Vu had fallen more than ten feet and died instantly. But I couldn't accept this as truth. I continued to wake up every morning, put on my slippers, and head next door to see if my best friend and make-believe older brother could come out and play. A few months of Vu's mother slamming the door in my face was enough for me to accept that he had gone away forever.

On some level I must have understood what happened all along, because I refused to eat tomatoes—my absolute favorite food—until the day my mother gave some to me on the boat. By then, more than six months after the accident, I understood that I no longer had an older brother.

I still see Vu today when I sleep, especially when I'm lonely and depressed. I see convoluted segments of the tragedy that broke my innocence: his face looking back at me before the fall and a woman in black clothing crying. Sometimes, he speaks to me; he is still young, and I have aged. When I wake up, I can't remember what he has told me, just as I have no recollection of the feelings of guilt and shame I must have felt when he died. These feelings are stored away in a forgotten capsule, never to surface again. I miss picking tomatoes, rolling abandoned car tires, and catching dragonflies with Vu, the older brother I barely had.

The boats are rickety and slow. They are filled beyond capacity and sag under the weight. I deduce what led to our quick

departure from snippets of conversation around me. In planning our escape, my father and his coconspirators had stocked each ship with enough food, gasoline, and water to last a month at sea. But someone had tipped off the Communists, and so the group was forced to leave Vietnam early. The men who had planned the journey didn't have time to find an adequate navigator. No one knows precisely where we're headed, but the goal is to make landfall in Hainan, an isle in southern China that is known to accept refugees.

Our boat is sixty feet long, and it's packed with well over three hundred people. Some have been wounded by the soldiers' fire, and they stay below deck with family members who care for them. Others are heartsick over being separated from family members who ended up on the other vessels—no time to be choosy when you're dodging grenades. They spend most of the time crying, praying, and mumbling as if they are actually talking to their separated family members. Most of us stay up on deck, where the air is clean and fresh. Our only form of communication with the other boats is a string of lightbulbs rigged to rusting flagpoles.

After we've been traveling aimlessly for three days at sea, the wind starts blowing. The gentle rocking that had soothed me to sleep each night gives way to a torturous series of ascents and elevator drops. Our boat is meant for fishing in the sheltered, iridescent waters of the South China Sea, and the open ocean shows the vessel no mercy.

By nightfall on the fourth day, the ocean has turned into a swirling, dark abyss. Large whitecaps surround the deck as my father makes his regular rounds. But he sees light from only one boat next to ours. He yells out for the boat that used to be on our right. Perhaps the rain and wind have blown out their lights. No response. He yells again, but there is no way they can hear him in this storm.

Pa returns below and gathers everyone's attention to explain

the situation. "It's getting dangerous up above. I think we are on the edge of a typhoon. The visibility is so poor that I can't see one of the boats."

As he points to the right, indicating the missing vessel, I hear people gasp and scream. Their family members are on that boat. Mothers beg the raging sea to show mercy for their children. A few of the men leap up and head for the stairs.

"What the hell are you going to go up there for!" Pa screams. "Do you know how windy it is? You're going to get swallowed up by the storm and spit into the ocean like a watermelon seed. Nobody goes up top until the storm passes."

The group follows Pa's orders, and we spend the night huddled in the darkness of the hull, packed into the belly of the ship like a can of sardines. People lie head to toe. It's impossible to move. Every other moment is punctuated by the sound of someone vomiting from seasickness. There's no bathroom, so there's no place for being bashful; people respond to nature's call where they sit. It isn't long before the stale mix of urine, feces, and vomit creates a suffocating stench.

The open ocean grows more violent as the night drags on. Like an oncoming army, the swollen waves line up for miles and slam our boat in turn. Butterflies swarm my stomach with each ascent up the face of a passing wave, only to leap back in my throat as we freefall down the back of another forty-foot monster. Everyone shrieks as we drop. Our boat smacks the water with a dull, painful thud, each descent bringing it one step closer to coming apart. The wooden hull groans deeply, and people cry to one another that we're going to sink like the other ships. The swells are so large now that they crest over the railings. Each thundering wave sends a rush of white water across the deck that spills through the gaps in the boards above—dousing us in a frigid bath of salty water.

I see Pa and the other men running about with buckets to keep the water out of the hull. When he comes near, I cry out to him.

"Are the waves going to break our boat in two?"

"Quit crying and take care of your sister . . . Live up to your responsibility as big brother. You will see worse than this."

The storm continues through the night, and the next morning, a few men poke their heads above deck and report—as we had feared—the boat to our right is gone. The boat to our left is still with us, though it looks low, as if it might be taking on water. It's too stormy to tell for sure. The men on our ship are busy all day bailing water from the hull. The next night is no better than the first, but we somehow make it through. Pa is the first on deck the following morning, and he reports that the ship on our left is gone.

By mid-afternoon, the swells begin their retreat, and visibility improves. It's obvious where the other ships have gone; they've taken our brethren to the bottom of the sea. Our crowded vessel feels lonely; its cadenced rocking offers no solace beneath the setting sun that has assuaged an angry sea.

Nightfall comes, and everyone finally sleeps. Pa lies down next to us for the first time since we left Vietnam. He hasn't eaten for three days. Anxiety suppresses his hunger, and he smokes the last of the dry cigarettes in an attempt to keep his mind sane. Eventually, we all doze off together.

I feel like my eyes have been closed for five minutes when I hear Pa yelling. "Everybody, wake up! Our boat is sinking, our boat is sinking! Wake up! Wake up . . ." Pa is on his feet, stepping across people like stones to rouse the other healthy men. The whole boat is tilted to one side. Half the lower level is blanketed by a foot of swirling salt water.

"Quickly, all of you. Throw everything overboard," Pa shouts.

"But what are we going to eat?" a gaunt old man cries.

"Would you rather drown today or starve tomorrow?"

Silence.

"Form a line, then. Now!" A vein pulsates wildly in his neck.

The men pass along huge bags of rice and five-gallon con-

tainers of water. Once our rations reach the men on deck, they toss the bags and containers overboard into the ocean. The supplies hit the ocean with loud splashes and quickly sink from view. Despite their weight, some of the rice bags float around us.

The water rises rapidly as the men work, and they are waist-deep before their task is done. A teenager with long, dirty hair finds a leak, and they load the remaining bags of rice on top of the hole. It slows the surge of water but fails to stop it. The men find other leaks and realize it's no use; our hull is fractured.

The hull continues to fill. Everyone heads for the deck. People crowd every dry space that has not succumbed to the rising water. They pray and cry and yell at the terror of impending death. Like most everyone else on board, no one in my family knows how to swim.

My father doesn't quit. He takes the men below to find the buckets, and they form another line to bail water. It's a losing battle. The water continues to rise, forcing the line up the stairs and out of the hull. I can see the water now from the deck, lapping up against the entry to the hull. Our boat will soon join the others.

Pa is the last man to emerge from the hull, soaking wet from head to toe. He pauses for a moment, looking out into the sea that has sealed his fate. Pa comes over to join Ma, Quy, and me, squats down, and wraps us tightly in a soaked blanket. It feels good to have Pa's arms around us. It calms and quiets us amid the chaos. As the night marches on, everyone watches in passive terror as our boat begins an awkward tilt toward the crack in the stern. People scratch farther and farther up the bow as it inches skyward. It's cold and dark, and the huddled masses stare with dread at the black ocean waiting silently beneath us.

A white light shines directly upon us. People stare into it, blinking and confused—as if it's their imagination or maybe Lord Buddha here to take them into the great beyond.

A garbled, loud voice speaks to us . . . in Cantonese: "What are you doing out here? Who are you?"

The wake from the long steel hull of the Hong Kong naval cruiser rocks and rolls what's left of our boat. People start to scream and cry. Those who aren't holding fast to something wave their arms.

Pa knows some Cantonese. "We're right here! Help us, our boat is sinking!" he screams at the top of his hoarse lungs.

The ship pulls close and shines more floodlights upon us. Their silence is isolating.

"Hold up your children! Show them the women and children," Pa shouts to the others. Babies rise like flags from the huddled masses, and a few fall into the water with their parents in the process. Their parents hold them and cling to the sides of our boat. Others struggle to pull the pairs to safety.

The voice crackles again on the megaphone, and I can see officers arguing on the platform. "Women and children only."

The sailors throw rope ladders down to us, and women begin climbing up the ropes with their babies strapped to their backs.

"Go, Big Head, go." Pa pushes me to the ladder behind Ma and Quy, urging me to leave with an insult about my duty as the "Big Head," or older brother. I cry and climb.

When I get to the top, I look down and see the men following us. They're climbing over each other on the ropes like ants trapped in a bathtub.

"Women and children only!" The captain's voice echoes on the loudspeaker.

The sailors rush to the side of the boat and help the women aboard, struggling to keep the men at arm's length. When the women get to the top, the sailors drop one of the ropes into the water—with six men dangling from it. Between my tears, I see Pa staring up at us.

My father leaps for one of the ladders and climbs up with the other men. He's quick to the top and begs one of the sailors to let him speak to the captain. When the sailors refuse, he reaches down with one hand and pulls off his belt. He holds it toward

the sailors who reel back as if he's trying to pass them a dirty diaper.

"There are twelve pieces of gold in there, sewn into the belt," Pa explains in broken Cantonese. "You can keep it if you let me speak to him. Even if he sends us back to drown, it's yours. Otherwise, it goes with me to the bottom of the ocean."

The sailors pull my father aboard. He asks to speak to the captain. It's against the law for the Hong Kong navy to rescue Vietnamese refugees, and my father knows this. The sailors concede to his request.

Pa runs across the deck of the navy ship, yelling in Vietnamese to our group, "Give me your gold, your jade! Any valuables you have stashed . . . pass them to me. This is our only chance."

People reach into their mouths, pull jewelry from their necks, and unwrap their babies to reveal stones hidden in the bundles. Pa scurries around with his palms outstretched, and people fill them with small treasures: gold, jade, silver, and diamonds. Pa walks the bounty over to the captain and pulls his hands apart above the desk, spreading the jewels across the map.

"This is all we can give you, other than our lives," Pa says.

The captain stares Pa in the eye; the other officers stand idly behind him. He won't accept our bribe. He waves his hand toward Pa. "Keep your belongings to yourselves."

The captain looks back at his officers and barks a final order as he marches back to his cabin. "The men can come with us."

"Thank you, sir," Pa speaks with his head bowed.

Then he turns and shouts to our group. "We're saved!" He even smiles.

The men race onto the deck to join their wives and children. Mothers cry, fathers sniff the cheeks of their firstborn, and we all turn to watch the last of our ship pass silently beneath the surface.

## chapter two

# TRUE HOLLYWOOD STORIES

Looking to the future from the top of our apartment building in Hollywood, California.

The moment our feet touch soil in Hong Kong, Pa pulls us aside from the rest of the confused boat people. He huddles Ma, Quy, and me together, squats on his haunches in the center of our circle, and speaks in a stern, albeit hushed, tone, "We are not the only ones here." Pa glances nervously between us to see if there is anyone within earshot. "A flash flood of Vietnamese have forced their way into this country, and we are the last to the

table." He throws a penetrating stare in my direction, "Our life here will not be like our garden in Da Nang."

We spend the next few weeks in a dizzying transfer between tent cities—each as filthy and overcrowded as the last. Though Vietnamese, the people in the tent cities aren't like the folks back home. They're needy and ravenous, always fighting for the last grain of rice or the next bucket of frigid, silted bathing water. Quy and I spend our days clung tightly to Ma like monkeys, while Pa roams each new tent city to "figure things out."

Our final resting place is a glimmering, marble-encrusted palace that Pa calls an "upscale hotel." We share living quarters with the hotel staff, have a small room to sleep in, and are given two boxed meals a day. I don't understand why yesterday I was eating rice soaked in squalid water from a rusted can, and now I'm treated to generous portions of Szechuan beef, seasoned rice, and steamed broccoli, plus a glistening green can of 7Up to wash it all down. I'm transfixed by the hot water that gurgles from the hotel showerhead, and Ma lets me play in the throbbing stream each night until I turn into a prune. By day Pa tells us we're lucky; with refugee camps bulging at the seams, the Hong Kong government has begun lodging the overflow anywhere it can find space. By night Pa grows suspicious of the sudden privilege that's been handed to us. As I lay down to sleep, and he and Ma are consumed by the whispers of adult conversation, he compares our treatment to a final meal before execution.

My father had ample reason to be suspicious. This wasn't the first time he had fled the Communists. When he was just five years old, living with his father on the island of Hainan in the South China Sea, Chairman Mao's Communist Party took hold of the country with an iron grip. Crops and livestock were plundered to feed the Communist soldiers, and Hainan fell into the throes of famine. Pa and his father, a medicine man, resorted to eating

insects and tree bark to stay alive. In happier times, Hainan's inhabitants had visited Grandpa to have their ailments cured, but none of his special remedies could alleviate hunger. Scores of people died from starvation and disease, including Pa's mother. To save him from a similar fate, Grandpa sent his son on the ferry to Vietnam with the address of family members scrawled on a folded sheet of paper.

Pa begged people on the streets of Vietnam to guide him to the address listed on the paper. He made it to his uncle, but his uncle had a family of his own to care for. He considered Pa an unwarranted burden, worthy of his abuse. He fed Pa the scraps from his family's table, which Pa considered an improvement on the tree bark and insects he had eaten back in Hainan. As Pa grew older and stronger, his uncle's physical abuse got the better of him. At the age of twelve, figuring he could do better on his own, Pa hit the streets of Vietnam and left the house for good.

The streets became Pa's home. He slept in alleys, abandoned houses, and temples and on park benches. At first, he ate from the trash and scraps left on the tables of outdoor restaurants, but Pa began to thrive once he learned how to hustle. He befriended an old street vendor in Da Nang who was known for his piping hot banh bao, a steamed bun stuffed with meat. Pa couldn't resist the aroma of the banh bao, which crept into the alley where he slept each morning, so he tried to strike a deal. The old man had trouble walking, and he couldn't sell the banh bao beyond the confines of his front porch. Pa offered to sell thirty banh bao a day for the old man in the city, as long as he would promise a full stomach and some pocket change in return. So, each morning, Pa followed the aroma to the old man's door and found a loaded tray of freshly steamed banh bao waiting for him. Pa took the banh bao into Da Nang and used his circumstances as a selling tool. "Please help this orphan earn money for school by buying these buns," Pa would say to the people who passed, or, "I'm an orphan without a father or mother. I'm doing this to survive. Please buy one."

Before long, Pa was selling banh bao faster than his patron could make them. When the old man was dying several years later, he scorned his wife and family and passed his secret recipe on to Pa. With the old man's recipe in his possession, Pa never went hungry again. But he also never stopped hustling. He financed the expansion of his banh bao business by working other odd jobs. He was a busboy, a waiter, a watch mechanic, and even a pimp. By the time he was twenty-three, Pa was fairly wealthy and very well known in Da Nang, owning a collection of bars, hardware stores, and nightclubs. He had overcome the confines of his circumstances to rise from rags to riches. But now that we'd left everything behind in Vietnam to flee the Communists once more, life had quickly returned to rags again.

With Ma, Quy, and me nestled safely in the hotel, Pa hit the streets of Kowloon to get the scoop. He found distant relatives who had fled Vietnam a year prior and now called Hong Kong their home. They told him that life in Kowloon was hard but safe. Since they didn't speak Cantonese they were forced to resort to manual labor to make a living. Pa learned where he could find a job and how he could get his family on the waiting lists for Heaven. American religious organizations had set up shop in Hong Kong to find converts in exchange for sponsoring their emigration to America. Pa didn't believe in Heaven, but he longed to provide his family the same opportunities described by the American soldiers during the war. Being an atheist didn't stop him from joining all four religions to better our chances of getting sponsored. Each week he shuffled us among Buddhist, Catholic, Protestant, and Baptist services, and he and Ma constantly took visits from evangelists who would stop by our hotel to preach to us.

We celebrate my fifth birthday in the palace with boxed meals, kisses from Ma, and a birthday gift of bubble gum in cartoon

wrappers. The next day, Pa and Ma come home from work early to tell us that, of the four Gods, Buddha has answered our prayers. We'll be leaving soon for America. Pa spends a good chunk of our savings to buy dress-up clothes for our trip to the Promised Land.

In the early morning darkness, on the day of our exit from Hong Kong, Ma stuffs me into an undersized corduroy suit, clip-on tie, and a pair of floppy, shiny dress shoes that are so big my feet try to slip out of them with every step. I don't complain. If Heaven is where we're going, Pa wants to make sure I have a chance to get in. To get to Heaven, we have to fly, and I'm awestruck by the sight of the shiny Boeing 747 airplanes parked neatly in a row. We stop at our gate, and the sun reflects so brightly off the airplane's nose that it hurts my eyes. It can't stop me from looking. They'd have to tear my eyes out to keep me from soaking in the magnificence of this winged machine.

"Airplane, Ma! Airplane! Are we going into that?" I ask, jumping up and down with excitement.

Ma scarcely hears me. She looks dead tired, with Quy asleep on her lap. We board the plane, and I run my hands along the stiff undulating fabric covering my seat. It smells new and fuels my excitement. I know for sure now that we're going to Heaven. We've clearly been chosen for this special journey. Pa doesn't seem so certain. I can see him chain-smoking nervously near the bathroom while he speaks to another refugee man.

"Are you hungry, son?" Ma asks as she balls up some sticky rice with beef jerky bits in her palm.

"No. I want to see the rest of the airplane."

"Your chance will come. Eat this; if you don't, they won't let you out of your seat." She tricks me into eating.

We sit on the runway for close to an hour in the sweltering summer heat.

"I'm hot, Ma." I yank off the clip-on tie and begin tugging at my sweat-soaked shirt collar.

"Don't take off that tie. Your father wants you wearing it when we get to America. Here, drink some soy milk to cool off."

With my belly full and my body exhausted from the heat, my eyes begin to feel heavy. As much as I force my eyes to stay open on the flight, the monotonous hum of the jet engines lulls me to sleep shortly after takeoff. I drift in and out of sleep for most of the flight, until a familiar hand gives a firm yank on my arm. It's Pa and he says we'll soon be in Heaven. All I can see out the window is darkness, so I drift off again. Ma always told me that we fall into a final slumber before awaking in Heaven, so I know that we've finally made it.

"Of all the places Uncle Sam can throw a refugee family to assimilate into American society, they choose this?" Pa says as he surveys our apartment. It's an ancient seven-story brick building on Western Avenue in Hollywood, California. It reminds me of the buildings I've seen in black-and-white gangster movies, complete with rusting fire escapes and long, dark hallways. As we step into the lobby, we're greeted by the smell of urine and mold. As Pa attempts to communicate with the man behind the counter, I can see commotion down every hallway. An old black woman with sagging breasts stands in the doorway of the room two doors down and yells at a man in a tattered wifebeater: "Get the fuck out of my face." She follows her statement with a heavy slam of the door. I'm not sure what her words mean, but I can tell they aren't nice, and I savor the powerful effect they have upon the man, who wanders off dejected, muttering under his breath.

The elevator is broken, so we hike the stairs up to our studio on the top floor. On the way up, I'm introduced to the diversity of our building's tenants. It doesn't take me long to distinguish which ethnicities live on which floors. The strong smell of fresh corn tortillas and roasted serrano peppers flows from the floors

housing the Mexicans, Puerto Ricans, and El Salvadorans. A thick and savory aroma of heavy butter, fried chicken, and corn bread comes from the black families' homes, and, of course, the intensely familiar scents of fried fish, garlic, and, jasmine rice waft from the units housing the Vietnamese, Laotian, and Thai families on our floor. I learn quickly that hunger doesn't discriminate between these aromas; sometimes, when times are hard, I long to join my neighbors to share in their meals and taste their delicacies. Instead, I obediently consume what my father can afford—rice with canned sardines and fish sauce, usually three times a day.

Downstairs, the doors to the two rooms closest to the elevator hang open most of the day. Their identical décor is sparse—metal bed frames that are rusting and broken, dilapidated mattresses without sheets, and stained burgundy carpet littered with colorful balloons. Sometimes the balloons even creep out into the hallway, where they'll lay undisturbed for days on end. I can scarcely believe my good fortune. I now know why everyone back in Hong Kong told us that America is Heaven.

One morning Ma and I walk downstairs to ask the building manager why our plumbing won't work. While Ma labors to communicate with him, I scurry to the open door and snatch up a long red balloon from the mangy carpet. As we walk upstairs I blow hard into the hole but can't inflate my testy balloon. The outside is as sticky and filthy as the carpet I pulled it from. I can tell someone else has been blowing on my balloon because the inside is moist and tastes salty. I wonder if they had the same problem blowing it up that I'm having, but I won't put it back. I love my red balloon. I pull it from my lips to smile at Ma as she opens the door to our apartment. She smiles back and seems happy that I've found a toy to play with.

I play with my balloon for days on end in absolute bliss. I still can't inflate it, but I bite, suck, and chew on it enough to remove the grime and restore its bright red luster. It's my most cherished

possession until Pa comes home one evening from *figuring things out* and spots me playing with it.

"Don't put your mouth on that!" Pa bellows, grabbing the balloon from my hand. "Someone's dick has been in this!" He shakes the balloon at me while he yells and the ends wiggle out from both sides of his clenched fist. He turns to Ma and his explanation transforms her bewildered look into one of horror.

I pout in the corner while they talk and point at my balloon. Pa and Ma come over and tell me that I can't play with it because it's not a balloon and it's dirty because people stick their dick in it. I don't understand why someone would stick his dick in a balloon and I don't believe them. They can't tell me it's not a balloon. There's a hole on one end to blow it up with, there are many different colors, and even different sizes. Pa just doesn't want me having any fun in Heaven.

I can't be separated from my beloved balloons, so I take a clandestine approach to honoring Pa's demands. I snatch balloons from the rooms downstairs every chance I get, and I'm careful to stuff them into my pockets when Ma and Pa aren't looking. When Pa is around, I keep them out of his sight. Sometimes Ma catches me playing with them. She always snatches them away from me and swears she's going to tell Pa about his disobedient son. I don't believe her, but I do notice Pa keeps a closer eye on me when he's home.

One day Pa comes home and charges right into the bathroom where he catches me playing with a large, ribbed black balloon. He tries to yank it away from me, but I hold on to it tightly with my teeth. I grit my teeth and purse my lips until they feel like they're going to explode from the pressure. Pa continues to tug on the balloon, pulling it farther and farther from my face. His face is as furious as mine is indignant. Pa's angered expression transforms abruptly into a massive, shit-eating grin. He releases the balloon suddenly and it snaps back into my moist lips with a loud pop.

Intense pain shoots across my lips, but I don't feel the sting for long. Pa follows with a hard palm that descends upon my cheek in a flash and sends my limp body flopping onto the floor. The bitter taste of blood fills my mouth as I lie there, my balloon on the other side of the room where it was catapulted by the impact. The balloon is still moist from my saliva, and it lies there glistening like a precious stone on our dirty industrial carpet.

It's the first time Pa has taught me a lesson with his heavy hands. I've seen them put to use before, to straighten up a drunkard who was harassing Ma in Da Nang. But never on me. It hurts worse than I ever imagined it would.

Pa must feel bad because the next morning he wakes me up to give me a present. It's the first one he's given me since coming to America, and he strokes my hair with his hand as I open it. It's a brand-new balloon that's still in the wrapper. I tear open the wrapper with glee and squeal when I realize that this balloon is red. It's a bit slimy and it reeks of rubber, but I love it—just as much as the one Pa took away.

"It's yours to keep if you can promise me one thing, son," he says, his hand still running rhythmically across the length of my scalp, "Promise me you won't blow on other people's balloons anymore. Because I bought this one just for you to blow on."

I bite on the balloon's opening and smile back in agreement.

"It's clean. Don't lose it." He pats me twice on the head and walks away.

I love my new toy and take it wherever I go. It's in my mouth at the market and in the thrift store. People stare at me and talk and point as I chew on my red balloon, but I don't care. They're just wishing they had a wonderful toy of their own. And I keep my promise to Pa.

Not that I'm able to leave the apartment much. Pa forbids Ma, Quy, and me from going out without him. The older I get, the better I understand Pa's depictions of how hazardous the prostitutes, gangs, and crack whores really are. I watch these

characters from our window as they play out a daily urban drama on the sidewalk.

It's never quiet around our building, particularly after darkness falls. The mayhem, commotion, and conversations increase in volume as soon as the streetlights turn on. We live on the top floor, where police helicopters shine their floodlights through the windows as they search the roof of our building. The roof is a crackhead and junkie haven with enough room and light for them to light up, shoot up, and enjoy the view. Our building manager allows this because he's a neighborhood dope man, pimp, and provider of stolen goods. All for a fee. He pimps prostitutes in the rooms by the elevator downstairs; when not in use, their doors remain open as a signal of their availability. Prostitutes who can't afford a room turn tricks for their clients on the roof for a lower fee. If you're not selling your body for money or smoking up the manager's drugs, you get the fuck off his roof.

All night long bottles fly from our roof and smash into the alley below. The Bird Man keeps a watchful eye on the streets below, and his piercing whistles invade my sleep. He whistles to let the dealers know when the cops are coming, and he strings shoes on the power lines in front of our building so the junkies know where to score. If you're still unsure of where to get your fix, the dealers that lean against our building will let you know. They call out to anyone walking by, "Need a fix? Pebbles . . . Pebbles . . . Pebbles. Mints? Tic Tacs? Sugar?"

And the drug dealers are competitive. As Ma, Pa, Quy, and I walk out of our building one afternoon, there is a young black man lying on the step in the fetal position. He's clutching his ribs and screaming. Dark blood flows from his side and pools in a crimson puddle. As our neighbors leave the building they step over him like he's not even there. One neighbor leans down as he steps over the injured dealer and spits, "You got what you deserved, bastard."

As I watch the pool of blood overwhelm the step and begin

dripping rhythmically onto the sidewalk below, I wonder why no one will help him. I also want to know what his wound looks like, so I step in for a closer look. Pa grabs my arm and pulls me back into the building. After fifteen minutes upstairs I hear the sirens, and the ambulance comes and takes him away. His blood leaves sticky black stains on the concrete that no one bothers to scrub clean.

I wake up alone in bed for the first time since we came to Heaven. I sleep on a full-sized mattress together with Ma, Pa, and Quy because our studio is too small to fit anything larger. And we couldn't afford anything more, even if we had the room. I'm usually the first one up, but today I know there's nothing worth getting out of bed for. Ma is a few feet to my left, cooking breakfast on the stove. Quy is sprawled across the floor at her feet, scribbling on a piece of paper. Pa left early, as usual, to look for a job.

The school year doesn't begin for a month, so I get to leave the apartment only when Ma and Pa take us to the supermarket, thrift shops, welfare office, or liquor store. I lay my arm across the windowsill and prop my chin up on it so that I can look down at the Puerto Rican kids playing soccer and jump rope in the alley below.

I miss Da Nang and long for the days when I could roam the streets freely with my best friend, Vu. In Vietnam, I didn't even have to ask to leave the house. Ma and Pa knew where to find me—either down the block at One-Eyed Lam's frozen-mango stand or up the block at Old Perverted Tuan's sesame glass-candy stand. And if I wasn't buying treats, I was definitely on my grandmother Ne's front porch eating them.

It makes little sense to me that I'm not granted the same freedom in Heaven. "Ma, can I go down to play with those kids?" I ask.

"No!" Ma snaps back.

"Why?" I whine.

Ma walks over and peers out the window. "Because those black kids will pick on you." She gets up, heads back to the stove, continues stirring the porridge, and says, "Do the homework your father assigned you. You can't be wasting your time playing."

Pa insists that I learn Chinese, so I have daily assignments that I'm forced to complete. But I want to be free, so I try to reason with Ma. "They won't pick on me. I'll make friends with them."

"No!"

"Why not?"

Ma offers her favorite statement of disapproval, "No is no."

"Why?" I ask again.

Ma continues stirring and speaks without looking up, "Don't ask why. If you really want to know, wait until your father comes home and ask him."

I turn and give Ma a sour look. A few moments later, I slither over to Quy and pinch her arm as hard as I can. Quy starts to cry. "Brother Lac just pinched me really hard," she sobs.

"You Monkey! Leave your sister alone."

Teasing my sister is one of the few things I can do to entertain myself. I feel suffocated and claustrophobic trapped inside this box all day. I don't have any toys beyond my balloon and a sack of marbles. No television. No coloring books. Nothing that captivates my attention-starved mind.

Quy finally stops crying and I return to bed. I lie on my back and stare up at the ceiling. My mind drifts off to distant places. I think of Vu and the days spent running free in the garden. Time flies by in a restful state of bliss.

Ma snaps me out of it for a moment. She stands over me waving a hand in my face. "What does a little boy like you think about that you don't hear me calling you?"

I don't have an answer for her.

"Now eat your breakfast before it gets any colder."

There's a lukewarm bowl of porridge sitting on the mattress

beside me. I run the spoon in circles around the middle of the bowl until Ma stops watching me. I haven't eaten much lately and my hunger is still missing today. I lie back down on the mattress and let my mind wander off to happier times.

Ma pulls me back to the here and now once more. She sits beside me staring out the window with Quy nestled in her lap. She is singing mirthless Vietnamese folk songs to my sister. The words stumble from her mouth as she chokes on bridled tears.

"Why are you crying, Ma?" I ask.

She looks at me, squeezes the tears from her eyes with her thumb and forefinger, and casts a motherly smile. "Do you miss Ne? Do you still remember your grandmother, son?"

"Yes."

"What do you miss about her?" She blows her runny nose into a tissue.

"Green-papaya salad with liver jerky."

"What else?"

"Her yellow-bean dessert . . . her sticky rice with pork . . . her candy . . . her steamed banh bao . . ." As I tell Ma what I miss about Ne, her quiet tears turn into little squeals, as though she's suffocating. I hate it when Ma cries. I won't cry along with her. Our suffocating box has sucked all the sympathy out of me.

"When can I see Ne again?" I ask.

"One day."

"Tomorrow?"

"One day, son . . . One day."

Ma stares out the window in silence. I don't disturb her because I know that she, too, is in a happier place.

My mother was the first in her family to leave Vietnam. My father was a capitalist and a soldier for the South, making him a marked man when the war ended. He was forced to leave the war-torn country, even if it meant leaving everything and everyone in his

life behind. The thought of leaving her parents, her nine younger brothers, and her baby sister behind was excruciating for Ma. Her family, especially her mother, Ne, depended on her.

Ma knew she would never separate from her children, but that required her to choose the family she built over the one that God created for her. Her family didn't believe that she would leave Vietnam, but when she asked her brothers to make the journey with us, they knew she was serious. Ma's family accused her of being disloyal and without honor. In the days before we made our escape, they disowned her and refused to acknowledge Quy and me as their blood.

A country crumbling into chaos ensured that my father's plans for escape did not proceed smoothly. Hustlers and criminals roamed freely, and they sabotaged his first two attempts, leaving him with little money. Pa spent the last of his cash on our third and final attempt. When someone tipped the Communists off to our group's plans, the journey became a do-or-die for everyone involved. We left the country immediately—more than a week ahead of schedule—in order to avoid capture.

With our exit hastened, Pa and I stopped by Ne's house before rendezvousing with Ma and Quy at the hideout. Pa pounded on Ne's door in a panic. My grandpa opened the door and greeted us with the skeptical indifference one normally reserves for solicitors.

"What do you want? Why are you still here?" Grandpa shouted.

"I'm here to pick up the gold nuggets Mother is holding for me in confidence."

"What gold nuggets? I don't have any of your gold!" Grandmother yelled from behind the door.

"What do you mean you don't have it?"

"I don't have it," was my grandma's muffled reply.

"Well, who has it?"

"I don't know what you're talking about."

Pa took a firm hold of the door, his knuckles white with tension. "Listen, I don't have much time. The boat is waiting for us and we need to leave *now*. For heaven's sake, please give me those gold nuggets . . . They're all I have left to feed my children when we land. *Your* grandchildren. Please, give me the gold now."

"No, I don't have it."

Some of Ma's brothers stood behind grandpa and joined the fracas. "We don't have it! Leave! Get out of our home!" they barked in turn.

With the support of his sons, grandpa struggled to shut the door on Pa. Pa released his grip on the door and stopped it from closing with his foot.

"Motherfuck! If you disown your daughter and me, that's fine with me, but have some heart and think about your baby grandchildren. I have nothing left. I spent it all trying to leave this place. I'm *wanted* by the Viet Cong. If I don't leave here, I'm dead. I'm *fucking dead*! Do you hear me? Now give me my *fucking gold*!"

"Then go die. You will anyways in the ocean. Go and die!" one of the uncles shouted.

"Motherfuck you!" Pa bellowed. "Who said that? Who? Show yourself and say it to my face you fucking coward!"

Time was running out. Pa had no hope of retrieving his gold. "Do you at least have the decency to give me a blanket to protect my children from the cold?"

"Take your foot out of the door and I'll go and look for one," Grandpa said.

Pa pulled his foot from the doorway and it slammed shut in his face. They never returned with a blanket.

Ma's tears are flowing yet again. I try to wipe them from her eyes, but this snaps her out of her nostalgia and she pushes my hand away.

"You cry too much," I say.

"Did you do the homework your father assigned to you yet?"

"I don't want to do it."

"Too good to learn Chinese, are you?"

"I want to go *play*," I whine.

"What did Pa say about leaving the apartment?"

"I want to go play with the black kids."

"Wait until your father comes home tonight. It's his first day on the job. What do you think he's going to do when he finds out that you won't practice your handwriting because he's not around?"

"I will be asleep."

"Mmmph. We'll see about *that*."

Ma waits up for Pa to come home. He told her he'd be home by eleven, but by the time two a.m. rolls around and he has yet to return, Ma is a nervous wreck. She paces about the apartment, muttering her thoughts aloud.

"Maybe the bus is taking longer than expected?

"Maybe he just took the wrong bus? No, Tran told him *exactly* which buses to take. He even wrote the lines down on a piece of paper.

"Maybe the restaurant stayed open late for a special guest? Maybe it's a famous movie star and the owner will keep it open as long as he wants . . . No, but he's only a prep cook . . . They wouldn't need him to stay."

She decides, just go down the hall and tell the neighbors.

Ma unlatches each of the door chains, unlocks the dead bolt, and opens the door. She stands in the doorway and peers down the dark hallway. There are no lights in the hallways, so it's pitch-black save for the glow emanating from our apartment. Pa has forbidden her from leaving the apartment without him. She thinks twice about this and snaps the door shut, locking the dead bolt and hinging the chains in rapid sequence. We don't have a phone, so Ma has no way of hearing from Pa. She joins Quy and me in bed, squeezes us tight and cries herself to sleep.

The sunlight creeps through the window and Pa still isn't home. Ma is at the stove making porridge for breakfast.

"Ma, where's Pa?" I ask.

"I don't know."

"Why?"

"I don't know, son. Now come and eat your porridge."

She feeds us porridge with pickled squash. I'm afraid so I eat every bite. As Ma is gathering up the dishes, the door opens—to a halt. The chains stop it. Ma rushes over to unhook them. Pa walks in silently. He throws his keys down on the table and lets out an exasperated sigh. His eyes are droopy and dark, and his lips are a gentle shade of magenta. He looks skinny in his fitted black leather jacket and polyester slacks. He walks past me to fix himself a cup of jasmine tea. As he passes I can smell a heavy blend of cigarettes and leather.

"Scoop me a bowl of that. I'm starving," Pa says.

Ma scurries over and fixes him a bowl of porridge. "For heaven's sake, where did you go all night?"

Pa walks over to the table, which rests about two feet off the ground, and squats down next to us to eat his breakfast. "Those fucking buses took me everywhere," he says between slurps of porridge.

"What do you mean? Tran gave you directions. You know which bus to take, where to get off, which streets to take—" Ma fires away until Pa sets his bowl down and throws her a stern look.

"Look, I did as he said, until I transferred to a third bus."

"Then?" Ma says.

"I was so tired that I dozed off. But I was quite aware of where the bus was going. Every time someone rang the bell to get off I would wake up. But . . ."

Ma listens attentively.

"But I got so used to hearing the bell that it didn't wake me up anymore. When I finally woke up I was at the beach."

"Did you get back on the bus to go back?"

"Of course I did."

"Then why—" Ma is anxious for Pa to get to the point.

"*Then* it took me to a city that had Korean writing on the buildings."

"Did you get off to ask those people for directions? They're Asian."

"You *idiot*; you think all Asians speak Vietnamese?"

Ma fixes her gaze downward and begins cleaning the dishes.

"So, I showed the bus driver my piece of paper and I asked him to take me home. 'Home, home,' I told him," Pa says as he reenacts the scene for us with his crumpled piece of paper.

"Did he take you home?"

"He was rattling off words to me like firecrackers and I didn't understand any of them. I just nodded my head and hoped he understood what I wanted. I sat on his bus for another hour, waiting for him to signal that I should get off, but he just kept driving."

Pa sips his tea and lights up a cigarette. He inhales deeply and pushes thick streams of smoke out his nostrils.

"It was well after midnight, and I was the only one left on that bus. The driver pulled into this big parking lot with all the other metro buses and turned off the engine. He looked at me back there and started to laugh. Then he told me to get off the bus. I showed him the fucking piece of paper again and he just pointed in all directions saying things I didn't understand. 'Go. Go. Go. No. No. No.' Something like that."

"Where were you?" Ma asks.

"I don't know. I just saw a lot of tall buildings and a lot of people sleeping on the sidewalk. So, I started walking. I kept walking and walking and then I saw some Chinese writing on the stores. Everything was closed. So, I waited around for a while until I could catch someone on the streets who spoke Chinese. I ran into a couple of people, but when I asked them for

directions they had no clue. So, I walked some more. And then—motherfuck—guess where I ended up?"

"Where?" Ma asks.

"The same fucking place where I started," Pa says, grinding his cigarette into the ashtray. "The restaurant where I work."

"For heaven's sake," Ma says with a smirk.

"I went all that way for nothing. Can you believe that?" He stands up, digs in his pocket, and pulls out five dimes, which he chucks onto the table. "I had five dollars worth of dimes in my pocket yesterday morning when I left for work. It only costs one dime to take a bus and another nickel for a transfer. That ought to tell you how many buses I took yesterday. Thank Heaven I had enough cigarettes to last me through the night. I don't know what I would do if I were to run out of cigarettes while stranded out there like that."

"But how did you get home?"

"I wasn't going to wait around for the buses to start running again, that's for damn sure. I know my own way home. So, I walked."

"But . . . Tran said the restaurant is thirty kilometers from here," Ma says with concern.

"Don't you think I know that, *stupid*? I walked every meter of it this morning. I don't need the buses' *help*. From now on, I'll get myself to work."

I don't see Pa much. He walks to and from work each day, which means he's gone when I wake up and he comes home long after I go to sleep. Sometimes, he wakes me up with his prickly beard when he sniffs my cheeks good night. On his day off, Pa is always willing to take Quy and me out to "play." Usually, it's a trip to the liquor store so that he can pick up a pack of Salem cigarettes, and today is no exception. I don't care where he takes us, so long as I'm with him.

On our way to the store, we run into a large black woman on the corner with big, poofy hair, a tight, pink miniskirt, and stiletto heels. She says something to Pa and he shakes his head as he walks by her. I can tell he's either scared of her or doesn't want her service. Once we're a few feet past her, Pa looks at me and says with a chuckle, "Fucking hooker."

"What's a hooker, Pa?" I ask.

Pa doesn't answer.

Pa takes us around the block two, three, and then four times before Quy decides she's had enough.

"How about you, Big Head? You had enough?" Pa asks me.

"I want to keep going." I'm already tired, but I'm not going back into that box.

We take Quy upstairs, and then Pa *really* takes me out. We spend five or six hours walking all around Hollywood. Pa must want to make up for all the times I begged him to take me out and he couldn't. Pa doesn't allow me to take a break during our stroll. He gives me just enough time to catch up with him and then he prods me along to keep moving.

"Keep moving! You wanted me to take you out to play, so let's go play."

"But I'm tired, Pa."

"You want to go play, right?"

I do. I want to be with my father. I miss those nights in Da Nang when he used to take me out and we took our time.

I also miss being free. Every time we go out in America, Pa has to *teach me something*.

"Now, don't stand too close to the curb while you're waiting for the light," Pa says. "If one of these cars is in a hurry and he makes a right turn, he will run you over."

Cars whiz by and we stand on the curb, waiting.

"Why do some people drive cars and others take the bus?" Pa asks.

"I don't know."

Pa smacks me across the back of the head.

"Wrong answer, Big Head. Some people drive cars and not buses because they're educated . . . Education gets you to places in this white man's land . . . It gets you far ahead in life . . . It gets you an office . . . an oak desk . . . People have to knock on *your* door first before they're able to talk to you.

"Look, Big Head, there's a fan over there on the curb next to the trash bin. Do you think it's broken?"

I shrug my shoulders to show him I don't care. Our apartment is already filled with items he's collected from the trash.

"Hurry, let's go see."

He grabs me by the hand and we walk over to the trash cans. As we approach the fan, Pa slows his walk and looks behind him to see if anyone is watching. He looks like he's going to steal something. He picks up the fan and sees that some of the blades are missing. He puts it back and climbs inside the trash bin. When Pa locates a bag of clothes, he starts looking over his shoulder again.

"Let's keep walking and wait until it gets dark. Then we'll come back and go through these bags. I see a pair of shoes in here that might fit you. You see them? Right . . . *there.*" He pushes on the side of the bag until the pair of shoes peeks over the edge of the bin at me. They're bright-yellow and worn with Velcro straps. They look to be more Ma's size than mine.

I stand there, half asleep and rubbing my eyes. The sun is setting, and a cool breeze whips my bowl cut against my ears. Like most every night, the Los Angeles sky melds into shades of gold and tangerine as the sun sinks beneath the horizon. I wish I could go home to eat my day-old rice with sardines. Instead, Pa drags me on to inspect more trash bins while we wait for darkness.

We don't find much. Pa takes his time inspecting each item until he uncovers what's ailing it. I watch him scrutinize an iron. He presses and clicks all the buttons to see if they work, even

though the iron is clearly not plugged in. I have no idea what he's looking for, and I'm too tired to care.

"This thing is brand-new. Why would anyone want to throw *this* away?"

"I don't know," I mutter.

"I bet the wires are severed inside the cord, right here."

Pa holds up the iron to reveal a crimp in the cord.

"I can cut the cord on either side and reconnect it. It'll be brand-new! We're taking this one with us."

"Pa, I'm sleepy," I moan.

He ignores me. After another hour, he decides to keep the iron and a belt. We head back toward the gold mine he discovered earlier.

"Do you remember how to get back to where we were, Big Head?" Pa asks.

"No."

"Why didn't you keep track?"

"Because I'm sleepy."

Pa brings the walk to a halt.

"What do you mean you're sleepy! I take you on these walks so you can familiarize yourself with these streets. What if I weren't here with you; how are you going to get home? What would you do?"

The thought of Pa not being with me in these streets scares me. I can feel tears welling up in my eyes.

"You need to remember where you're going at all times, and how to get back. I could be away at my job, and if your mother needs to go to the store, you need to take her there. You hear me, Big Head?"

Pa grabs me by the hand and we continue. He points at a swing on a tree.

"See that swing on that tree? Remember it."

He points at a yellow Volkswagen Bug. "You like that cute car?"

"Yeah."

"Remember that."

A few blocks over, he points to a wall that's covered with graffiti.

"We're almost there at the old trash bins. You know how I know?"

"No."

"Because of that big number eighteen on that wall. That's how I get around. Remember things that pop out at you. Are you listening to me?"

"Yes, Pa."

"Okay, now you can walk home alone without me. I'm leaving you now."

My face turns pale. I squint my eyes, getting ready to squeeze out a flood of tears. "No, Pa, don't go," I sob. "Don't leave me!"

"You can find your own way back home."

"No!" I scream.

"All right, all right, stop crying. I'm just teasing you, but I want you to understand my point." He chuckles as he rubs my head. "If you ever get lost and you're on your own, crying won't get you home. So, be cognizant of where you are at all times. You hear me?"

We get back to the trash bin. Someone has already been through it. The bags are torn open, and items are strewn all over the bin.

"We're late. Someone already took the fan. I wanted to take that pair of shoes for you . . ." Pa looks disappointed, but it doesn't stop him from rummaging through the bin again.

"There's nothing left. They took all the good stuff."

A bicycle frame that Pa had overlooked is still there, leaning against the wall behind the bin. It's the frame of a dirt bike, without handlebars, wheels, or pedals.

"I need *this*," Pa says with a grin. He holds the bike frame up above his chest to admire it. "I have everything I need to put

this bike together at home. I'm going to ride this bike to *work* tomorrow."

Before we head home, Pa lifts me up into the bin and makes me help him organize the mess. We bag and stack the trash neatly until it's exactly as we found it. Pa hops out of the bin, grabs me under the arms, and pulls me down to him. He takes my hand. He puts the other arm through the bike frame and hoists it onto his shoulder. He grabs the iron and belt and we stroll home.

Pa, the embodiment of capitalism, posing proudly in front of one of his warehouses in Vietnam before I was born.

# *A* IS FOR BOY AND *B* IS FOR CAT

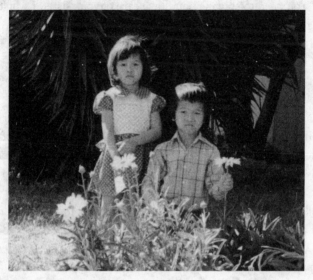

Quy and I in front of the new apartment on Sunset Boulevard.

**M**a drops the phone abruptly onto the base. The receiver emits a fragmented ring from the impact. Ma's wild-eyed and frantic, throwing a tattered wool sweater over her head as she dashes across the room. She searches frantically for some bobby pins, which she uses to fashion her hair into a frizzy black bun. She's wearing a loose cotton muumuu with a flower print that hangs so low that it hides the stripes on her tube socks. Her green plastic slippers click-clack across the tile with every hurried step she takes.

She runs over to the couch and grabs me by the shoulders. "Stay here and take care of your sister. I have to go."

"Where are you going?" I ask. "I want to go with you."

"You can't. I have to take the bus to go and see your father."

"But I want to go with you. I don't want to stay here . . . I'm scared."

"You need to stay here and take care of your sister. I won't be long. Don't leave the apartment, you hear me?"

I nod my head. "But where's Pa . . . ?"

"Now, come and lock the door behind me."

I follow Ma to the door and she snaps it shut without an answer. I set the dead bolt and latch the chain.

I've never seen Ma leave the house without changing into her "going-out" clothes. I look over at Quy, who climbs the back of the couch to watch Ma through the window. She cries and screams as Ma catches a bus on the other side of the street. It's dark outside, and this is our first time in the apartment alone. I don't feel capable of looking after Quy, but I try. I bundle up next to her on our turquoise pleather sofa, and she cries herself to sleep.

After a while I join Quy in slumber, but the silence of the empty house stirs me awake. I look around and see no one. I cry in the darkness for my mother and father. I peer out the window every time I hear the hissing breaks of a passing bus, but it's no use. People get on and off, but they are not my parents.

We've moved into a new apartment on Sunset Boulevard in West Los Angeles. Pa now makes enough to pay the rent in low-income housing, and our apartment is a small step up from the projects we lived in on Western Avenue. The traffic in front of our building is a tangled, teeming mess. Cars, buses, and ambulances tear by our building on their way to the freeway, and the evening rush hour is marked by gridlock. The ruckus outside makes me feel more alone inside this empty apartment. It's usually so loud and chaotic in here that I'm immune to the pandemonium out front.

The silence breeds fear. I unleash another heavy bout of sobbing, which wakes Quy up. She stares at me as though I'm her younger brother. I don't care. I keep crying while she plays with her My Little Pony.

The next thing I know, I'm startled awake by the ringing telephone. It sounds louder than usual.

"Ahlo?" I ask.

"Son, is that you!" Ma's voice assaults my eardrum. I pull the receiver away from my head.

"Ma! When are you coming home?" I scream into the phone. "Why are you taking so long?"

"Where's Quy?"

"Over here."

"Over here is *where*?"

"She's playing with her toy."

"I will be home soon."

"When?"

"Soon."

"Where's Pa?"

"He's in the hospital . . ."

*The hospital?* I think. I don't probe any further. I just want them to come home.

"Hurry. Come home. Hurry!" I plead.

"Soy milk and cereal are in the refrigerator. Eat some and give some to your sister. You hear me?"

"Yes, Ma."

"And your father says *do not* leave the house. Are you listening?" Ma is shouting through the background noise.

"Hurry."

"Bye, son."

I hear a click.

"Ma! Ma! Where are you? Ma! Ahlo? Ahlo?"

Silence.

Quy and I eat bowl after bowl of cereal and wander about the

apartment together until we can't keep our eyes open. Normally, I'd be picking on her, but tonight we're too scared to fight. I like to wipe boogers on her face so that she'll chase me around to get back at me. I drive her crazy, to the point that she fights back. When Quy's really mad, she's just like Pa. She'll charge at me and dig her fingernails into any piece of skin her tiny fingers can grab. I don't mind, so long as she doesn't touch my head, especially my face. When she touches my head, I become Pa. I wail on her with my fists in an angry blur.

Even though Pa hits Quy like he does me—and she's only a year and a half younger than I am—she's a girl, so I'm not allowed to hit her. When Ma catches me, she spanks me and calls me a "dead dog." Her spankings don't hurt, and they don't stop me from picking on Quy. Pa doesn't involve himself until things get out of hand. When he does, he comes on fast like a train. There's no use arguing with him. He passes a point of no return. His eyes go wide and his brows point into a $V$. He'll bite his lower lip as he grabs me by the hair and smacks my butt so hard that it gives me a headache. There's no warning and never an explanation. Pa can tell how much pain I'm in by the sound of my wail. I guess his hand no longer makes me wail like I used to, because I've graduated to heavier things. Shortly after my eighth birthday, he started using the broom handle.

Now, Quy falls asleep, so I turn on the tiny black-and-white television that Pa found in the Dumpster. It has no sound, and the metal hanger Pa fashioned into an antenna can barely pull a signal. I watch *Tom and Jerry* cartoons through the static, and the glowing screen makes me feel less alone and afraid.

When I wake up the next morning, Pa is in bed asleep. It's strange to see him lying there. He should be up already, at the dinner table drinking his tea and chain-smoking while he reads the paper. I climb onto the bed and lean over his face to see if it's really him. It's Pa all right, but he looks different. He's covered with bruises. There are Band-Aids all over his face and a mas-

sive piece of gauze taped securely around his neck. All of Pa's bandages are stained with blood, and he has gashes around his eyes that are sewn together with black strings. His right eye is covered with a pirate's patch.

"Pa, wake up!" I shout.

He groans and his eye stays closed.

"Shhhh . . . let your father sleep," Ma whispers.

Pa hears the two of us talking and opens his left eye. He looks at me and tries to say something, but his words are garbled.

"Pa, where did you fall?" I ask.

Pa nods his head twice and closes his eyes.

"Lac, let your father rest." Ma grabs me by my waist and pulls me out of the bed and into the living room.

"Did Pa fall somewhere?" I ask.

"Some people hit your father yesterday after work. He almost died."

Ma's suggestion is incomprehensible. Who would dare hit Pa?

The evening prior, my father was riding his bicycle on the outskirts of Chinatown. He had just completed his shift at work and was on his way to a friend's house near Dodger Stadium when he came upon a brutal, winding hill that was too steep to ride. As he walked his bike up the hill, he passed five big cholos—Mexican gang members who were sitting on a retaining wall that ran along the sidewalk. The year was 1984, and cholos greased their hair back and wore hairnets. My father had the tendency to stare blatantly at people he found interesting or funny-looking. He noticed the tattoos on their arms and associated them with gang markings. This peaked his attention further and caused him to stare harder.

"Hey, you got a lighter, homes?" one of the Cholos asked with a nod of his head.

My father didn't understand. He spoke very little English, so he shook his head no and kept walking.

"A lighter, homes? You smoke?" The gangster walked toward my father. He pointed to the pack of cigarettes in Pa's front pocket and made a gesture with his thumb like he was lighting a Bic.

"Oh, yes . . . yes, a match," Pa said in Vietnamese.

He reached down to pull the book of matches from his pants pocket, but when he looked up the other gangsters were off the wall and coming at him with PVC pipes. The guy who asked for the lighter put Pa into a headlock and dragged his little body over the wall and into the corner of a parking lot, away from the street. A flurry of fists, pipes, and feet proceeded to wail on Pa's head and torso. He felt hands searching for his wallet and tried to scream as they pulled his leather jacket over his head. His scream was followed by a blunt blow to the head that knocked him unconscious.

When my father awoke, the gangsters were removing the watch he'd worn every day since receiving it for his wedding. They released his wrist, and one of the gangsters straddled my father's chest and pulled out a screwdriver. As the gangster thrust the screwdriver down into my father's throat, Pa snapped his head to the side to avert the jugular. The wound wasn't mortal, but Pa gurgled and choked all the same, in the hope that playing dead would make the gangsters go away.

A few minutes later, Pa's watch, wallet, and leather jacket were gone with the gangsters. He trailed blood as he walked the rest of the way up the hill to his friend's house, where they called him an ambulance.

I couldn't sleep a wink last night. Ever since Pa regained his strength, all my parents can talk about is school, and today is my first day. I'm terrified. Ma and Pa tell me it's going to be great and I'm going to learn a lot, but I don't believe them for a second.

My first two years of American school were a horrifying exercise in alienation. The school near our old apartment on Western

Avenue was so much dirtier than the schools in Vietnam. No one spoke Vietnamese, so I learned very little English. At first I was excited to have the chance to play with the other children on the rooftop during recess, but my enthusiasm soon withered. The English-speaking kids wouldn't play with me for very long. As soon as they discovered that I didn't speak English, they stopped including me in their games. All of the kids who spoke Spanish played together, so I tried to join their games. Every time I came near them, they would dance and point at me, laughing and singing, *"Chino, chino, japonés, come caca y no me des."* I couldn't understand the meaning of the words in their song, but I knew they were teasing me.

So I played by myself.

Everyone is still asleep because the sun has yet to pierce the horizon, but the noise is already growing in the street out front. I watch the people passing our house on foot and in cars, and I wonder if they even went to bed last night. Maybe they're all nervous and scared like me. I lie on the couch and dig my nose into it until Pa gets up.

Pa is still banged up from the men who hit him. The cuts on his face and neck have grown scabs that are dotted with globs of pus. The doctor gave Pa antibiotic pills to fight the infection, but we Vietnamese only have one remedy for all things painful and infectious—Tiger Balm. An analgesic rub that smells and works a lot like Vick's, Tiger Balm has a unique blend of camphor, menthol, and cloves that produces an aroma to tingle your nose and trick you into believing in its healing power.

Pa cringes as he spreads the oily ointment across his scabs. I watch in awe as he replaces the bandages on his face. He looks so tough and brave, like a boxer tending to his wounds after a bout. He always says that first impressions are important, and he doesn't want to look too beat up when he meets my teacher.

He considers the first day of school a special occasion, and he's taken the day off from work just to walk me there and back.

He dresses me up in a suit. It's a gloomy fall day, so he rubs Tiger Balm on my chest before putting on my shirt and blazer, to make sure I'll keep warm.

"I'm proud of you, son," he says, adjusting my tie. He's rough as he jerks it back and forth, and my shoulders sway with each tug. "You're experiencing the one thing I've wanted my entire life—a free education."

Pa plasters my cowlick down with Vaseline. He puckers his lips together as he concentrates on parting my hair in the straightest line possible down my scalp. When he achieves his goal, he puts his hands on my shoulders and admires me for a moment with a smug look on his face. It looks like he wants to give me a kiss, like the white people do on TV. I turn my head and look away.

The walk to school is six miles, so we leave an hour and a half before first bell. When we arrive, there are children swarming the playground. Pa smiles and points to the monkey bars and the handball court. I don't know what they're for. I look at the children running around and am horrified to discover that I'm the only one who is wearing a suit and tie.

Pa snorts and swallows his phlegm. "I guess in America the older children don't wear a suit and tie to school like they do in Vietnam." He is disappointed.

A black kid runs pass me and notices my outfit. He runs over to his friends. They all look different from one another—different skin colors, different hair texture, different height and weight. The variation scares me. They point at me and laugh. All of a sudden, I can feel the Vaseline around my forehead and ears. I hide behind Pa's legs.

"Don't be scared," Pa says, grabbing me out from behind him and pushing me toward the other children. "Pa's going to come back in a few hours to pick you up. Make friends with the other students and make sure you listen and cooperate with the teacher."

"Stay with me. Don't leave . . ."

"You're a big boy now. I don't want to hear or see you cry. Big boys don't cry. You hear me?"

"Yes, Pa." I try not to cry by sucking my lips through my teeth. My nostrils flare, and my eyes begin to blink rapidly. I'll do anything to keep the tears from flowing. I want Pa to tell his refugee friends that I was a good boy and I didn't cry on my first day of school. That's what Pa and his friends do—they obsessively compare their children's progress in America. Some of them have boasted that their kids have "adapted to the white lifestyle *right away.*"

The school bell rings and the teachers come out to greet us. They're holding up big signs with words and numbers on them. Though the letters of the Vietnamese alphabet resemble those of the English alphabet, Pa has a hard time reading the words. He runs up and down the playground, dragging me by the arm behind him. As he approaches each sign he compares it to the name our social worker wrote on a scrap of paper. My teacher's name is Mrs. Coeffe, but Pa can't find her sign. When some of the teachers begin taking their students into the classroom, he decides to ask for help.

He turns to the other adults on the playground and asks, "Café?" while pointing at this slip of paper.

A large black man with a clipboard and a whistle around his neck stops and looks at the piece of paper Pa is holding.

"Mrs. Coeffe!" he screams, pointing at me. "Room 6! Here's one for you."

Mrs. Coeffe waves us over. Her students are assembled into a neat, single-file line. Pa grabs my hand and drags me to her. He walks right up and shakes her hand firmly. I can't believe it. He looks like a dwarf standing in front of her. Her giant meat hook of a hand engulfs Pa's. She points at Pa's face and asks him something he doesn't understand. Pa grins and nods his head anyway.

Mrs. Coeffe looks down at me. I run behind Pa's legs and can feel the tears welling up behind my eyes.

Pa turns around and whispers to me sternly, "Go. Greet your teacher, Lac."

I approach Mrs. Coeffe reluctantly. Her hair is blond and puffy like the hair of the lady from *Charlie's Angels*. She kneels down next to me and I'm transfixed by her teeth. They're long and flat and blindingly white. Mrs. Coeffe reaches out and shakes my hand. Her fingers feel like a bundle of bananas are wrapping themselves around my wrist. I shut my eyes tight and begin to weep. Pa pats me on the back and tells me to say, "Ciao, tay," for "Greetings, teacher."

"Say it. Greet your teacher," Pa says again.

I feel ashamed for crying, but I'm too scared to open my eyes. Pa grabs me by the shoulders and spins me around.

"Shut up right now! You stop your crying or I'm going to beat you right here!"

Pa spins me back around and I open my eyes. He holds me by the shoulders while a horrified Mrs. Coeffe fumbles a cartoon sticker off of the roll and onto my blazer. She takes my hand and leads me to the front of the line. I look back at Pa and wipe my tears away.

In the line I notice that all the other kids have stickers on their shirts, too. As Mrs. Coeffe marches us to the classroom, we pass another line of children. At the very front of the line I see another Vietnamese kid who just like me is wearing a blank expression on his face. Though his teacher is smaller and more normal-looking, his class doesn't seem very fun—they don't have any stickers, and their teacher doesn't have a permanent smile frozen on her face like Mrs. Coeffe. The Vietnamese boy is short like me, and his hair is cut into a bob just like mine. He stands knock-kneed and holds a small glass marble up toward the sky, turning it and watching the light glimmer through it. I remember how Vu and I used to hold dragonflies up to the sky like that to admire their colorful wings.

In homeroom, Mrs. Coeffe makes us recite the Pledge of Al-

legiance and sing "God Bless America." I don't understand why the white children insist on screaming each word as if Uncle Sam himself might hear them. They remind me of the Viet Cong who would sing at the top of their lungs as they marched through the streets of Da Nang.

I understand very little of what goes on in homeroom, but fortunately I don't spend much time there. At ten a.m. I'm taken down the hall to the English-as-a-second-language class.

I'm greeted by our ESL teacher, Ms. Ping, a short, pudgy Chinese woman with pasty skin who waddles about the classroom like a penguin. The classroom is populated mostly by Mexicans, though there are a few from Central America, Armenia, and Asia. Ms. Ping takes me over to my seat, which is next to the Vietnamese boy I spotted earlier this morning. He's still playing with the same marble and looks eagerly in my direction as I take my seat.

"Lac . . . you will sit . . . here," Ms. Ping says, pursing her lips to exaggerate the pronunciation of the English words, "next to Johnny."

"What's your name?" the boy asks me in Vietnamese.

"Lac."

"Lac what?"

"Lac Su."

"You Chinese?" he asks with a disapproving look.

"No, just my dad is. I'm from Vietnam."

"Oh," Johnny says, going back to his marble.

"Are you Vietnamese?" I ask.

"*Ya.*"

"Then how come the teacher called you Johnny?"

"My dad made me change it last year because all of the white kids made fun of me."

"Why? What's your real name?"

"Phat . . ." he says, looking down. "Phat Bich."

"Oh, I see," I say. But I don't. I think Phat Bich is a fine name and don't see why the white children would want to make fun

of it. Pa's friend's name is Phat, and he owns his own furniture store.

We've made fast friends because we're the only Vietnamese kids in ESL class.

Ms. Ping's derisively easy English lessons fuel my disgust for her. I learn more English listening to Pa's radio than I will in her silly classroom, so I toy with her every time she shuffles over to my desk for a lesson.

"Now, Lac, what is the letter *A* for?" Ms. Ping asks with a squinty smile.

"F-f-f-feeeiiiissshhhh," I sputter in my thickest Vietnamese accent, while Johnny giggles behind me.

"No, fish starts with an *F*," Ms. Ping persists. "Now, tell me a word that begins with an *Aaaaaaa*."

"Say 'boy,'" Johnny tells me in Vietnamese with his hand in front of his mouth.

"B-b-b-boy."

"No, Lac, I'm sorry. Boy begins with a *B*. A word that begins with *A* is a-a-a-apple, or a-a-astronaut. Let's try another one. What's a word that begins with the letter *B*?"

"Say 'cat.'"

"Cat."

Ms. Ping is finally at a loss for words, and her blank expression makes me giggle. The laughter gives me away, and it doesn't help that Johnny is bowled over facedown on his desk, snorting as he tries in vain to hold it in. Ms. Ping makes the both of us repeat "*A* is for apple, *B* is for boy, *C* is for cat" twenty times before we can leave for recess.

Out on the playground, Johnny and I try to tag along with the white kids. They seem so confident and in control of their world that we want to be with them. But they don't want us around. Every time we come near, they pull their eyes back into a slant and yell things like, "Ching chong, ching chong," or, "Kung fu, Bruce Lee . . . hiya!"

I'm so happy to be around other children that I don't mind their teasing much. And with Johnny around, rejection doesn't make me feel so alone. Johnny, however, can't take it. A good 50 percent of his English vocabulary is curse words, so he responds to the constant teasing with broken phrases that make the white kids run to the teachers, "Fuck! . . . Fuck yoo! . . . Mudderfuckah you! Fuck yoo, sista. Fuck you, fodder. You shit, poosy. Fuck yoo!"

We move on to the Spanish-speaking kids, hoping they might let us join their soccer game. But every time we come near, they stop playing to sing and swing their hips in unison, exaggerating their words, *"Cheeno, cheeno, hop-on-a's, comb a cocka ee no me days!"*

Their singing infuriates Johnny, who runs through his usual loop of profanities. But his curses don't faze the Spanish-speaking soccer players, and they sing their song over and over again until we leave.

As we walk away from their game, Johnny speaks to me in Vietnamese, "You know what their song means, Lac?"

"No."

"It means, 'Chinese, Chinese, Japanese. Eat shit and don't give it to me.'"

# BRAIN FOOD

Pa making sure I smiled for the camera.

**W**ake up, Big Head," Pa says, shaking me by the shoulders.

I sit up in bed and wipe the boogers out of my eyes before heading out into the living room. Pa is sipping tea and smoking a Salem at the dinner table. Ma is in the kitchen, cooking rice.

"Big Head, you up already?" he asks with a silly grin on his face.

I'm not sure what he wants me to say. It's rare for Pa to be home when I wake up, and even more unusual for him to be in such a great mood.

"Are you hungry, son?" Ma asks.

"No."

"Don't eat anything. Just save your appetite for lunchtime," Pa says. "I want to take our family out to an *American* restaurant."

*Pa wants to take us out to a restaurant?* I wonder. I look over at Ma, who shrugs. We've never been to a restaurant, let alone an American one.

"Which restaurant do you want to go to, Big Head?" Pa asks as he ruffles a stack of colorful paper. "Our social worker put these in our mailbox. She says we can buy food with them."

I grab the stack from Pa's hands and flip through it. It looks an awful lot like money—green ones, brown ones, even purple ones.

"Pa, you have a lot of money!" I squeal.

"You see, isn't Uncle Sam good to us?"

Pa's goofy grin is suddenly contagious. Ma and I wear ours proudly.

"He knows we're struggling. So he decided to give these to us. I want to take the whole family out to buy our first restaurant meal with them. Where do you want to go, Big Head? Tell your Pa, and I'll take you there."

"I don't know." I give Pa a sheepish look. I don't want him to see how badly I've been wanting to go to the restaurant.

"Hmmm . . ." Pa nibbles on his bottom lip as he thinks. He thrusts his drooping cigarette toward the ceiling. "I've got it! How about that place around the corner? You know, the one with the fat boy in red overalls."

"Yeah, I want to. I want to," I say while jumping up and down. I know exactly which restaurant he's talking about—it's Bob's Big Boy. We always stop there on our walks but never go inside. Pa usually sits on the bench and smokes a cigarette while I play on the statue.

"You better start getting ready, then. Go take a bath and put on your suit."

"I don't want to wear my suit."

"Then you can't go to the restaurant. We are going to be eating with white people. If you don't look nice they will look down upon you. I'll be wearing mine, too."

I belt the Bob's Big Boy jingle while I'm getting ready, "At Bob's Big Boy, we love good food, just like you do!" They play it incessantly on the radio. It's my favorite English song and one of the few for which I know all the words.

My family saunters down to Bob's Big Boy in our best clothes. The hostess smiles and takes us to our table. She's tall, her skin is pasty, and she has shiny yellow hair. A moment later our waitress comes over. I can scarcely tell her apart from the hostess—she's also pale and towheaded and towers over our table. The two of them remind me of Big Bird from *Sesame Street*. I spin around in the booth and look toward the hostess stand to make sure they aren't the same person.

"How's everybody doing today?" the waitress asks. Her frizzy blond hair is held up by a pencil. "Can I get you anything to drink?"

"Lac, what did she say?" Pa asks me in Vietnamese.

"Drinks . . . She wants to know if we want any drinks."

Pa looks at the menu and recognizes the Pepsi logo.

"Peep . . . seee," he orders proudly.

"Okay, how many would you like?" the waitress asks.

Pa looks to me immediately.

"How many drinks, Pa?"

Pa smiles and holds up four fingers, "Fauw."

"Four Pepsis it is. I'll be back in a jiff."

Pa looks around the restaurant to see what other people are eating. Ma holds the menu up close to her face, laboring in vain to decipher the food in the pictures.

The waitress returns with our drinks.

"There you are, four Pepsis. Now, what can I get you all to eat?"

"Excuse me, miss, can you tell me what this is?" Ma asks the waitress in Vietnamese.

The waitress shakes her head, not knowing what to say.

"Is this cow meat or pig meat?" Ma continues in Vietnamese.

"Why the hell are you speaking Vietnamese to her? She's white!" Pa spits.

The waitress looks over at Pa. She's uncomfortable and visibly confused. Pa resorts to his favorite method of English communication: he points at items in the menu, nods his head rapidly, and smiles from ear to ear.

"I'm sorry, sir. Which one of these do you want?" The waitress points to the various pictures in the menu and Pa nods for every one of them. "I'm going to bring you four hamburgers with French fries. How about that?" She looks at me and winks.

Minutes later, the waitress comes back with four massive plates, each holding a juicy half-pound burger, a mound of French fries, and coleslaw. Ma and Pa look at the plates in front of them like they are from another planet.

"What is this?" Ma asks and breaks the silence.

Pa looks equally puzzled. "This looks like bread . . . this like lettuce . . . this tomato. What's this brown thing on the bottom? Is it meat?"

Ma lifts the bun with her thumb and looks at the "brown thing," like it's an insect hiding under a rock. Pa picks the hamburger patty up to his nose and smells it.

"It smells like meat," he says, with Big Boy special sauce smeared across the tip of his nose. He looks in my direction, "How do you eat this? Should we ask them for chopsticks?"

"No, Pa . . . Americans use *forks* and *knives*."

Pa surveys the restaurant to see how the other patrons are eating their burgers. "Ugh, *that* is disgusting. What a bunch of savages—they're eating these things *with their hands*!"

I love the fries, and so does Ma. They're crispy and salty, and they feel good in my mouth. We eat the bread and the lettuce and

drink our soda. Pa tries to eat his burger like the white people. It's too big for his mouth. The lettuce and tomato spill out and flop back onto his plate. He asks Ma to wrap our hamburger patties in a napkin to take home with us.

The waitress comes by to check on us. She has too many other tables on her mind to notice the debacle in front of her. "You doing all right?" She smiles and nods, so Pa and Ma do the same. She reaches into her apron for the check and slides it onto our table. "Just take care of this whenever you're ready."

Pa picks up the bill and surveys it carefully. He reaches for his wallet and takes out twelve dollars worth of crisp, colorful food stamps. He counts the food stamps out—two purple and two brown—and places them on top of the bill. He leans back contentedly in his seat and interlocks his fingers atop his belly.

"Did you enjoy your food, Big Head?" Pa asks.

"I liked the fried potatoes."

The waitress swings back by our table to pick up the check and sees the food stamps arranged neatly atop it.

"I'm sorry, sir. We don't take food stamps," she says, sliding the colorful coupons across the table to Pa. "Cash, check, or charge."

Pa nods and smiles. The two look at each other, smiling, for several seconds. Pa slides the stamps back in her direction.

She leaves the stamps on the table in front of her. "Cash only, sir. Cash, check, or charge."

Pa struggles to keep his gaze—and his smile—fixed upon the waitress as he speaks to me in Vietnamese, "Tell her I don't need any change, son. The extra is a tip for her, for the excellent service."

The waitress looks to me as I struggle to make out the words, "Um, he don't want it. For you . . . Take it. Thank you."

Pa stands up, picks the food stamps up off the table, and hands them to her with both hands. "Youl, youl," he says, placing the stamps tenderly into her fingers and clasping both his hands around hers.

Again the waitress looks in my direction. This time she points the stamps at me and the words fly out of her mouth like bullets from a machine gun, "Tell your father I cannot take these. Restaurants do not—they cannot accept food stamps as a form of payment."

I look at Pa and shrug.

She turns to Pa and waves the stamps in his face, "No, no, no stamps. Cash only. Do you have money?"

"What is this lady saying?" Pa asks.

"She's saying your favorite word . . . 'No, no, no,' about something . . ." Ma teases.

Pa laughs along with Ma in spite of himself. The waitress's frustration boils over, and she walks away in a huff. A minute later, a short chubby man in a suit comes over to our table. He's balding with a trimmed beard, and he walks with an air of authority. He rattles off something to the same effect as the waitress, before reaching into his wallet and pulling out a crisp five dollar bill.

"This is cash—dol-lars," he says, flicking the bill with his thumb and middle fingers and over-enunciating the word. "Do you have any dol-lars?"

"Lac, I have enough money at the house to pay them. Tell the man that I will go home and return with his money," Pa instructs.

"We give money. Father go home; bring you dollar," I struggle to explain.

"Oh, Christ, just forget it!" the manager chirps. He plops the five dollar bill onto the check, takes the food stamps from the table, and stuffs them into his wallet before removing another five and two ones, which he plops onto the table to complete the check. He picks the cash and bill up off of the table, waves them in front of Pa's face, and walks away.

Wary that things may not be settled, we stay put in our booth until the manager returns and escorts us out the front door.

"Go, go, go!" he says, shooing us along with his hands.

Pa waves his hands about as we walk past the giant plastic Bob's Big Boy toward home. "These crazy white people with their 'No, no, nos' and their 'Go, go, gos!'"

Because Ma and Pa constantly compare me to the children of their refugee friends, they are particularly preoccupied with my lack of progress in school. They think I'm a slow learner. They *never* think about how lonely I am in America. They're oblivious to the recurring nightmares I have of our escape from Vietnam. They confuse my cautiousness for a lack of desire. They see my desperate attempts to gain attention as the actions of a spoiled American brat.

In the evenings—once I've completed the homework my teacher assigned at school—Pa drills me in math and Chinese. His tools are an ever-increasing mound of flash cards and a blackboard that is fastened onto the wall adjacent to our dining table.

"What's this one?" Pa says. He's holding a note card toward me that reads "$14 \times 7$."

I bite my lip and stare down at the table. I try drawing the problem on the table with my finger but lose track when I move to carry the two and can't remember the number below it.

"I don't know," I say. I run my finger frantically across the table, struggling to retrace my steps.

Pa slaps the card down onto the pile. The force of his hand pushes the bottom half of the cards out across the table and into my lap. "This is going to be a long night," he says with a piercing stare. "Look at all the cards you have left to learn." He opens a fresh pack of Salems and lights up a cigarette.

My stomach grumbles. Pa won't let me eat dinner until he's satisfied with my performance. Like most nights, the rest of the family is already off to bed. The hunger makes it hard to focus

during Pa's lessons. The delicious aroma of Ma's cooking lingers in the kitchen. It doesn't help. It's after midnight before Pa gives up on me and lets me go to bed—without dinner.

He grows so dissatisfied with my concentration during his lessons that he introduces me to a young green flexible bamboo shoot. While we go through the flash cards, he lays it on the table next to his right hand. When I get one wrong, he picks the shoot up and whips me on the forearm or across the shoulder. Pa takes the bamboo shoot with him to the chalkboard. If he catches me dozing while he's writing Chinese characters on the board or droning on about life lessons, he whips me across the neck and chest.

With the bamboo shoot in hand, Pa is like a firecracker with a testy fuse; I can tell when the flame has burned the fuse down to nothing, and I wait with apprehension for him to pop. He chain-smokes and twitches his legs while he asks me questions. When I struggle to find the answer, he breathes hard, grinds his cigarette into the ashtray, and waits. If my answer is wrong, he goes to work on me with the bamboo shoot. When I cry, the blows grow harder.

To avoid more whips, I learn to endure the pain without crying. While he whacks away I surrender; I allow my body to grow numb. I can see him swinging. I can feel the wind across my face from the bamboo shoot traveling through the air. I can feel it thumping in rhythm against my chest. But I don't feel the pain.

I don't know quite what being smart is in his eyes, but I want to be that for him. Instead, I am his dim-witted son—the slow and naïve Big Head upon whom he can unleash his frustration.

He breaks three shoots across my body in the first week. When the shoots fail him, he uses anything he can get his hands on—the plastic rod from the mini blinds, a spatula, a rice bowl, a fishing rod, my notebook, a radio antenna, a wooden yardstick, and a broom handle—before settling on an extension cord as his weapon of choice. The extension cord is long and flexible. It

won't break, and the blows unleash a painful wound that stings now and burns later.

I don't feel any smarter from the beatings. They make me move like molasses for fear of taking a step in the wrong direction. I haven't even completed the third grade, but Pa wants me to become a man. The small doses of nurturing that I've learned to wait for and cherish are no more. Like sandy cliffs along the seashore, they've eroded away with time.

It's Friday afternoon and I'm working on my regular homework at the table. My mother is building an altar on a small end table behind our front door. I drop my pencil as she moves through her neurotic ritual. First, she lays down a shiny, metallic pizza tray. She places a small red plastic plate directly in the middle of the tray. On the plate she lays four massive navel oranges in a square. In the space at the center of the square she places a small packet of Chinese sugar cookies. She fills a ceramic teapot with oolong tea and sets it next to the plate along with two miniature tea cups.

Ma kneels before the table with her hands pressed together like a priest. She closes her eyes and begins an incantation, "Great ancestors, we welcome your spirits today. Please have some cookies, tea, and oranges. Our family does not ask for much, but today, we have one small request. It's our son, Lac. Why is he so slow? He forgets things, he looks confused all the time, and I catch him staring into thin air thinking about who knows what. It's like he's retarded. All we're asking is for you to grant us the small favor of making him smarter. It hurts me most to see his father beat him all the time for his stupidity. Please make him smarter so he doesn't have to endure any more beatings. That's all we ask, great ancestor of ours." She looks desperate and distressed. I try to make her feel better by staring straight down at my paper, with my pencil poised.

I wrap my homework up as Ma serves dinner. Since it's Friday, I don't have to sit through one of Pa's lessons. We sit in the living room after dinner, and Pa begins working on a watch. There isn't any junk in the house for him to fix, so he just takes things apart, cleans them, and puts them back together again. He needs something to do.

"Big Head is so fucking *slow*," Pa says while removing a screw from the watch with a miniature screwdriver. "He will never be able to keep up with those white children at his school."

"Maybe it's just a phase and he'll grow out of it," Ma says.

This line of conversation makes me nervous. I run my fingers back and forth along the seam in the couch.

"Ha! I doubt that," he says without looking up from the watch. "You haven't . . . and we know he got this from you. There's no way *my* genes produced such a stupid child."

Ma slides Quy's pajama top over her head. "Do you remember what Lanh did with his kids? They, too, were slow, but look at them now."

Pa has the shade off the lamp and is holding the watch next to the bulb, examining it through a jeweler's loupe. Ma's suggestion captures his fancy enough to pull him away from his project. "He got help from that medicine man over in Chinatown, didn't he?"

"Yes, he did. Do you think it might help Big Head?"

"It couldn't hurt. Lanh's kids are at the top of their class." Pa looks warily in my direction. "I'll go and see the medicine man tomorrow morning to find out what he thinks."

Pa shakes me awake the following morning. His hands are cold, and he smells like cigarettes. He must have been outside. "Get up and come into the kitchen. Your mother cooked something special for you."

Something special for me? My birthday isn't until September. Maybe she made that mackerel stew! I throw the covers off

and run out into the kitchen, barefoot and in my pajamas. Ma is stirring a steaming kettle. My excitement builds. I don't know why she's making stew for breakfast. And then I smell it—the aroma of ginger and Chinese herbs. It's the scent that lingers in our apartment when someone is sick. It's not the smell of good grub.

I grab a chair from the dining table and drag it across the kitchen over to the stove. I scramble up onto the chair and peer into the bubbling clay pot.

"It's almost ready. Don't ask me what it is." Ma's voice is stern.

I stare into the boiling, brown liquid. A thin layer of brackish sediment forms a foamy ring around the rim of the pot. The steam releases a scent that's reminiscent of the herbal stores Pa drags me through in Chinatown.

"Lac, go sit down at the table. I'll bring it over to you when it's ready."

I sit at the table and wait, fork in hand. After a while, Ma kills the burner and puts a lid on the pot. She picks the pot up with a pair of oven mitts and carries it over to the table. Quy runs over from the living room and takes the seat next to me.

"I want some," she squeaks.

"I made this for your brother," Ma replies.

Quy flops back onto her haunches and frowns. Ma removes the lid, blooming a mushroom cloud of steam above the table. Quy gets a whiff of the vapor and casts me a disgusted look. She runs into the living room and plops onto Pa's lap. Pa puts his paper down and joins us at the table.

"You don't have to eat it all but just eat a good amount." Ma says as she digs into the pot with a pair of serving spoons.

"It will make you smart and take away all of those stupid demons from your head that keep you from memorizing your multiplication tables," Pa says with a hand on the back of my neck. "And the more you eat, the smarter you'll get."

Ma lifts the spoons up out of the broth. She cradles a throbbing round lump of pink flesh between them that's about the size of a softball. She dumps it awkwardly onto my plate. It lands with a splat. I can tell that it's meat, but it's nothing I've ever eaten before. The oblong hunk of flesh is riddled with blood vessels and deep crevices that look like tendons. I lean over my plate to sniff it. The smell is so pungent that my head snaps back.

I look up at Ma and Pa with a grimace.

"You see, I told you he'd be too scared to eat it," Ma says.

"Shut up. You're making it worse," Pa mumbles, his face frozen in a forced smile. "Look Big Head; it's good for you . . . I'll even eat it."

Pa takes the spoon, stabs it into the top of the flesh and forces a spongy piece loose. He blows on it to cool it down and then puts it into his mouth. He smiles and chews gingerly, "Mmm . . . It's sooo goood. I feel big and strong and smart already." Pa looks over at Ma and they both smile and nod their heads at me like puppets. "The herbs mask the taste of the brain. You can't even taste brain; it's all herbs. Here, you try it."

Pa scoops another piece and points the spoon in my face. I purse my lips and shake my head. I'm not eating brain. I scoot my chair back and stand up to leave.

"Sit back down and open your mouth!" Pa shouts. "I'm going to beat you right now if you don't open your mouth and eat this cow. Now!"

I look over at Ma, hoping she'll save me. "Eat it," she says. "You're so slow; you need these vitamins to make your head work better."

Quy opens her mouth wide, which makes Ma chuckle. "You see, your little sister's not afraid. Give her some to try."

Pa feeds Quy what's in the spoon. Her face turns sour as soon as he pulls the spoon from her mouth. She spits the piece of brain out onto the table.

Pa's eyebrows slant into the shape of a *V*, and his forehead

wrinkles. He scoops the piece off of the table and shoves it back into Quy's mouth. "You said you want to eat it, now eat it."

Quy chews it three times rapidly and then swallows it. "It's so bitter!" she cries and then runs out of the room.

"All right, Big Head, it's your turn."

I take the spoon reluctantly from Pa's hand and stab it into the brain, which shakes back and forth. I scoop out a small piece and look at it, resting there on the spoon. *This was inside a cow's head.* I picture a cow standing in our kitchen, looking at me with its deeply set, dark-brown eyes.

I slide the piece into my mouth. The spoon clanks against my teeth on the way out. I close my mouth and the piece of brain is mashed between my tongue and the roof of my mouth. It's soft like mashed potatoes, but it tastes like liver. The piece of brain becomes grainy as it melts in my mouth. It's more sweet than salty. Sweet and bitter. *I don't want to eat sweet cow brains.*

I force another piece into my mouth.

"Good, good. Eat some more. Eat the whole thing." Ma's eyes are wild.

I shake my head with my mouth full. I know there is no way I can eat the whole thing.

"I don'th *like ith.* Ith sthmells like medithine," I mumble in English with steam escaping my mouth.

My parents exchange confused looks. I nod and smile, praying that my English has impressed them and they can now appreciate what I'm learning in school.

"He says it tastes like medicine," Quy calls out in Vietnamese from the living room.

"That's why it's good for you," Ma says.

"I don'th wanth anymore."

"He says he doesn't—"

"Eat!" Pa interrupts, slamming his fist onto the table.

I can feel the tears welling up behind my eyes.

Pa offers a bribe. "If you finish the whole thing, you can go outside to play."

*Go out to play?* I give Pa a massive, brain-stuffed grin. This is a fair trade.

I spend the next half hour gorging myself on cow brain. I scoop and stuff massive chunks down my throat, only to gag and retch half of them back onto the plate. I have to eat the whole thing to go out and play, so I scoop them up off the plate and try again. I munch away with my eyes closed, inhaling deeply before each swallow.

I'm forced to eat a boiled cow brain every Saturday morning until I finish the third grade. A couple of weeks into the summer, I break out in hives after eating one, which makes it my last. As far as I can tell, I don't get any smarter from the effort.

# CRAZY

Crazy got hold of me last night.

Quy extends her limp hand in a halfhearted gesture of compliance as we head for the door. I clasp my flaccid hand with hers. We walk out the front door and lumber down the steps and onto the sidewalk toward school.

"Keep a close eye on your sister, Big Head," Pa yells from the doorway. "I don't want to come home from work and hear you failed in your duty as a big brother."

Quy and I are dressed in matching puffy blue and yellow bomber jackets that were handed down to Pa by another refugee family. I look back at Pa and Ma and smile to reassure them.

The moment we're out of site, Quy and I yank our hands apart in a simultaneous demonstration of disgust. Quy's friends have gathered down the block, and she sprints over to join in their giggling.

I stop a couple of houses away from them and wait for Johnny to arrive. I get to thinking about the directions Pa showed me the previous day. That was our first day of the school year, with Quy beginning the second grade and me entering the third. Pa walked the two of us from our apartment to the campus. But upon our arrival, he revealed that he was simply showing us how to get to our new school. We'd be on our own from then on. Many of the other children in our neighborhood take the bus to school, but Pa is too mistrusting of the bus system to put us on one. Before he left us at school, Pa reminded me several times that it's my duty to protect my sister and that he'd be keeping a close eye on my performance. I can't get that thought out of my head while I wait for Johnny.

The air is unusually cold and crisp for a fall sunrise in Los Angeles, and the biting morning wind makes our noses red and runny. As Johnny and I wander through the streets on our six-mile trek to school, we entertain ourselves by blowing "smoke" from our mouths. We laugh and snort as each warm breath condenses into a rising stream of vapor.

We pass building after building on Sunset on our way to school. Johnny and I are so busy chatting and fooling around that the storefronts blend together in a sickening barrage of pastel stucco. I'm surprised to see that we're lagging so far behind Quy and her friend; they're a good fifty yards ahead of us, turning the corner onto St. Andrews.

As Johnny and I near the corner, a shadowy figure lurking beneath the awning of the last façade catches my attention. The figure rocks nervously from side to side as we pass the building. Before we can turn the corner, he leaps out from the shadows and stops us in our tracks. He's a young Mexican man wearing cutoff

jean shorts, a black hooded sweatshirt, and corduroy house shoes without socks. Johnny and I take a quick step back in response to his presence, bumping into each other awkwardly.

The man stands there sizing us up in silence. He scratches hard on the left side of his neck with his right hand and fumbles about inside the large pocket on the front of his sweatshirt with the other. His bloodshot eyes protrude so far out the front of his head that they look like they might just pop out and fall onto the sidewalk. They move rapidly in every direction—peering behind us, across the street, and over his shoulder.

The strange man frightens me, so I step into the street to get away from him. He pulls out a small, dirty Swiss army knife, grabs me by the jacket, and lifts me back up onto the curb. He swings me around by the jacket and pins me up against the wall, the base of the knife held tightly against his stomach and the blade pointing at my face.

"Run, Johnny!" I scream.

Johnny just stands there frozen in place, with his arms raised in surrender.

A steady rush of cars passes us on the street, but no one bothers to stop or even honk their horn.

"How much money you got?" the stranger asks, breathing into my face. His breath is stale and moist and it smells so bad that it makes my nose tingle. He doesn't look like the bums I usually see on my way to school. His clothes are freshly soiled. His face is filled with bumps and rashes that look like pimples that refused to pop. His neck is scratched raw and covered with scabs. There's a huge gap between his yellow front teeth, which hang from bleeding gums. His chapped, cracked lips are bordered by a thick, white ring of dried saliva.

"No money . . . no money," I tell him.

"Don't fucking lie to me, Chino," he grunts.

I think about the dollar Ma gave me yesterday, but I can't remember if I grabbed it from my dresser. I can feel the prick

of the five-dollar food stamp Ma had shoved in my shirt pocket on the way out the door. She wants me to stop by Ron's market after school to pick up green onions and sugar. I don't intend to disappoint her.

He pats my pockets with one hand and holds the knife to my face with the other. He finds the dollar bill in my jacket.

"What's this, little Chino? I thought you had nothing." He puts the Swiss army knife back into his sweatshirt and pats me some more with both hands. He reaches into my shirt pocket and finds the food stamp.

"What else you got, liar?" he shouts in my face.

"Nothing," I say, more angry than scared. Now I won't be able to buy a Big Stick and a bag of Pop Rocks from the ice cream truck after school.

"Take off your shoes."

I step on the heel of each shoe and flick it off. He takes a look inside my shoes and then rubs down each of my feet. Disappointed, he yanks on my collar to see if I'm wearing a necklace. "How 'bout you, *flaco*?" he asks, turning to Johnny.

"I got nothing," Johnny replies while patting himself down and pulling out his pockets.

The stranger must believe him because he takes off running around the corner and up St. Andrews—the same direction Quy and her friend are walking to school.

Anger rushes over me. I run to the corner to see where he's headed. He's speed-walking down the street. Several blocks down, I catch a glimpse of Quy's blue and yellow bomber jacket. I need to protect her. I take off running down the adjacent block so that I can warn Quy before he gets to her. Johnny runs, too. Johnny's legs are longer than mine, and I struggle to keep up with him. Johnny and I cover block after block before I catch sight of Quy and her friend on the other side of a gas station. We cut through the pumps and I run up to my sister, wheezing.

"What?" she asks, annoyed.

I place my hand on Quy's shoulder and look up and down the block. The stranger is nowhere in sight.

"Get away from me!" she shrieks, wriggling out from under my hand.

Her friend giggles and they run off down the block toward school. I spot the stranger lurking in an alley on the other side of the street. He leaves us alone, and we make it the rest of the way to school without a problem.

I tell Ma when I get home that I lost her food stamps.

My regard for Quy grew with the arrival of my baby brother, Vinnie. He was walking by the time I finished the third grade and was a dream come true for me. I finally had a live-in friend to fill some of the void left by Vu. When I was at home I'd spend every minute with Vinnie, waking up early each morning to play with him before I left for school. Ma taught me how to change his diapers, feed, and burp him.

I savored my time with Vinnie because I knew that it might not last. He wasn't my first baby brother. A couple of years prior, when we lived in the studio apartment in Hollywood, my mother had become pregnant. Toward the end of the pregnancy, she and Pa came home bubbling with excitement—the baby inside Ma's belly was a boy. A boy named Zeal. I'd finally have a little brother.

I pestered Ma incessantly to go ahead and just poop Zeal out, but she would just laugh and remind me that people can only poop when they need to. Pa was working at the restaurant in Chinatown, and I wasn't in school, so Ma and I had plenty of time trapped inside the studio to think about the baby.

Our tiny apartment was infested with vermin, which made an excellent distraction from my impatience. I would hunt the rats, roaches, and daddy longlegs that swarmed the place. The rats were too fast for me to catch, so I focused on the insects, which

were much slower and less intelligent. The roaches that carried eggs were my favorite target. Roaches store their eggs in a casing that hangs from a female's back. I'd stab it with a pencil and watch the mother take off without her young. The eggs inside the pouch looked like little brown Tic Tacs. I'd take each one out and drop it in a jar. Most would die before hatching. Some were born inside my glass prison.

Most evenings, Pa would come home from the restaurant and work himself into a rage over the rats and insects scurrying across our apartment floor. At first, he would wander the studio like a madman, spraying the pests with Raid. When that didn't stop them, he laced the studio with rat poison and used fumigators. Pa loved to spray. He'd bite his lip and pop the caps off the fumigators like they were grenades. Then he'd sit in his chair and smile as a thick fog engulfed the apartment.

The fumes that lingered in the apartment left me chronically sickened and fatigued. My sinuses dripped an unusual, pepper-flavored mucus, and I developed a violent cough. Thinking my illness was the common cold, Pa rubbed Tiger Balm on my throat, chest, and in my nostrils. It didn't help.

Ma got the worst of it. The fumes made her throw up often, and she had trouble breathing. Pa had her hold a wet towel to her nose to "filter out the pesticide" for Zeal. His advice seemed to help Ma with the vomiting and breathing, but the poison held dire consequences for my little brother. When Zeal was born, he was rushed by ambulance from the French Hospital in Chinatown to the massive Children's Hospital in Los Angeles. Zeal's little, misshapen lungs just didn't work well enough to give his body the oxygen it needed, and the doctors at Children's couldn't make them right. My newborn brother never made it home from the hospital. The doctors said the Raid was the culprit. The crib that Pa had pulled from the Dumpster—and had been so careful to fix and polish to perfection—sat empty in our apartment collecting dust for nearly two years, until the day that Vinnie came home.

_____

Our new apartment was much bigger than the old studio—a solid nine hundred square feet versus two hundred and fifty—and my father often took people in. Some stayed for a day or two, while others joined us for weeks and months at a time.

I hated having an extra mouth at the dinner table. It meant our meager meals were split into smaller portions to feed our guests. I'd go to sleep hungry unless I filled the extra space in my stomach with condensed milk. The government gave the milk to us in abundance, but it gave me diarrhea every time I drank it. I'd drink it anyway to fill my belly.

The most random people passed through our home. One time, it was a Chinese bum. Pa brought him home and had him park his grocery cart full of black plastic trash bags on the side of the apartment. I'd never seen an Asian bum before and assumed they didn't exist. Pa and the bum would share sob stories until the wee hours of the morning. The bum didn't stay long—just enough to eat for a couple of days and clean himself up. Pa gave him some old clothes to change into, including a beanie my grandma Ne had knitted for me in Vietnam. Pa said he needed the beanie more than I did. After the bum left, Pa made me clean the dirt rings he had left behind in our bathtub.

And then there was my cousin Crazy.

Crazy was in his mid-twenties when he made it over to America. My father let him stay in our apartment until he figured out how to make it on his own. Crazy stayed with us for eight years.

We called him Crazy for obvious reasons. He had an abundance of odd habits, including his refusal to cut his nails with a clipper. Instead, he would chew them off with his teeth. Crazy would sit on our sofa with one foot resting comfortably on the floor and the other one in his mouth. Although my father smacked me whenever I picked at my nails, he never said a word to Crazy.

Crazy stood just five feet tall and wore his jet-black hair in an overgrown bowl cut. His eyes were small and tight, and he'd often sit on our sofa with his hands on his knees, watching. I hated the way he'd follow me around the room without moving his head. His eyes would pursue me from beneath those tight eyelids like a crocodile waiting for its prey.

Crazy continually tried to get Pa to join him in sampling the hookers that hung out in front of our apartment.

"Come on, Uncle, it'll be fun. I'll even pay for you," Crazy pleaded.

"Nah. I have kids. I can't be doing that. Plus, I've been reading in the paper about this new disease called AIDS. They say you can die from it."

"It's nothing your potent sperm can't kill."

"You're right, but still. Why don't *you* go? They're all waiting for you out there on the corner." My father giggled with a look in my direction.

Crazy couldn't keep his hands to himself, whether it was with the hookers or anyone else. He touched people, even those he just met, in inappropriate places. One time he poked at my mother's breast.

"You can't do that!" Pa scolded. "You're lucky it's just your aunt; if you do that to a white person, they'll call the police."

"I'm just playing."

"You can't play like that. Don't be crazy, Crazy."

One time when we were watching a Lakers basketball game on TV, Crazy slapped Pa's ass after Kareem had sunk a skyhook on Robert Parish. Pa grabbed Crazy by the arm and pulled him close to his face.

"You know who the fuck I am?" Pa shouted. "You touch me or anyone in my family again, and I will kill you. You hear me?"

Crazy stared back into my father's face for a moment before fixing his gaze on the floor. Apparently, he wasn't *that* crazy; he understood that my father *would* kill him—on a moment's

notice. But something in Crazy's eyes made me believe that he would break his promise someday.

At first, I thought Crazy was playing some kind of joke on me when he'd secretly pinch my penis through my pants as I walked pass him. But now he does it so much that it makes me uncomfortable. I'd like to tell Pa, but I'm afraid. So instead, I tell Ma how he's always grabbing me.

"He's crazy. Just ignore him," she says.

"I tried to ignore him and he won't stop," I whine.

"He's just trying to play with you. He's older than you, so you can't tell him what to do. You need to show respect for your elders."

"But I don't like it."

"Show respect, Big Head."

"I'm going to tell Pa."

"You know what will happen if you tell your father?" Ma cocks her head and puts a hand on her hip.

Silence.

"He will get very angry—so angry that he might kill Crazy. And then the police will come and they will put your father in jail forever. Do you want that to happen?"

I shake my head.

"Then show some respect. Crazy is older than you, and he's just playing with you."

The next evening, Pa insists I take a shower with Crazy in order to save water. I don't mind showering with Pa, but I'm terrified to go in there with the crocodile. Still, there's no use in trying to disobey Pa.

Crazy thinks bathing together is a great idea. He heads straight to the bathroom and hops in the shower. I gently push the door open with the tips of my fingers and enter the bathroom. Droplets of condensation are already cutting their way

through the fog on the mirror. Just like Pa, Crazy is whistling and singing behind the curtain. I hang my towel on the rack and turn to enter the shower. Crazy stops his song. My stomach sinks—I can see his piercing eyes staring at my naked body through the crack in the curtain. Showering with my cousin isn't going to be like showering with Pa at all.

I step into the tub and grab the bar of soap. Ma or Pa always scrubs me when I bathe, and I don't want Crazy to do it. He stops washing his hair and insists on helping me. I refuse.

"I'm going to wash your hair then," Crazy says.

He squirts shampoo into his hand and works it into a lather on my head. Crazy has a funny way of washing my hair. He stands behind me and caresses my scalp with tendril-like fingers. He scrubs my hair so tenderly—even more gently than Ma. It feels like he's petting a cat.

"Hurry, I have shampoo in my eyes," I screech. My eyes are burning.

"You shut up. Your hair is dirty. I need to clean it good," Crazy says.

Crazy leaves the shampoo in my hair and begins scrubbing my body. I don't like the way he rubs my shoulders. He works his way down my sides. He reaches around to rub my stomach and his hairy penis pokes me in the back. My body grows stiff, and a wave of panic rushes over me. When his hands make their way down to my penis, I leap out of the shower so abruptly that the curtain almost comes with me. I slip and fall onto the bathroom floor. I grab my towel from the rack and run down the hall with soap all over my body and shampoo bubbles in my hair.

I run into my parent's room but they aren't there. I dry off, dress myself, and head out into the living room, where Pa is sitting in his chair puffing a cigarette and reading the Chinese newspaper. I can hear Crazy singing his song again in the shower.

I stare at Pa, wondering if I should tell him. He's laughing

about something he read, his cigarette dangling from his lips. I want to tell him, but I can't get Ma's words out of my head. *He will get very angry—so angry that he might kill Crazy. And then the police will come . . .*

I manage to stay out of Crazy's clutches by hopping in the shower with Vinnie; Ma bathes him every evening before Pa gets home.

On Halloween, the sugar rush keeps Vinnie and me up late. But Vinnie passes out the moment we crawl into bed together. I lie there behind him, thinking. I'm starting to doze off when I hear Crazy come home from work. He takes a shower and comes into our room. But instead of sleeping in his bed, on the other side of the room, he crawls into ours.

Crazy curls up behind me and spoons me. I pretend I'm asleep. His hand drifts down my chest and slides under the elastic waistband on my pajama bottoms. Crazy begins fondling my penis. I push his hand away with my elbow. He continues to fondle me and makes grunting noises in my ear, so I push his arm away harder. I'm too terrified to speak. I continue to pretend that I'm sleeping and hope he will go away.

Crazy snuggles up even closer. He crawls over me to spoon my brother. I feel Crazy struggling as he searches for an entry to Vinnie's pajamas. I crawl over Crazy and lay between him and my brother. He pulls my penis out of the opening in my pajama bottoms and begins stroking it.

Erections are a novelty that I enjoy. I get them watching the *Price Is Right* models in their bikinis. I get them when the prostitutes out front flash me their breasts. Erections are warm and tingly and they make me feel like I'm floating. This one is different. It's cold and suffocating and painful. I lie there like a lifeless corpse that's being devoured by a starving vulture. And then, suddenly, Crazy stops touching me, rolls over, and falls asleep. I lie awake most the night, hugging my brother and crying.

## chapter six

# HEAVY JAVI

Shakey's Pizza Parlor. I was never there for the pizza.

I don't consider our neighborhood on Sunset Boulevard a poor one. The lawns are green and manicured, daisies and pink roses grow in the spring in front of our building, and the people are interested in their neighbors. The real poverty is *inside* my house—where I go to bed hungry most nights, where I'm starved for affection, and where my father's unpredictable anger has us walking on eggshells.

Things are different outside. The people I meet all look and act so differently from my family. They show interest in me and treat me kindly. There's the Armenian man downstairs who can

eat an onion like an apple, the itchy Haitian woman who sells her body to buy crack, and the elderly Vietnamese couple next door who beg Pa to give them my urine, so that they can drink it and grow younger. Even the Vietnam veteran living in the apartment further down, who uses racial slurs like "gook" and "wet back" so freely, asks me how school is going and gives me candy. The people in our neighborhood think I'm the cutest kid on the block, and that keeps me coming back for more.

But Pa usually wants me to go outside to play with the Asian kids. He doesn't trust whites, which to him means anyone who isn't Asian. The few Asian kids on our block bore me when I try and play with them. They act too much like my family, and the only things they like to play with are Chinese jump ropes, kites, and paper ninja stars.

Lately, however, I haven't had to worry. I play with whomever I want because Pa is far too sick to keep track of me. His illness started a few months ago, when Ma was still pregnant. He had a constant aching in his stomach, which she joked was sympathy pain. By the time she gave birth to my baby sister Bo, Pa was already bedridden and unable to work. Tiger Balm and Chinese herbs do little to quell his pain, and he refuses to see a doctor. He just lies there groaning and vomiting a gooey brown liquid into an old paint can by the bed. He's so sick that he can't even smoke his beloved cigarettes anymore.

Ma is with him day and night. Between caring for Pa and Bo, she hardly notices when I come and go. I spend the bulk of my afternoons and weekends in Shakey's Pizza Parlor across the street from our apartment. Shakey's is the main hangout for all of the kids in the neighborhood. There's always a dozen or so of us in the parlor, and we watch a bulbous Mexican kid named Javier play *Spy Hunter*. Javier acts like it's his game. He waddles into Shakey's, goes right up to the machine, and pushes whoever is playing out of his way. All of the kids in Shakey's are so scared of Javi that we just watch him play and

cheer him on. I don't know where in the world he gets all of those quarters.

Javi is the same age I am, but he must weigh twice what I do. And he's a filthy animal. He always wears the same outfit—a pair of black Levi's, a cream colored T-shirt that was once white, and a black hooded sweatshirt that he throws to the ground when he gets too sweaty playing, which is pretty much any time he's pumping quarters into that machine. Sometimes I'll get distracted from cheering Javi on and just watch the beads of sweat work their way down the rolls on the back of his neck. He must not even feel them beneath all of that skin. When he runs out of quarters and drops his arms to his side, it pulls the rolls in his neck taut, revealing stripes of dirt that have accumulated within each crevice. The most distinct is the scent of corn tortilla his body emanates.

Javi's mission in life is to get the high score on the *Spy Hunter* machine in Shakey's. He'll burn through an hour or two just slurping on an RC Cola from the all-you-can drink soda fountain and beating on the *Spy Hunter* buttons. The thick glass protecting the game's screen bears a crack from Javi's frustration. There are ten slots on the high-scores page, and "Javi Loco" is inscribed in every one of them except for the coveted top spot. The highest score belongs to "Trucker." We don't know who Trucker is, but every time Javi posts a score that's anywhere near the high score, we'll come in the next day after school to discover the bar has been raised even higher.

When Javi gets excited playing *Spy Hunter,* he'll reach out and smack whoever is watching him right in the face. The other kids cry and move away from the machine when this happens, but I stand pat while my ears ring and my vision blurs. The meaner Javi is to me, the more I want to be his friend.

"You going to take your nunchucks out and fuck me up now, Chino?" Javi asks after running his palm upside my kisser.

"Nope," I say, still watching what I can see of the screen.

"That's what I thought. Now, go and get me another drink. *Apúrate!*"

Javi hands me a plastic cup with melting ice and a chewed-up straw. I take it over to the soda machine and fill it to the brim with RC Cola, just how he likes. I walk back to the machine and set Javi's soda down next to him. He picks it up and slurps it down without acknowledging the favor. I cheer him on until he destroys his last car and the screen flashes "Game Over."

"*Pinche, Spy Hunter!*" Javi yells, smacking the side of the machine with one hand and the side of my head with the other.

I look at him and smile.

"*Qué es tu problema, Chino?* You like getting hit? Eh?" Javi laughs with a snort at his own joke.

I keep smiling and reach into my pocket. I open my hand to reveal two shiny quarters.

"*Horale, Chino. Me caes bien,*" Javi says as he rips the quarters from my palm. Even in Spanish I can tell his words are laced with sarcasm.

I can't wait to get him some more quarters.

Javi isn't my only friend in the neighborhood. Whenever he isn't at Shakey's, I hang out on my friend Frog's porch. Frog's building is right next to ours—and right across the street from Shakey's—which makes it a perfect place to pass the time.

Frog's brothers call him that because of his small chin and round, puffy cheeks. His cheekbones are so round that I thought he was sucking on Gobstoppers the first time I met him. Frog also has a very lazy eye, which makes him look like he's tracking a bug to eat while he's talking to you. He is twelve, like me, but we go to different schools.

Frog's older brothers roll with the Kingsley Street Gang. They're always drinking and smoking weed on his porch, and they like to hang out with us. I like hanging out with them, too.

They're like a big happy family—always playing music, laughing, and telling stories on the porch. They give each other tattoos with a sewing needle and a bottle of Indian ink. I don't think they have real names. Even Frog's mother calls her sons by their street names: Sleepy, Cricket, Owl, and Casper.

Frog and his brothers don't call me Lac. They like to call me Little Chino or Chinito. Chino is a member of their gang who is Mexican like them but is really short and has slanted eyes. He's serving time for stealing a car, so they let me borrow his street name.

The camaraderie of the boys in the Kingsley Street Gang intrigues me. If it wasn't for Frog, I would never have a place in their tight-knit circle. I'm intimidated by their face tattoos and their baggy clothes. They don't seem scared of anyone or anything—like Pa. I'm unassuming around them, my eyes fixed on the ground as I wander across their porch to see if Frog is home. I sense heavy eyes probing me, like pit bulls waiting for their master to unleash them. Despite my insecurity, nothing bad ever happens to me when I'm around them, except for the occasional racist jokes aimed in my direction. But even the teasing makes me feel accepted.

The Kingsley boys are always pressuring me to smoke weed and drink with them. It's tempting—especially when I see Frog get so happy sipping from his brother's tall can—but Pa's angry face scares the sirens away. I decline and lean into their peer pressure by making fun of their vices.

I tell them, "Vietnamese don't drink beer. We drink snake wine and rice vodka."

"*Horale*, Chino, go and get some snake wine *de tu papi* for us, then," Sleepy says. "For now you can hit this *yesca* though."

"We don't smoke weed, we smoke opium." I continue, pulling the sides of my eyes back with my index fingers, "Make you feel better. Make you eyes small like me!" The porch erupts in laughter. Even Sleepy laughs so hard that he drops his joint. Making

Sleepy laugh is no easy task. He was shot in the back by a rival gang and lost his ability to walk. He spends most of his time rolling around the porch in a wheelchair with a scowl on his face.

The more I hang around Frog and the other Kingsley boys, the more I want to be like them. I try to dress like they do, but I can't afford the clothes they wear. So, I dig through Pa's wardrobe to find the closest thing I can. The faded blue jeans I borrow from him are bell-bottoms, but they're big and baggy enough in the waist to bear some resemblance to gang attire. Frog lends me his pair of Nike Cortez and insists I wear them because "gangsters don't wear Pro Wings." He even tucks a black bandana into my back pocket to pull it all together. I stuff my "gang" clothes into a plastic bag and hide them before going home. No matter how sick Pa is, I know it'll be the death of me if he finds out I'm spending time with the white people and dressing like them.

Even though I'm a puppet—a term for a non–gang member who is unschooled in the way of the streets—the Kingsley boys let me play the part.

"What's up, Chino?" Cricket asks with his shoulders swayed back and his thumbs hooked through his belt loops. "Where the fuck you from, *ese*?"

I stand up to respond and notice Javi walking on the sidewalk on his way to Shakey's. I puff my chest out at Cricket and throw my hands up defiantly, "*Puro* Kingsley Street Gang, *vato*! Where *you* from, *ese*?"

My gangster drawl leaves the Kingsley boys in stitches. I look over at Javi, who stands there with his mouth agape at the sight of me hanging out with the Kingsley Street Gang. But staring at gangsters isn't a smart move, as Pa learned the hard way. Javi's curious eyes catch Sleepy's attention.

"What up, *vato*?" Sleepy says, wheeling himself in Javi's direction. "*Qué es tu problema?*"

Javi puts his head down and tries to keep walking, but Cricket

and Owl jump the railing and cut him off. Cricket leans in close and speaks inches from Javi's face, "What the fuck you staring at, homes?"

Javi looks scared. He mutters something unintelligible, with his gaze fixed on the teardrop tattoos beneath Cricket's left eye. Kingsley boys earn a teardrop by getting shot or shooting someone.

"I can't fucking *hear you*, fucker," says Cricket.

"L-L-Lac . . . I was looking at Lac," Javi says.

*He knows my name! I can't believe he knows my name.*

"Ay, Chinito, you know him, homes?" Sleepy asks.

I look over at Frog for guidance. He scratches his chin to disguise that he's shaking his head no.

"Yes, he's Javi. He is my friend," I tell them.

"Then you better come up here and have a beer with us, *gordo*," Casper says, placing Javi in a playful, yet painful, headlock and dragging him up onto the porch.

The boys crack open a beer and hand it to Javi. He takes a swig and wipes his mouth on his sleeve. Javi looks around at everyone with a shit-eating grin. He just might like hanging with the Kingsley boys more than playing *Spy Hunter*.

"*Oye*, why you so fat, *ese*?" Sleepy rolls up to Javi and pats his gargantuan belly. "Don't you do no exercise, homes?"

"I exercise," says Javi.

"Let's see it, then, *ese*. Do some push-ups right now," Casper says.

Javi peers up sheepishly from behind his Budweiser tallboy. When he sees that they really want him to hit the deck, he acts like he's too busy drinking his beer.

"*Vente, cabrón*. You can't kick it with us if you don't do no push-ups," Sleepy says. He grabs Javi's can from his hand and motions toward the ground.

Javi flops onto his knees and gets into the push-up position. The boards in the deck vibrate and groan with his every move.

His belly hangs so low that it touches the deck with his arms extended. As Javi bends his arms and lowers his face to the ground, his belly is squished against the ground by the weight of his body.

"*Uno . . . dos . . . tres . . .*" Javi counts out the push-ups.

Each successive trip to the ground sends Javi's belly gushing out the bottom of his sweatshirt like silly putty. He can't make it past four and a half. Javi's arms throw in the towel and send him crashing down, chin first, onto the deck. The Kingsley boys are laughing so hard that tears are coming to their eyes.

"Okay, *güey*, maybe you're not so good at push-ups," Sleepy says, struggling to compose himself. "*No hay problema.* I bet I know what you're good at. You're good at eating, no?"

Javi nods, athirst to prove himself.

"I got something for you," Sleepy says before wheeling himself up over the threshold and into the house. He returns a moment later with a sixteen-ounce bar of government cheddar. "You think you can eat this, *ese*?"

"Easy. That's nothing." Javi says, wiping the sweat that glazes his forehead from the push-ups.

Javi grabs the block of cheese from Sleepy, rips the plastic wrapper off with his teeth, and takes a massive bite. He smiles and chews with his cheeks puffed out like a chipmunk smuggling nuts. He swallows fast and chomps down on the cheese again. I sit down next to Sleepy to watch Javi work. He stands tall, his arms hanging down at his side while he chews. I watch what's left of the cheese dangling in front of me. Javi's bite marks are large, semicircular wounds that glisten with saliva. There are grooves in the wounds where his crooked teeth cut through the cheese. Javi works the block into a small piece that he pops into his mouth. He punctuates the feat with a forceful, pungent belch.

"That's pretty good, *gordo*. How 'bout another one?" Sleepy asks.

"I can eat another one," Javi says.

Sleepy wheels into the house and returns once again with a large bar of government cheddar. Javi tears into it just like the first. It's gone in five minutes.

"*Horale, gordo. Aquí está número tres.*" Sleepy reaches his hand down into the gap between his thigh and the wheelchair. He pulls out another bar of cheese and hands it to Javi.

Javi takes a concerned look at the cheese. "You want me to eat *another* one?"

"You wanna do more push-ups, *ese*?" Casper asks.

Javi opens the third bar of cheddar delicately and takes reluctant bites. The boys slap him on the back and egg him on to eat faster. Javi works his way through half the bar before grabbing his stomach unexpectedly. "Ugh, I don't feel so good. I can't eat no more," he pleads.

"You wanna kick it? Then you gotta finish it," Sleepy reminds him.

Javi glances at the faces surrounding him on the porch. He stares at the cheese like it isn't even food. He takes another bite.

"*Horale!*" The Kingsley boys whistle and cheer.

Javi takes another bite and retches the moment it hits his lips. He cups his hand over his mouth in a fist and chokes it down, gagging between chews. The boys go nuts when Javi finishes his last bite. Javi looks at Sleepy, who flips his palms up as if to show that he doesn't have any more cheese for Javi to eat. For a moment Javi looks relieved and thrilled to be hanging out with the Kingsley Street Gang.

Then his face turns green. Javi reels back abruptly into the porch railing; the plastic wrapper from the last bar of cheese slips through his numb fingers and falls to the ground. Javi's eyes grow wild with panic. He lurches to his right and then his left like he's going to run. He flips around, grips the porch railing with both hands, and projectile vomits most of the three pounds of cheese onto the sidewalk. I'm bewildered by this turn of events and worried about Javi, but it throws the Kingsley boys

into a fit. Cricket laughs so hard that he falls off the end of the sofa onto the ground.

Javi doesn't even get a chance to turn around and see our reaction. He clutches the back of his jeans with both hands, arches his back, and dances around on his tippy-toes. A horrific smell wafts across the patio.

"Oh, shit!" Cricket yells, leaping up and pointing at Javi. "It's coming out the other end, too, *ese!*"

Javi tiptoes his way off the porch and into the street, gripping his ass the entire time. He cuts down the block and disappears into an alley. I've never seen such a guffaw—most of the Kingsley boys have dropped their beers or kicked them over during the commotion. Sleepy's joint is drowning in beer in the middle of a warped patio board. Frog is beaming, having finally seen the bully get his due. I turn the hose on and spray Javi's puke into the street.

"Yeah, Chino. Clean that shit, homes. That cheese smells like shit," Sleepy says.

Sleepy cracks open a fresh beer and takes a pull off it. I watch him while I spray. He looks heroic sitting there in his wheelchair, all tatted up, with his gun tucked in the waistline of a pair of baggy Dickies.

Sleepy notices me eyeing him. "What the fuck you looking at, Chino?"

"Is that a gun?" I ask, wanting to see it.

Sleepy finds my curiosity amusing. He taps Cricket on the arm, "Look at this puppet, ay, he wants to know if I carry a *cuete.*"

Cricket's expression makes me scared.

"Come here, Chino, you want to hold it?" Sleepy asks.

I want to hold it, but I'm scared. Pa's angry face is all I can see. I know he's stuck in bed, but I look over my shoulder toward our apartment just in case.

"Come on, *puto*, let me show you," Sleepy says.

I turn the hose off and put it down. I walk over to Sleepy, and

he pulls a black gun out from under his waistline. He pushes on the gun, which makes it click, and a black sleeve falls out of the handle.

"Here, Chino, take it. It's empty."

I reach out with both hands and take the gun. My hands drop a few inches the moment Sleepy lets go of it. It's incredibly heavy for its size.

"Is there bullets in it?" I ask.

"Fuck no, *ese*! I don't let no puppets carry a loaded gun for no reason . . ."

Cricket snatches the gun from me and stuffs it into the waist-line of my pants. "That's how you carry it, Chino," he says.

"Like *this*?" I ask, pulling my shirt over the gun.

"No, like *this*, fucker . . ." Cricket says, tucking my shirt back in so the gun shows. "You want everyone to see it."

"If anyone asks where you from, say Kingsley Street and show 'em that fucking *cuete* like you're ready to squeeze . . ." Sleepy says, "like *this* . . ." Sleepy leans back in his wheelchair, with his right hand by his waistline and his left hand in the air, flashing the Kingsley Street gang sign with his fingers.

I try to mimic him, but his reaction suggests that I've got it all wrong. Now Casper comes over, grabs me by the left ankle, and places my leg further out in front of the other one. Some of the other boys start to whistle and cheer. Apparently I'm the center of attention.

"There you go, Chino, now throw up a *K* with your fingers, *vato*!"

Frog cranks up the volume on the boom box until Zapp's "More Bounce to the Ounce" is blaring. The woofer hits the low notes with a dull thud that vibrates the porch beneath our feet. The Kingsley boys gather around me and dance the two-step. They throw their fingers in the air, flashing the sign of the Kingsley Street Gang. I do the same with one hand, but I need the other to keep Pa's baggy bell-bottoms up.

# THE NAKED TRUTH

Sprouting like a bean.

With Pa bedridden for so long, I've had complete freedom to roam the neighborhood and make friends. The tighter I get with Frog and the Kingsley boys, the more I long for the affection of the one fat friend I can't seem to crack. I saw Javi in Shakey's the day after he shot out all the cheese. He went right back to bullying the kids at Shakey's, but he doesn't terrorize Frog and me the way he used to. He'll let me stand alongside him while he plays, so long as I'm funding his game. Javi will even throw a word or two of *Spy Hunter* wisdom my way while

he plays. It's not like I'm his new best friend or anything, but at least he isn't smacking me upside the head anymore.

I've been trying to get to know Javi better while he plays, but the only thing I've gotten out of him so far—other than some game tips—is smack talk about the other kids in Shakey's. I'll laugh along as Javi shovels out insults, but as soon as I hand over the quarters, our bonding time screeches to a halt. He continues with his game as though I'm barely there. It's getting to the point where Javi doesn't even use his own quarters to play anymore. When I have money, *we're* playing *Spy Hunter.* I don't mind because Javi's reliance on my money gives the impression that we're tight. No longer am I standing behind the pack, peeking over shoulders to get a glimpse of the action. Javi wants me right beside him.

I have a bulletproof plan to win Javi over—we're going to beat Trucker's high score. If I'm not watching Shakey's play, I'm off trying to make money so that I can get back into play. I draw graffiti art pictures that I sell at school for two bucks a pop. Sleepy gives Frog and me money for ice cream sometimes, and I give mine to Javi. I also get money from Sleepy for doing favors. I'll run over to Shakey's and get Frog to come home for a buck, or even fetch things from inside the house when Sleepy is too stoned to wheel himself around. And then there's the food stamps—I've discovered I can get people to give me cash for them at the market.

I need to hurry and get Javi that high score while I still can. Three months ago, Pa decided he'd had enough of the pain in his stomach. Instead of lying there with his arm across his forehead, groaning—as he'd done every day for weeks—he fell out of bed in the middle of the night screaming. He finally wanted Ma to take him to the hospital. Since Ma doesn't drive, and it was too late for the RTD buses, one of Pa's friends picked us up and took us to the hospital.

The French Hospital in Chinatown was the nearest facil-

ity that would take Medi-Cal, my family's meager government health insurance. It's eighteen miles from our apartment. We had our own ambulance siren inside the car for the journey, and from the way Pa was screaming, I was surprised he kept it up the entire way. Ma, Quy, and I sat in the backseat of the car, with Pa stretched out across our laps. He writhed in pain the entire way. I'm just glad that Vinnie and Bo stayed home, even though they were with Crazy, so they didn't have to see Pa like that.

When the hospital staff heard Pa's screams, they wheeled him straight into surgery. After several hours the doctors came out and told us they had removed his horrifically infected pancreas. They didn't tell us they'd taken Pa's hope for the future along with it.

Pa was up and out of bed six weeks later. With the doctors putting him on permanent disability, and his body no longer able to digest food properly, he hobbled on broken glass. Now I steer clear of him as much as possible, and can see the intense irritation in his eyes every time I look out the window to see what's going on across the street. As weak as he is, I'm certain he can muster enough energy to beat my ass, so I do what's expected of me, retreat to my room, and make quick runs over to Shakey's or Frog's house when he sleeps.

"Move . . . Let the Chino in!" Javi knocks the kids around him down like bowling pins, while maintaining focus on his game.

"Sup, Javi . . . Look at that! You almost beat Trucker."

"Where you been, Chino? You got *feria*?" Javi asks.

"What's *feria*?"

"*Money*, fucker. You got quarters?"

"Just three."

"How we gonna beat the high score with just three quarters?" I wonder that myself.

"Go get more quarters. I'm gonna beat Trucker. Go!"

Where am I supposed to get more money? I can't go in the house and get food stamps. They are in my parents' room, where

Pa is resting, and if he wakes up, I'm toast. I make my way through the crowd and rack my brain for ways to make a quick buck. I could sell my urine to the elderly Vietnamese lady next door. It's been quite a while since Pa had me pee into a teakettle for her to boil and drink as tea. He doesn't charge her for it, so there's no way I could do it without him finding out. He would flip. Or he might get a kick out of my hustle. Truth is, I don't really know what Pa will think. He's unpredictable that way. Since he's in a surly mood lately, I decide against taking a chance.

I walk out of Shakey's and spy my Swahili neighbors eating Funyuns on their porch. Frederique and Francette are there. They're cousins, and their families live in the same apartment. They don't speak French, just Swahili and English. I walk over to Frederique, because I know I can get her to give me some money. She's the older of the two cousins, a little taller than Francette and a lot darker. She's fourteen years old and horny as hell. Thing is, she's a bit of a tomboy and likes to play basketball with me. Her stepdad bent a piece of rebar into a ring and hung it above their garage door. We play in her driveway some nights before dinner.

I found out that Frederique has a thing for me a few weeks ago during a game of twenty-one. Guarding her is a challenge, because she's a good foot taller than I am. On one possession I manned up behind her to keep her from getting to the basket. Usually she just runs around me, but this time she bumped and rubbed her body against mine. She just stood there bent over, dribbling with her back to the basket and grinding her ass against my crotch. When I stole the ball during her slow play, she became extra aggressive. She ran up behind me, and her defense became a seductive offense. Reaching in for the ball became playful caressing.

"You like that? Huh? You like that?" Frederique asked with a whisper.

"Like what?"

"Me guarding you like this?"

"I dunno . . . Just play ball."

"Are you hard?"

"Whatever . . ." I said, embarrassed. I was hard.

"Let me see your erection."

"What?"

"Just pull your pants down and let me see."

"No! Why?"

"I want to see what it looks like."

"No."

"Come on . . . Just show me really fast."

"Whatever, just play ball. If you beat me, then I'll show you."

She'd played easy on me for too long that night and couldn't overcome my lead.

"Hey, Frederique, can I borrow a couple of dollars?" I ask. "I want to buy some basketball cards. The new Star Magic Johnson card is out."

She makes a smacking sound with her mouth as an incredulous way of telling me, *Chinaman, please, I ain't got no money for you.*

"Come on, Rique, I'll pay you back, *pleeaasee . . .*"

"With what? How you goin' to pay me back if you borrowing money from me?"

"I don't know . . . I'll figure something out. I really want those cards."

"You *never* pay me back. You still owe me for them stupid graffiti markers."

"I *will* pay you back. Just give me four dollars."

"Four dollars? You said two!"

"Let me borrow four. I want to make sure I get Magic Johnson."

"No!" She walks off the patio and heads into her family's apartment. I follow her back into her room.

"Come on, Rique . . ."

"You crazy?"

"I'll give you something you want . . ."

"What?"

"I'll show you my thing. It's hard right now . . ."

"Stop playing . . ."

"Seriously. It's hard right now."

"Let me see . . ." she says with a huge grin. She rests her fingertips gently on each side of my rib cage and looks down at the bulge in my pants.

"I'll show you if you give me four dollars."

"I don't have four dollars. Besides, I've felt your little Asian thing already."

"You want to *really* touch it?"

Her eyes widen.

"You'll let me touch it?"

"For seven dollars."

"You said four!"

"Seven to touch it with both hands."

I unzip my pants and pull my penis out to close the deal. She reaches for it, and before she gets her hands on it, I turn around and stuff it back in my pants.

"Seven dollars."

Frederique rolls her eyes and smacks her lips, which is suddenly the cutest thing in the world.

"You make me sick . . ." she says before rummaging through her desk to get my seven dollars.

I run back across the street to Shakey's and exchange the bills for quarters. It's getting rowdy over in the arcade room—everyone is cheering for Javi. I make my way over to the machine and side up next to him.

"What took you so long, Chino?" Javi yells at me without looking up from the screen. "I almost died!"

I watch him drive for a moment. His score is up over 100,000.

I've never seen it this high. He's only 20,000 points away from Trucker.

"Juanito gave me two quarters to keep going. You need to pay him back. How many quarters you got?" Javi asks.

I reach into my pocket and retrieve two quarters for Juanito. Then I pull out a handful to give to Javi, but leave a few jingling in my pocket for later. I count the stack of quarters in my palm. "Twenty-one quarters . . ."

"*Horale!* That's a lot of quarters, ay. You going to let me have 'em?"

"Yeah, sure."

Javi looks over at Juanito and gives him a little grin. "This Chino's cool, ay. He gives me money all the time."

"All right, Chino, you down, homie!" Juanito bursts. "Javier's going to beat that score. Watch!"

The higher levels are increasingly difficult. Javi dumps quarters in as fast as the machine will take them.

Another boy nudges my arm, "Can *I* have some quarters?"

"Hell, no! He only gives *me* money. Right, Chino?" Javi says.

"Yeah . . ." I agree, which gets Javi back concentrating on his game. Behind his back, I slip the kid a couple of quarters from my pocket, which he accepts warily.

Javi's car bobs and weaves across the screen. He destroys an enemy's car with his machine guns, and his score climbs past 120,000. He hits 121,000, and his car veers into a tree and explodes. He snatches his last quarter off the glass and drops it into the machine.

"Just three thousand more points, Javi!" I gush, patting him on the back.

"I know, I know . . . Shuddup, I'm trying to concentrate," Javi spits. This hushes the entourage gathered around the machine.

It's surreal to see Javi's score climb so close to the high of 124,142 that's remained so doggedly at the top of our screen every time we play. Finally, Javi surpasses it. The high score is

his. It ticks along in unison with his points tallied on the left side of the screen. We all go nuts.

Javi's last car explodes into a ball of fire. "Fuck!" he beats on the machine. "You have anymore quarters, Chino?"

"No, I'm out."

"Fuck!" Javi bangs harder on the glass.

"We did it! You got it—you beat Trucker," I say.

The high-scores screen flashes, and Javi enters "Javi Loco" in the top slot above Trucker. I look at him, a little scared, and say nothing. I don't want to give him any more quarters.

"Come on, Chino, let's celebrate," Javi says, beaming. He fills his cup with RC, and we head over to one of the tables near the game room. All the other kids follow and fight for a seat at the table. Javi lets me sit next to him. He slurps on his soda and basks in the glow of his victory. "Did you see those missiles I got to blast the Mad Bomber with?"

*"Simon . . ."* Juanito confirms. "I knew that was the only way to kill him."

A fat white man walks right by our table and into the game room, holding a pitcher of beer and a cup. His gray hair is an overgrown mess of long curly tendrils that dangle out from his mesh cap and dance along the collar of his faded T-shirt as he walks. And he walks with purpose—right up to the vacant *Spy Hunter* machine. He takes a good look at the screen, and then smirks in our direction. I don't see many white people in my neighborhood, and I wonder if all white men have overgrown stubble and handlebar mustaches like him. He looks like an older version of the one white man in our building—a Vietnam veteran who calls us "spics" and "gooks" when he tells us to get off the grass in front of his building.

"Javi, Javi . . ." I tap him on the shoulder and try to get his attention. He doesn't pay any; he and Juanito are too busy recounting his victory.

The man at the machine is already playing. He takes long

swigs from his beer between levels and hammers away on the controls. I can hear the faint sound of the machine's signature tune, "Tommy Gun," as he plays. I hear him crash, and the game-over music plays. He takes the opportunity to refill his beer, then lifts the side of his shirt to reveal a four-barrel coin dispenser hanging from his belt. He taps the lever without looking, and a quarter drops neatly into his hand. He pushes it into the slot and continues his game.

I stand to get Javi's attention, "Javi, I think it's *him*."

"What are you talking about, Chino?"

I point to the man in the tight jeans and the snakeskin boots who's playing our *Spy Hunter* machine. "It's Trucker."

Everyone at the table watches him in silence. He reaches to his waist and pops out another quarter.

"Fucking ay, it's *really* him," Javi says.

The man pops the quarter into the machine, looks right at us, reaches for the bill of his cap, and nods. We watch in horror as he plays and plays and plays. When his pitcher of beer goes empty, he whistles and motions to the manager behind the front counter. On cue, the manager brings him a fresh pitcher of beer and takes the empty one away. The stranger plays for another hour, making his way through a third pitcher of beer. When he's finished playing, he smirks at us again and makes his way to the counter to take care of his tab. Javi and I are the only ones left. We leap up from the table and run over to the *Spy Hunter* machine. The high-scores page is flashing with the name Trucker in the top slot. He's beaten Javi's score by more than 50,000 points.

Trucker walks out the front door toward the parking lot. Javi and I run over to the window to watch him leave. I expect him to hop into an intimidating, black big rig, or maybe even a beer delivery truck, but there isn't a three-axle vehicle to be found in the Shakey's parking lot. Javi and I share a befuddled look as Trucker digs in his pocket for his keys and unlocks the door to

his vehicle—an ice cream truck. He slides the door open, steps inside, and walks over to the driver's seat. As he starts up the engine, the high-pitched melody of "The Entertainer" begins blaring from the rooftop speaker. Trucker pulls out of the parking lot and makes his way down Sunset, the music growing as dim as our hope for a high score in *Spy Hunter*.

"Go get some more quarters. I'll be here tomorrow after school," Javi says. "You better be here." Javi grabs his sweatshirt from the table and gulps down what's left of his soda. He taps me on the forehead as he makes his way toward the door. "Don't forget . . . tomorrow . . . get a lot of quarters. All right, Chino?"

"I'll try." The three quarters I've been toying with in my pocket don't feel like much anymore.

I walk out of Shakey's alone, stewing upon my dwindling options for coming up with more money. Javi and I are becoming fast friends now that I supply the quarters; I just don't know how much longer I can keep up with the demand. I should get to finishing up the pieces of art I've been working on. But how on earth am I going to do this by tomorrow?

I look across the street and see Pa on Frog's porch, talking to Sleepy. What could they possibly have to talk about? Snake wine, rice vodka? I hope it's not about the gun Sleepy let me hold! A rush of anxiety comes over me, but then I see the two of them laughing. I don't understand. Pa tells me to avoid hanging out with those "bad white people," but then he's on their porch yucking it up like they're old pals. From afar, Pa's four-foot-eleven-inch frame looks as thin as the beam he's leaning against. He's lost an incredible amount of weight since getting sick. Sleepy leans from side to side in his chair as he talks, like he wants to stand up but can't. I run across the street and walk up beside Pa to catch a piece of their conversation. Pa, as usual, has a cigarette dangling from his lips. Sleepy grabs his own from behind his ear and asks Pa for a light.

Pa leans down and flicks his Bic under the end of Sleepy's cigarette. "What happen you? Why you chair?" Pa asks, referring to the wheelchair.

Sleepy puffs on his cigarette to make sure it's lit. He blows smoke out the side of his mouth, "Got shot, homes."

"What?"

"Shot . . . with a gun." Sleepy makes a pistol shape with his fingers.

"Why? They . . . Who shoot you?" Pa tends to yell when he's excited, especially in his broken English.

"Gang bang." Sleepy looks away, perturbed. I don't think he likes talking about his accident.

"What?! Gang?!" Pa probes on, undeterred.

Sleepy takes a while to answer. He looks in the other direction and smokes his cigarette.

"What's gang?" Pa continues.

"Gang bang, homes. For my *calle*, Kingsley Street, homes. I got shot by someone who wanted me dead."

"Oh . . . no good. Why you gang?"

"I don't know, homes, it's just the way it is."

"They go jail?"

Sleepy simpers and looks at the ground, like he knows something we don't and isn't going to tell us. "It's over. It's been taken care of." Sleepy looks over at me and shrugs. I'm in no place to stop Pa from asking him so many questions.

"Oh . . . danger. Very danger!" Pa continues.

"Fuck, ay, I don't know. Let it go, homes. It's over. Let it go."

I don't think Pa understands the nature of the Kingsley Street Gang's retaliation against rival gangs. Pa doesn't know the rules of the streets here in America—one big reason why he got jumped a couple of years back by those Mexican gangsters. He's definitely blind to the meaning behind the tears tattooed under Sleepy's eye, but he finally seems to get how much Sleepy resents this line of questioning.

"No more sex for you," Pa quips, mercifully changing the subject.

"Fuck that, homes, I still get pussy." A smile comes back to Sleepy's face.

"Noooo . . . you lie," Pa teases and points his finger at Sleepy.

Sleepy thrusts his torso in the wheel chair as though he has a girl riding his lap. "Right here, homes."

"Oh . . . *vellie goood.* Happy wit girl . . . you."

I contain my amusement while Pa and Sleepy share in the joke. I don't dare let on what I know about sex. The last time I asked Pa why there are so many prostitutes on our block, he told me that I shouldn't be asking about them, and that he'll tell me when I'm a little older. Then he stopped me and said, "Whatever you do, don't stick your dick in any of those hookers. They might have Aay." I know he meant AIDS, but I don't know why he thinks I'd want to stick my penis inside anyone.

I stare at the ground while Pa and Sleepy go on about sex, and I notice that Pa is carrying two bags of groceries. *That's how I'm going to get more* Spy Hunter *money.* Now that this month's food stamps have arrived, all I have to do is trade Ma's stamps for cash with the people at the market. The last time I did this, I walked away with enough cash to buy myself a new pair of house slippers, the same ones that Frog and the Kingsley boys wear. My plan fills me with manic excitement, and I walk away from Pa and Sleepy toward our apartment. All I can think about is that yellow raincoat where Ma keeps her booklets of food stamps.

"Hey, Big Head! Can't you see I'm holding these heavy bags of groceries?" Pa yells in Vietnamese, stopping me in my tracks. "Take them inside the house to your mother." Pa is no longer the chatty cool neighbor.

On my way to our apartment, I get goose bumps just thinking about what I'm going to do. The threat of Pa finding out, although terrifying, makes the whole endeavor that much more

exciting. I open the door and take the groceries into the house. I'm greeted by the aroma of garlic and peppered mackerel. Ma is in the kitchen fixing my favorite dish.

"It has been a while since I've cooked this for you. Are you hungry?"

"I could eat the whole pot."

We have something good to eat for dinner tonight because our food stamps just arrived. We'll be back to sardines and crackers by the end of the month.

"Doesn't the smell of peppered fish remind you of your grandmother?" Ma asks.

"Ya, but not as much as the smell of mango."

"Son, I forgot to ask your father to buy fruit from the store."

"That's okay. I don't like fruit."

"It's not for you . . . I need fruit for Vinnie and Bo." Ma's tone grows more serious. "That's why the government gives us the stamps, so that we can buy nutritious things for your little brother and sister to eat."

"Oh. I can run to the store and get fruit for you," I say with a coy shrug of my shoulders.

"What a good brother! Vinnie likes bananas and Bo likes plums. If the plums are too ripe, then get her some grapes. Quy will share with them. Let me go grab you some food stamps." She releases the spoon that she's using to stir the pot and reaches behind her back to untie her apron.

"That's okay, Ma. I know where they are."

"You do?" Her voice trails off behind me as I scurry down the hall toward her bedroom.

I head straight for the raincoat in the closet. Pa will be home any moment, and I want him getting as little wind of this as possible. I reach my hand inside the large pocket on the side of the raincoat and feel an envelope. I pull it out and discover it's filled with stacks of crisp, colorful food stamps. I'm so excited that

it's hard to think straight; this will please Javi to no end. I rip a five-dollar blue stamp, for the fruit, along its serrated edge and a ten-dollar stamp for me.

I run back down the hallway toward the front door.

"How much did you take?" Ma shouts from the kitchen.

"Five dollars."

"That should be enough. Hurry home for dinner!"

I slam the front door shut. Pa is coming up the walk.

"Where are you going?" he asks. "It's dark outside."

"To the store to get Ma some fruit."

"Now? It's dinnertime."

"It'll be fast, Pa. I'll be right back."

"Don't lie to me and go play with your friends. You better get back here right away."

"I will, Pa."

I run all the way to Ron's Market and head straight to the produce aisle. I snatch up the fruit Ma wanted and wait in line, in agony, to pay for them. The cashier rings me up and I take my bag out to the front of the store. I stand next to the coin-operated horsey ride and wait. The first few people to whom I offer my stamps give me disappointed looks. Ten minutes pass and I'm so anxious that I start pacing in front of the door. I'm thinking about giving up and heading home when an old Armenian woman strolls up with her grocery cart.

"You again," she huffs.

"I have ten dollars of food stamps. Do you want them?"

"For how much?"

"Eight dollars."

"Too much."

"Six dollars."

"No. I'm scared of police."

"I'm not going to tell the police."

"No."

I'm running out of options, "Okay, five dollars."

"No. Why you do this? You young boy," she says, looking me in the eyes.

"I need cash to buy books . . . for school."

"Are you sure? I think you buy drugs."

"No way! I say 'nope to dope and ugh to drugs.'" I sarcastically recite the mantra from my school's D.A.R.E. program.

"For school? Are you sure?"

"Yes."

"Then I go inside Ron's to buy you books."

"Ron's doesn't have the books I want."

She stares into me, trying to read my face to see if I'm lying. I give her my best innocent poor-boy look. As she's analyzing and I'm posing, I can't help but notice a massive chocolate-brown mole on her nose that has three strands of hair blooming from it.

"Okay, for school I give you three dollars."

*Three dollars? That's only twelve quarters.* With that little coin, Javi would barely make it past Phase 3 on *Spy Hunter,* if he were lucky.

"My book costs six dollars."

"No. I only have *three* dollars."

"Okay, four dollars." I smile. "I want to be a doctor when I grow up. This will help me." I should quit fibbing while I still have a shot at her money. That last comment sounded really fake.

"My son Rafael wants to be doctor, too. What school you go to?"

Rafael? Not the same Rafael Kavorkian from my class, I hope.

"Uh . . . I go to Grant."

"My son go there, too. Who your teacher?"

Shit, it is the same Rafael.

"Uh . . . Ms. Taylor." I give her a fake name.

"Oh. Rafael in Ms. Flarethy's class."

I know.

"Okay, I give you four dollars," she says, breathing heavily

and digging through her oversized purse, "but for books, not drugs."

I make it home for dinner without a hint of suspicion from Ma and Pa. Ma even pats me on the head for being such a good brother and running out to buy fruit for my siblings.

But four dollars isn't enough to beat Trucker. It takes ten before we're on top again, then fifteen, and then twenty. Javi and Trucker up the ante with higher and higher scores. It goes on this way for weeks. Selling food stamps makes the money come too easily. I'm becoming Javi's cash whore. It's getting hard to see much difference between myself and the prostitutes on our block—we both do things for money that we then pass on to someone else.

I think I'm almost there. Last week, Javi brought me over to his house to show me his basketball card collection. His mother even made me a bean burrito and homemade *horchata*. I'm also hanging out with him at school every day. Javi lets me cut in line at lunch, and he always picks me to be on his team when we play *socco*—and his team always wins. After a long cold winter of solitude it feels like things are warming up—it feels like I belong. But I know this bond comes with a price.

I don't keep count of how much I've been taking until I overhear Ma lamenting how much we're spending on food.

"Did you take sixty dollars from our food stamp booklets this month?" she asks Pa.

"When?"

"Most of it this week."

"I don't take your food stamps. You give them to me when I need them."

"I thought I had more money, but when I counted it out today we're going to be short for the month. Where does all the money go?"

"Maybe you spent them but forgot you did. Just keep track of how much you're spending."

Their conversation makes me nervous, but not enough to stop funding Javi. The next afternoon when I come home from school, I make sure Pa isn't around and head straight for their bedroom. I open the door to the closet and stick my hand in the pocket of Ma's raincoat. It's empty. I check the other pocket. Empty. My neck grows hot and my mouth dry. I scour her closet and poke my hand in every pocket in her wardrobe. Empty. I look down at the floor and spy a trash bag stuffed with hand-me-downs. I pull the bag toward me to survey its contents and uncover a pink ceramic piggy bank resting beneath it.

I get up from the floor and lock the bedroom door. I peek into the slit on top of the piggy bank, but there's only darkness. I look for a way inside and notice a piece of paper taped to the side of the pig. The paper has Chinese characters on it that I don't understand. I shake the pig, and the shuffling sound it makes tells me it's filled with paper. I flip the pig over and there's a round plastic stopper at the bottom. I pull it out and cash pokes out the hole. It's real money. I grab the corner of a bill and pull it out. It's a twenty.

I contemplate taking another. There are so many greenbacks inside the piggy bank that Ma will never find out. I pull out a five and then a single. I'm relieved to be free from selling food stamps and run across the street to share the good news with Javi. By dinnertime, most of the money has vanished.

Because of his operation, Pa can't work at the restaurant anymore. He's too stir-crazy to sit around the house all day, so he rides his bike to friends' houses and does odd jobs for people. He fixes watches, electronics, anything people need, and he doesn't leave their house until he's done. That gives me a lot of time to play *Spy Hunter*. I'm taking so much money out of the pig that Javi doesn't even have to ask anymore. I'm digging in the pig every day or two and don't even bother with the singles anymore. The look on Javi's face when I present the money is worth every dollar in the world. It goes on this way for weeks.

———

It's Saturday afternoon, and Pa is at the dinner table fixing a Betamax player and teaching me how to write in Chinese. Parts are strewn across the table, and he's digging in the mouth of the player with a screwdriver in the hope that it will cough up a tape. I write on the chalkboard and blurt each character aloud. When I make a mistake, which is often, Pa corrects me and sports an increasingly dissatisfied look. The stubborn tape holds the bulk of his attention. I'm too jittery to concentrate. I know Javi is across the street playing *Spy Hunter*, and I want to know how he's doing. When we got to Shakey's yesterday afternoon, Trucker had upped our high score by a good 50,000 points. Twenty dollars in quarters wasn't enough to beat it.

"*Yào*," I say, stroking the chalk across the board to form the next letter.

"No," Pa scolds me in Vietnamese, eyes widening, "the pronunciation is *Yāo*."

Pa puts the screwdriver down and looks in my direction with furrowed brows. He's on the brink today. His lower lip starts to quiver, and his legs twitch with nervous anticipation. He doesn't say another word. He's like a balloon that's ready to burst—every mistake I make at the board is another breath of air exhaled inside him. I turn back to the board and start on the next letter. I don't want to see it coming.

The doorbell rings. It's Pa's old friend Chao. I call him Uncle Chao out of respect for his age. The two met in Vietnam at one of Pa's bars. Chao would loiter there for hours, chatting and sipping on soda water. Thank God he's here. Pa hasn't seen him in weeks, and they have much to catch up on.

Pa gets up from the table to greet Uncle Chao, and his expression turns from hostile to warmhearted. "We'll finish this later," Pa tells me, pouring Uncle Chao a cup of tea.

I lay the chalk down in the sill and run off down the hall

toward Pa's bedroom. I pause in the doorway. Ma is feeding Bo on the couch in the living room. Pa is already lost in conversation. I can hear him at the table, waxing pessimistic about his future because of the surgery. I tiptoe my way over to the closet. Pa's angry face is all I can see. I shake it off. I pick the piggy bank up and fumble with the plug. I stick my finger in the hole and feel around. I pinch the first bills I feel against the side of the piggy bank and slide them out. It's a ten, a twenty, and two fives. I stuff them into my pocket and cork the piggy bank. I look over my shoulder to make sure no one is coming and then slide the piggy bank back into the corner of the closet. I walk softly down the hallway and out the front door.

Out front, Frederique and Francette are talking to their friends on their porch steps. I ignore them and dash down the block to the light where I can cross over to Shakey's. Frog and the Kingsley boys are on his porch drinking beer and smoking weed.

"*Qué honda*, Chino!" Sleepy yells. "Where you going, *ese*?"

"To Shakey's . . . to play video games."

"Tell your old man I got laid last night, homes," Sleepy continues, thrusting his pelvis skyward, "right outside your window, *ese*."

The laughter dies down as I make my way across the street.

I enter Shakey's and walk toward the front counter. The manager sees me coming and pops the cash register drawer open. I change my bills into quarters and stuff my pockets with them. I have to hold them shut to keep the quarters from spilling out on my way to the game room.

Javi is playing *Spy Hunter*, and his score is already approaching Trucker's. *With all this money, Trucker is never going to catch us.* Javi is in the zone; he's sweating out of every pore. He's so far along in the game that I don't even recognize the level he's playing. I stand there feeding the machine quarters. Javi lets me take the controls so that he can go take a piss and refill his soda. He's back in a hurry.

"Did you die, fucker?" he asks.

"No."

"Better not fuck up my game."

I'm so enthralled by the game that I lose track of time and space. Javi's score climbs 50,000 points above Trucker's, then 100,000, and then 150,000. I cheer and holler, pounding Javi's shoulders in triumph with each new level passed.

"Fuck Trucker!" I yell. "Javi is the man!"

A heavy hand taps me on my right shoulder. I don't turn around.

Another tap, harder this time.

"What? I'm playing. Leave me alone," I say without taking my eyes off the screen.

The hand clutches my shoulder and yanks me around. It's Pa. He's quiet and collected. I don't think he's ever been here before. Judging by the look on his face, I don't think we're going to sit down for pizza.

"Let's go home," he says. His voice is placid.

"Is it dinner already?" I ask, trying to make conversation.

Silence.

"I got the high score on this game, Pa." Maybe he'll be proud of me.

No response.

"Is Uncle Chao still at the house?"

He walks me across the street and right past the crew on Frog's porch without saying a word. Pa opens the door to our apartment and waits for me to walk in. Ma and Uncle Chao are sitting in the kitchen. Ma looks disappointed. The empty look on Uncle Chao's face tells me I'm in for the worst. Pa slowly unbuttons his shirt. He pulls his arms out of the sleeves and walks it over to the kitchen table. He lays the shirt on the back of a chair and approaches the china cabinet, slowly, methodically, like he's involved in a royal ceremony. He reaches up behind the lip at the top of the china cabinet and fingers around until he gets ahold of

what he's after—his bundle of whipping rods. He splashes them down onto the kitchen table. The rulers, tree branches, and extension cords skid to a stop, but the fishing and mini-blind rods roll off the table onto the floor.

"Lay down on the sofa," Pa orders.

Ma can see the terror on my face. She looks away. I look over at Uncle Chao. He fixes his gaze upon the floor. I can't help but cry at the pain I'm about to endure. Before the tears can fall from my eyes, Pa storms through the kitchen, grabbing a half-inch eucalyptus branch from the table on his way by. He grabs me by the hair and slams me face down onto the sofa. The whipping starts while the sofa cushions are still vibrating from the impact of my body. The flexible branch slices through the air with a high-pitched whoosh. It feels razor-thin as it pops against the back of my bare legs. Each blow from the branch shoots stinging tendrils up my back and makes my ears ring. Pa gets into a rhythm and the blows grow more frequent until there is no discernible pause between the smack of the branch against my brown skin and the hiss of the next blow. I turn my head toward my father and watch him move in slow motion. He bites down hard on his lower lip and swings with both hands, his eyebrows pointed in a downward arrow that signals the direction of the blows. The lacerations raise the flesh in crisscrosses on the backs of my legs. He strikes my legs until no virgin flesh remains. The impact of the blows grows dull and impersonal; I feel less of each new layer he adds to the wounds.

After five minutes of leveling my flesh, Pa stops. I lie there and watch him. He is drenched in sweat. His face is pale. His shallow breaths are interrupted by wheezing and coughing. He sits down in his chair with his hands on his knees. Then he leans back and reaches into his pocket for his cigarettes. He shakes a cigarette out the end of the pack, puts it in his mouth, and lights it. He takes a long drag and fixes his eyes upon me. My wounds are growing hot, throbbing and burning with the beat of my heart. My frozen tears find the courage to fall.

Pa relaxes a little after making some progress on his cigarette.

"Where are you getting the money to play video games so much these days?" he asks.

My head and neck grow cold. *He's going to call the police and have them take me to jail.* From the description of the Kingsley boys, jail doesn't sound like a good place for me.

"My Mexican friend gave me the money."

"What?" Pa leaps up out of the chair. "Where did you say you got the money?"

"My Mexican friend . . ."

Pa throws his cigarette onto the floor and grabs a ruler from the table. He pins my shoulder to the couch with his left hand, turns the ruler sideways, and uses his good hand to strike me in the ribs with the sharp edge. I close my eyes. He swings his arm around like a windmill, bringing the ruler down against my side over and over again until it breaks. He tosses what's left of the ruler and goes into the kitchen. He returns with Ma's wooden broom. He snaps it over his knee—near the end with the bristles—and holds the shaft above me like a sledgehammer.

"I'm going to ask you again . . . Where did you get money to play video games?"

When my father asks me a question, I am to answer him in a timely and obedient manner. Silence.

He thrusts the broomstick down with both hands and cracks me in the side. It knocks the wind out of me. I fold up like a chair and suck for air.

"WHERE?" he spits.

Wheezing.

He cracks me again.

"WHERE? TELL ME WHERE!"

He waits until I catch my breath. I lie there, clenching my stomach, and I look up at him. I look him in the eye. The veins

are bulging out of his forehead. His mouth is ringed with saliva. I'm too scared to speak. I curl into a ball.

Pa wails on me like a piñata until his arms quiver and shake. He leans down close and spits his angry words into my face, *"Where did you get the money?"*

"I took the money from your closet."

*"What?"*

"I took it from the closet."

*"Where?"*

"From the piggy bank."

"Did those white kids tell you to steal?"

"No."

"How much did you take?"

"I don't know."

*"You don't know?"* Pa paces in a tight circle, the broom handle pointed skyward. He looks like he's about to let me have it again.

"I don't know, I swear I don't."

He leans down in my face again and lowers his voice, "Five *hundred* dollars. That's how much you stole from your mother. Your *mother."*

I sit in silence. His words make me feel ashamed.

"Don't you feel shame for stealing from your own family?"

I don't know what to say.

"Don't you feel any shame or remorse at all? It's bad enough to steal, but from your own *family?"*

I'm silent. Dizzy.

*"Motherfucker!"* Pa screams. "Are you trying to be hardheaded with me, you dead dog?"

Pa picks me up by the flaps of my shirt and rips it off of me. The buttons go flying in every direction. "Take off your clothes!" he spits.

"Take of all your clothes *now!"*

"Why?" I moan like a drugged-up heroin addict.

*"Why?* I'll show you *why!"*

Pa's eyes widen again. He grabs me by the waist and slams my shorts and underwear to the ground.

Uncle Chao gasps. My naked body feels big, standing there in front of him and Ma, like it fills up half the room.

"Okay, brother," Uncle Chao intervenes, "you don't need to make him take his clothes off. Just tell him what he did wrong."

"*Shut up!* Don't tell me how to discipline my child, or you'll be next!" Pa snaps back.

Uncle Chao sits down and places his face in his palms.

"I'll show you what shame feels like . . ." Pa grabs me by the nape of the neck, like a cat, and drags me toward the front door.

Sensing what's about to happen, I cry out for Ma and try to break away from him. He pinches my skin tighter and pushes me forward. I scream and wail. Ma cries for me in the kitchen but dares not leave her seat.

Pa rips the door open. The bright sun blinds me. The cool breeze whipping against my skin confirms that I am utterly and completely naked.

"Now, *this* is what shame feels like," he growls through clenched teeth as he shoves me out the door onto the patio.

I cry and scream and beat on the door with both fists, pleading with them to let me in.

Pa cracks the door, "Think about this the next time you want to steal."

Like the woman who lifts a Volkswagen to rescue her baby, adrenaline floods my body and I force the door open with incredible strength. Still, standing there on the sill, I'm no match for my father's resolve to teach me a lesson. He palms my face like a basketball and forces me to the ground. The door slams shut and the dead bolt turns. I pound on the door and scream until my voice is gone. With the piercing sound of my cries no longer echoing in my ears, I can hear and feel the buzz of a busy afternoon on Sunset Boulevard behind me.

Pa opens the window and yells out to the street in Vietnam-

ese, "Look everybody! We have a thief here! Come look at him! A thief! A thief!"

The elderly Vietnamese couple next door walks out onto the patio when they hear the commotion. I can hear doors and windows opening all over the building.

Frederique comes out of her apartment, and her eyes go big as quarters the moment she sees me standing there. "Francette, come out here quick! Lac is naked!"

I cover up my penis, which is shriveled from the cold like a dried prune, with one hand and beat on the door with the other. When this fails to improve my situation, I kick and claw on the door with my bare feet. I hear whistling and cat calling from across the street. Frog and his brothers have come out on their porch to see what all the fuss is about. Sleepy rolls out behind them and yells across the street, "What the fuck you doin', Chino? Go and put some clothes on, *ese!*"

A small crowd of awestruck neighbors forms behind me.

"Ma! Ma! Let me in," I sob. I slide down the door, defeated, and land in a heap. "Pa . . . open the door. I won't steal *anymore . . .* I promise!"

Javi and company walk out the front of Shakey's. They spot the commotion and give chase across the street. They force their way through the crowd of my whispering, finger-pointing neighbors. My vision blurs. I can barely make out Javi's face as he stands above me, laughing hysterically and clutching his jiggling belly. The pain in my body pales in comparison to the deafening echo of Javier's laughter.

Ten minutes later, Pa opens the door. His shirt is back on and he looks normal again. He looks down at me, ignoring the crowd. I slither between his legs and the door into the safety of our apartment. Pa tells me to put my clothes on. He spends the next two hours lecturing me and explaining the rationale for my punishment. Nothing sinks in. I'm too tired, beaten, and shell-shocked to absorb the message. Pa keeps talking and talking. He

rubs Tiger Balm on my wounds. Then he gets up and walks over to the bedroom. He returns with the piggy bank.

"Read this." Pa points at the Chinese characters on the note taped to the side of the piggy bank.

"I don't know those words."

"Yes, you do. I taught them to you."

"I don't remember."

"Of course you don't! You're too busy stealing and playing video games to remember anything I teach you."

I nod my head.

"I wrote this for your mother . . . to motivate her to save more money. Sometimes, we skip meals just so that we can put more money in it."

I survey the piggy bank in Pa's hands. He fondles it tenderly and stares off into the distance. His eyes hold a rare glimmer of hope. "What does it say?"

"It says, 'Children's college fund.'"

# ALHAMBRA

Quy poses with Pa's ladybug-red Chevette, our family's first car.

I'm sitting in the backseat of my father's first car—a ladybug-red 1976 Chevette. The car is ten years old, but it doesn't look half its age. Pa bought it from a Mexican guy that parked it in the grocery store lot with a For Sale sign. The Chevette set him back four hundred dollars, and there's no question it's his most prized possession in the world. It's hot as hell in Los Angeles, even though it's December. A thick layer of smog blankets the city. The backs of my legs stick to the diaper-brown vinyl upholstery.

Pa tests each of the switches and knobs in his new car. It's

an optimistic gesture for a man who's never driven a car before.
Crazy is riding shotgun. Pa steps on the gas and all fifty-one
horses beneath the hood do their best to lurch the car forward.

Crazy points out the windshield as he instructs. "Turn, turn
. . . left . . . right . . . stop!" Then, he panics. "Stop! Stop! You're
going to hit the garage!"

Crazy's screaming gets Pa flustered—the neighbors are
watching. We still haven't made it out of the side yard.

"Motherfuck! Why are you screaming?!" Pa screams. "Let me
see you try driving this thing, you fucking dead dog! Now, shut
the fuck up!"

Crazy turns bright-red and keeps his mouth shut. The neigh-
bors are still watching. Pa has managed, somehow, to wedge the
car sideways between the side of our house and the neighbors'
garage. With inches of breathing room between his bumpers and
an unfathomable ding, he ekes the car back and forth. Ten min-
utes of this and we're no better off than when we started. My
father is the last person on earth to ask for help.

Pa turns off the engine, gets out of the car, and slams the door
hard.

"Don't just fucking sit there, come help me push this thing
out. You, too, Big Head!"

Pa steers through the open window while Crazy and I push
the car back and forth. Four or five rounds of this and the Che-
vette is pointing toward the street. Pa hops back into the car and
fires it up. He's too anxious to step on the gas again, so he sits
with his elbow hanging out the window like the white people do.
I don't want to be in this car when he hits the busy streets.

With the car still in park, Pa revs the engine. If you could only
see his face you might think he's driving a GTO. He shifts into
drive without putting his foot on the brake. The clutch cracks
and the car jerks forward violently. Pa stomps on the brake and
we skid to a halt.

"What did you tell me to push the gas for?" Pa scolds Crazy.

"To make sure we have gas running through the engine. To warm up the car." Crazy reaches for an explanation.

"Get the fuck out of my car!" Pa reaches over and pulls the latch on Crazy's door. "Leave! You're bad luck. I can't learn how to drive with you in this car."

"But I didn't . . ."

Pa unbuckles Crazy's seat belt and pushes him out the door. "Leave, I said!" Crazy gets out and stands beside the car. "Big Head! Get up here with me."

I wish Crazy would leave more than this car. He has a job and enough money to live on his own now; he shouldn't even be living with us. Shit smears to new places, I guess.

"Put on your 'seek bell,'" Pa says to me in English.

I reach back to grab the shoulder harness but don't know how to put it on. I've never ridden in the front seat of a car before. Pa triple-checks the shifter to make sure the car is in park before reaching over to help me. Crazy folds his arms and taps his foot. He gives me a dirty look. I respond in kind.

Pa leans his little head over the steering wheel and tries to move forward again. He pushes on the gas with his right foot but won't take his left off the brake, so our progress is jerky and painful. My head snaps back and forth against the seat as we inch our way down the long drive leading up to our complex. Pa rattles off driving advice to me the entire time, his head never leaving its place above the steering wheel. His knuckles are white from the death grip he has on the steering wheel.

When we get to the end of the driveway, Pa decides he'd better practice going in reverse. He moves the shifter forward a click and looks over his shoulder. He struggles to keep the car straight. We zigzag our way back up the driveway with Crazy running behind us, waving his arms about to correct our direction. I chew on my fingernails. It's strange to see Pa so uncertain about something and looking so nervous. *Pa can do anything*. His vulnerability makes me anxious.

After a few more trips up and down the driveway, Pa relaxes a little. "You see, I told you driving a car isn't hard. What's so difficult about moving this steering wheel to make the car go where you want it to go? Like anything you want to perfect, you just have to practice it over and over again."

"Are we going to drive in the streets now?"

"Not yet, son. I still need to get used to the two feet down here. One is to make the car move and the other is to stop it. They aren't natural to me."

I hope Pa takes the whole family out in the car once he learns to drive. It'll be just like the white people do on television. Except Crazy—he can stay home.

"Where did Crazy go?" Pa wonders aloud.

"I don't know. I guess he got tired of standing around."

"Good. He's bad luck. I almost crashed twice with him in the car," Pa says. "With you next to me, I'm driving perfectly."

My heart starts racing uncontrollably. Was that a compliment? I feel elated and uncomfortable at the same time. It's unnatural for him to speak so highly of me.

"Anyway, it's a waste of time for you to be sitting in here with me. Go inside and get your Chinese books. You can recite prose to me while I learn to drive. We'll learn together."

I run into the house to get my books. We've already been here a month and I still can't believe we live in a real house, just like the Brady Bunch and the Cosbys. It even has a yard with a mature sycamore and our own garage.

After he caught me stealing, Pa decided that Hollywood was no place to raise a family. And when Pa says it's time to go, it's time to go. We were packed up and out of our apartment within the month. All he told me was that we were moving east of Chinatown. He said Alhambra's a place where other Asians dwell—a place where I'll be protected from the white people.

I didn't tell any of my friends that I was leaving. I moved through my last day at Le Conte Junior High like it was any

other. No "see you soon." No "keep in touch." No "good-bye." I sat through each period, waited for my teacher to sign my transfer slip at the end of the day, and I was gone. I didn't tell anyone in the neighborhood, either. Just hopped in my uncle's car and off we went. Some things are better that way. A secret is easier to keep when you know you're never going to see someone again. A friend will flutter like a feather when the wind blows.

Pa says Uncle Sam has been gracious in light of his disability and the additions of Vinnie and Bo to our family. That means we can afford to rent a home in a nicer neighborhood where we can be around our own people.

I don't see what's so great about living in a neighborhood full of Asians. They're everywhere in Alhambra: in the markets, at the gas stations, and on the streets. Even our mailman is Asian. On the surface Asians might not seem so bad, but they remind me too much of my family. At least in Hollywood, whenever I'd had enough of my family, I was able to leave the house to be with other people—people who didn't remind me of the ugliness of my own.

Our new neighbors are friendly enough, sure, but they're different than the people back home in Hollywood. Alhambra is quiet and tame. Gone are the buses roaring up and down our street, the incessant police sirens, and the ghetto birds flashing their bright lights in our windows at night. There aren't any prostitutes and drug dealers hanging out on the corners. Things feel safe here—neutered and sterile, but safe—like the whole place is devoid of passion and self-interest.

My parents are like fish in water here. All of our immediate neighbors are Vietnamese or Chinese. Asian markets, herbal stores, and restaurants are within walking distance. My parents are no longer apprehensive and guarded when we walk down the streets. They'll even stop and talk to complete strangers. They share recipes and meals with our neighbors and grow vegetables and herbs in a small garden. Vinny and Bo have friends their age here, and our neighbors watch them when my parents run er-

rands. I haven't seen Ma and Pa this happy since we left Vietnam. For my sake, I hope that Pa stays this way.

I grab my stack of Chinese books off the kitchen table and run outside to rejoin Pa in the Chevette. He takes a final drag off his cigarette and flicks it out the window. A quick turn of the ignition and pull on the shifter, and I'm reciting Chinese prose while we put up and down the driveway. Pa focuses on his driving for more than an hour before he speaks.

"You've been studying hard, haven't you?"

I look up from my book. "Uhh . . . yes, father."

"I can tell. You haven't made a single mistake."

I turn my head away and pretend to look out the window. My broad smile is not something that Pa would want to see.

When I first enrolled in the new junior high school, I was relieved to see a bunch of Mexican kids roaming the hallways. It turns out Alhambra isn't all Asian—the Mexicans just live on the other side of town. I guess that's where I need to go to make some friends that aren't like me, since the Mexican kids at school are indifferent to my chummy advances.

The girls at school are the nuts I'd really like to crack. Puberty is hitting me hard these days. Sometimes I'll pop a wood in class for no reason and have to stay at my desk when the bell rings until it goes away. Summer is near, and the string tank tops and short-shorts the girls are wearing aren't making things any easier. It seems like they know I'm watching them, the way they bend over to pick things up or brush against me when they walk by my desk. If Frederique still lived next door, I'd be in for some trouble. Man, you don't know what you have until it's gone.

Pa's strict rules and curfew make it hard for me to meet girls. For one thing, he says that if he finds out I'm involved with one, he'll kick my ass. He's always reminding me that I shouldn't be thinking about girls until I graduate from college.

"Girls and education don't go together," he says.

"Why don't they, Pa?"

"Because a woman is the most wicked thing in the world, next to money. Men do stupid things—they'll even die—for the dollar and that irresistible stink hole." Pa points his finger against my chest. "The sanest person you know will become lost and irrational the moment he sees cash or smells pussy."

"*Really*, Pa? Why do people do that?"

"Don't worry about why. Just put your family first and your education above all else. Without them, you're just another poor, stupid Vietnamese refugee living in the white man's country. You'll spend your whole life picking up trash for the white man if you don't finish school."

I still want to know why someone would lose his mind over a woman, but Pa lets me go outside so that I'll stop asking questions.

I hop on my Huffy and pedal away from our house. Cruising the neighborhood on my bike has become one of my favorite things to do since we moved. I don't care where I go; I'm just happy to get away. I ride west toward City Terrace and my surroundings begin to change. Tree-lined suburban streets transform into broken sidewalks and dilapidated buildings sagging under the weight of time. Kids play soccer in the street. A *paleta* man stands and pedals hard to ferry his ice-cold cargo up the hill. He rings the bell on his bike to let the soccer game know that he's coming. It all reminds me of Sunset Boulevard. I feel like I've come home again.

I stop at the liquor store and pick up a lemon Jolly Rancher and a bag of *saladitos*. I pull the bag open and slip a *saladito* into my mouth. The salt makes my tongue curl and my lips pucker. I pedal slowly along, sucking hard on it until I can taste the sweetness of the prune. Small, boxy houses crowd the street. Their tiny yards are enclosed in warped chain-link fence and are overgrown with weeds. Many have chickens strutting about and

pecking at the ground. This neighborhood is oozing with life. I wish Pa would have moved us here.

I see three boys my age standing above their bikes, talking to each other at the street's edge. They dress like Frog, in white T-shirts, black beanie caps, and white tube socks pulled up to their knees. I tap my brake as I ride by and make eye contact with the boys. I want to stop and make friends with them. I give a quick nod to say, "What's up?" They return my salutation with cold stares and steely eyes. I keep riding.

I suck on my Jolly Rancher and pedal along, soaking up the scene. The walls around me are tagged with gang writing and the murals of graffiti artists. I recognize some of the gang names; it's a Mexican neighborhood, indeed. Code words, nick-names, font, and penmanship tell you who's who and remind you where you are. I see the name Chaka on some of the buildings. He's one of the new breed of graffiti artists who tag their name as many times, in as many places, as possible. They aren't gangs, but most taggers run in named groups. I hear Chaka runs solo. I stop and admire the audacity of his work.

I bunny-hop my bike off the curb and cruise into the next neighborhood. I hear mariachi music blaring in the distance. The familiar sound means someone is having a party. I seek it out.

I know I'm getting close when I can make out a garbled mix of voices and laughter. I hear different conversations going on all at once, people cursing in English and Spanish. I slow down and stop before I reach the house. The ambient sound and smell take me back to the Kingsley boys.

I creep up to the chain-link fence that borders their yard. Half a dozen cholos sit in a circle on plastic milk crates and patio chairs. Their heads are buzzed bald and they're all shirtless or wearing white wifebeater undershirts. Their brown skin is cov-ered in dark-blue ink—images and calligraphy that match the graffiti blanketing the neighborhood. The front yard has more dirt than grass, and it's littered with beer cans. A guy with his

back to me downs a beer, crushes it in his hand, and throws it onto the pile of empties lying at his feet. He has the letters *CT* tattooed onto the back of his head. It's most likely the initials of his gang.

A cholo with a baby face holds the group's attention with a story. "The fucking *payaso* thinks he's hard, ay . . . throws up his barrio."

"What you do, *ese*?"

"I threw up my hood right in that *pinche payaso*'s face, *ese*. Fuck his ass up right in front of his boys."

*"Simon, ese,"* the one with the tattoo on his head drawls to nods of approval around the circle.

"Then his homies step to me. But I don't move, homes . . . I ain't scared of those *putos*." Baby Face pushes himself up off his crate and stands tall with his chest puffed out and his chin held high, to show his homies just what he looked like.

"Then . . . what happened, ay? Fuck, get to the good shit, homes!"

"I took out my *cuete* and put it in his fucking face, homes." Baby Face pulls a nine millimeter from his waistband, cocks it, and points it in the face of an imaginary person. "Those *putos* ran away . . . fast!"

*"Horale!"* cheers erupt from the group. The culmination of Baby Face's story is met with raucous approval. Beers are held high.

I smile to myself because they're just like the Kingsley boys. The stories are not as much about what you did as they are about how you tell them. The gangsters take their homies right into the moment. Tell a good story to the gang and you're the life of the party. Tell one that's a buzzkill and they beat your ass. It's just how it works.

I miss having a seat around the circle. I wonder if these guys will take me under their wing like the Kingsley Street Gang. Maybe they'll even know about the Kingsley boys, and we can

share stories. I decide I'm going to give it a try, and my heart starts racing. I stand there on my bike, trying to come up with the best way to introduce myself. Before I get the chance, three spotted brown pit bulls come running out of the house. The dogs run down the porch, barking madly, and storm across the yard in my direction. Their muscular frames come skidding to a halt in the dust on the other side of the fence. Their vicious barks pound against my eardrums. One of the dogs has terrifying yellow eyes. It seems hell-bent on finding a way over the fence.

The cholos respond to the commotion by leaving their seats and walking over to me. The guy with the tattoo on his head is the last one to turn around. When he does I can see that he's blind in his left eye. A long, deep scar runs out of the socket and across his temple. He speaks to me first.

"Sup, Chino? What you want, *ese*?" he widens his eyes as he speaks, further revealing the sunken blind eye and its cloudy, white pupil.

He's trying to intimidate me, just like Sleepy did the first time I met him. I bet he's just playing. I *hope* he's just playing. "Nothing," I say meekly. "You guys having a party?"

"What, *ese*?" Dead Eye's voice sounds serious.

The other guys are smirking and giggling behind him. He can't be serious.

"You having a party?"

"Depends who's asking, *cabrón*. Go get the fuck outta here. Get your yellow ass back to Chinatown."

Now I know he's serious and I start to panic. His instructions make me feel suddenly and unequivocally out of place. I just stand there, without a clear thought in my head.

Dead Eye leans over the fence and barks in my face, "You stupid, Chino? Get the fuck outta here before I hop this fence and beat your ass." Then he waves the back of his hand at me, "Go eat some chop suey or somefing!"

My trepidation grows. I'm more tongue-tied than ever, but I

don't want to leave. I know I can win them over if I just get the chance. I'll have to loosen them up somehow. I try not to make eye contact with any one of them. They'll take that as me calling him out for a fight. So, I just look through them. I look through them and rack my brain for something clever to say.

Baby Face steps up beside Dead Eye and rests his forearms on the fence, "Where you from, Chino?"

I can't say Alhambra. I won't say Alhambra. I can't have them thinking I'm just another Chino from the other side of town. I blurt out the only thing I think can save me. "I'm from the Kingsley Street Gang."

My words are the catalyst for a nuclear reaction. The looks on their faces tell me I've made a horrible mistake. Baby Face is gripping his pistol before I've even finished the sentence. I turn and push on the pedals with all my might. Dead Eye scrambles over the fence and chases after me. I stand and thrust the pedals up and down to build speed. I look back and see Dead Eye running right behind me, reaching out to grab me with both hands. His tattooed paws are so close to my bicycle seat that my heart feels like it's going to rip out of my chest. Their street is on a hill with a shallow incline, and I'm headed in the wrong direction. It takes everything my shaky legs have in them to build a little breathing room between my bike and Dead Eye's pursuit.

I look behind me to see how I'm doing. Two skinny gangsters have caught up to Dead Eye and are running alongside him. Baby Face is behind them. He stops and whistles back at the house. Within seconds a whole mob of gangsters come running through the gate and out into the street after me. With a good twenty guys now in hot pursuit of my bike, a fresh rush of adrenaline gives my legs newfound strength. I put my head down and pedal away until I reach the top of the hill. The down slope on the other side of the crest is steep. I ignore the burn and pedal hard the entire way down the hill. I only catch a quick glimpse behind me, because it gives me speed-wobbles that almost send

me over my handlebars. The gangsters are at the top of the hill, panting with their hands on their knees.

I lean back on the bike and coast until I run out of speed. My face is drenched in a cold sweat. I stop out in the flats to catch my breath and get my bearings. I run my forehead against my sleeve. I've made it all the way down near the 10 freeway, and I need to find my way back east to get home. The purple sky and cool wind tell me that Pa is anxiously awaiting my return. I'm going to have to deal with him next.

I start up again and turn down a street to the right. I'll have to make a big loop to work my way back without cutting through the gangsters' neighborhood. I don't want to know what will happen if I bump into them again. I grow increasingly paranoid as I pedal my way down the block. My hypervigilant eyes wander and scan every detail of my surroundings. A shopkeeper hosing the sidewalk looks at me skeptically as I ride by. A woman yells at her children for walking into the street, and her hollering feels as though it's directed at me. Something isn't right. The street is uncrowded but it feels suffocating, like everything is closing in on me. I hear screeching in the distance and I don't know where it's coming from. Little kids on the corner stop their game of hopscotch as I approach them. And then I hear an unmistakable roar behind me. A black Chevy Monte Carlo comes screeching around the corner, its tires curling tendrils of white smoke into the air as they struggle to grip the asphalt.

*Fuck. It's them.* I pedal for my life down the street and don't look back until I hear the Monte Carlo coming up close behind me. I can see Dead Eye glaring through the windshield from the passenger's seat. The car inches up behind me until the hood emblem is inches from my bike. The car swings over into the left lane, and Dead Eye leans out the window with a wooden Louisville Slugger. The driver maneuvers him closer so that he can take a swing. Dead Eye reaches back with the bat and I cut to the right into an alley. I skid to a stop. My legs are shaking,

and my heart is thumping. My entire body tingles and it's hard to think.

I can hear the Monte Carlo screeching around the block. *Maybe they'll leave me alone. Maybe they'll circle until they find me.* I can't outrun a car. I spot the Monte Carlo cruising past the other end of the alley. Someone in the backseat sees me; I can see an arm thrust out the narrow back window. I turn and pedal out the alley the way that I came in. Tires squeal as the Monte Carlo flips a U-turn in the street and comes roaring down the alley toward me. I can hear the big boat rattling its way down the undulating passage as I exit into the street. On the other side of the intersection ahead of me is the entrance to the 10 freeway east. The light is red, but I pedal through the intersection anyway. Cars are coming at me from both directions, so I look down and pedal harder. I hear horns and brakes screeching on either side of me. I make it through the intersection and cruise down the freeway on-ramp. Before I make it to the end of the ramp, the Monte Carlo comes storming through the intersection, but it's dinnertime in Los Angeles and the freeway is jammed with cars. The gridlock halts the Monte Carlo halfway down the ramp. I head down the narrow right shoulder of the freeway and don't stop pedaling until I reach the Fremont Avenue exit. The cars on my left have scarcely moved during my journey down the interstate, and the gangsters are out of sight.

I don't know how long it will take the Monte Carlo to make the exit, or how they might guess which exit I took, but I'm not going to take any chances. I've never been happier to go home to Alhambra, and I pedal hard until I'm there.

# I LOVE YOUS ARE FOR
# WHITE PEOPLE

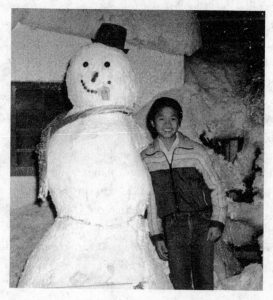

I love Christmas.

When we walk through the front door, the distant squeaking of rubber-soled sneakers against lacquered hardwood taunts me. This would be so much easier to tolerate if it wasn't open-gym.

"Pa, can I go play basketball?"

"No," he scolds me. "That's not why we're here."

"Can I go play after?" I beg.

Pa doesn't answer. He makes me get in line with Vinnie and

Quy and Bo and a bunch of little kids. I bet I'm the only fourteen-year-old on the planet waiting in line to see Santa. A black man plays Santa this year. The synthetic, bright-white beard he's wearing makes his teeth look yellow. Bo cries at the sight of him. Vinnie runs back over to Pa.

"Pa, that's not Santa," Vinnie whines, tugging on Pa's jacket.

"Shut your mouth!" Pa snaps. "I see the Christmas clown right there . . . just like last year."

"But he doesn't look like that on TV . . ." Vinnie says and pouts his lips.

"He has presents, doesn't he? Now get back in line or you won't get any."

Pa walks outside to have a smoke. I look around and try to distract myself from the humiliation I'm about to get on Santa's lap. The YMCA here is so much cleaner than the one in Hollywood. It's just four miles from our house, but it took us over an hour to get here—the typical pace for a journey with Pa behind the wheel. He's so short that he drives with his head in front of the steering column, reaching up to grip the wheel and looking out between the spokes like the old lady in the "Where's the Beef?" commercial. Our trips in Pa's little red Chevette are conducted in the bike lane on the far right side of the road. They are marred by a merciless barrage of honking cars. Pa yells and curses back at them, convinced that he's done no wrong. He stops every few blocks to check his map—a tattered little number that's dotted in the red ink he uses to earmark the route. Pa can't read the English street signs, so the map isn't much help.

I'm next and Black Santa looks confused. He's expecting me to escort my siblings away and instead I'm hopping onto his lap. He fakes a smile for the elf that's snapping pictures.

"Oh, ho, no, aren't you a bit large for Santa's lap?" Santa's hat is off-center, exposing his cornrows.

I peruse the pint-sized children standing around me with a

quizzical expression. At five feet four inches tall, I'm short for my age, but I still tower over the tallest of these runts. There's no way Santa is going to buy this.

Once he realizes that I'm not going anywhere, Santa takes me through the routine, "And what is *your* name?"

"Lac."

"Have you been a good *boy* this year?" he asks, mocking my age.

"Yes."

"Ho, ho, ho. There you go. Now get your present and get out of here."

I grab a present from Santa's bag and slip out of the spotlight. Pa points Vinnie back to the bag and tells him to exchange it for a bigger one. Vinnie is afraid, so Pa walks him over to the bag and reaches in himself for the biggest box he can find. Pa comes up with the box and spots me hiding in the corner.

He yells at me in Vietnamese through the crowd of people, "Hurry and get back in line to get another present!"

I walk around to the back of the line. A Vietnamese family sitting along the wall smirks at me as I pass. Our holiday ritual is already halfway to disaster. At least this year's Santa is nice. The Asian Santas at the YMCA in Hollywood were always mean and nasty. Last year, Santa yanked me off his lap and asked if I felt shameful taking gifts from the little children.

"Here, let me hold your present so the clown won't think he gave you one already," Pa insists.

While I wait in line again, I watch Pa argue with Vinnie and Bo about whether or not they can open their presents. Fifteen minutes later, I'm at the front of the line again.

"And what is *your* name?" Santa asks skeptically.

"Um . . . Tuan," I say, looking down at the tightly knit industrial carpet.

Santa pulls my shoulders back so that he can take a good look

at my face. "You sure about that, kid? Wasn't your name *Lock* just a minute ago?"

I'm so embarrassed that I want to jump off his lap and run and hide in the janitor's closet. That isn't an option. Pa wants another present. So, I sit on Santa's lap in silence.

"Aight, lil' *Too-On*, it's Christmas. Go and get yourself a gift, then, pardner."

I get my gift and make my way back to Pa and the siblings.

"Wait ten minutes and then go back for another one, Big Head," Pa says.

*Why doesn't Quy have to go and get another gift?* "I have enough presents. I don't want anymore," I say.

"It's not for you, Big Head. Go see the clown and get another gift for your siblings. Here, take your sweater off." Pa grabs my wool sweater at the waist and pulls it over my head. "Now he won't remember you."

I stand there in my undershirt looking at the line. I'm a foot taller than any present-seeking person in it. Santa will remember me.

Pa puts his hand on the small of my back and pushes me toward the back of the line. "By the time you make it to the front, the clown won't remember you. You don't even look like the same boy. Think, Lac! Be smart. Go!"

I make a sour face at Pa and make my way over to the line. Fifteen minutes of misery and dread later, I'm approaching Santa.

He takes one look at me and waves his finger, "Ho, ho, ho— only one gift per person."

I return to Pa empty-handed.

"What happened?" Pa asks.

"He said one present per person."

"Did you tell him you got one already?"

"No."

"Then why didn't you get a gift?"

"He said only one present per person."

"Then tell him you didn't get one . . ."

"I didn't know."

Pa gives me a Bronx cheer. "You need to be more clever than that. Think on your feet, for heaven sakes! You're going to be swallowed whole by the real world, you're so retarded."

We leave the YMCA toting more gifts than the Chevette's tiny cargo space will hold.

I head over to 7-Eleven after school to meet my friend Arturo and show him my new graffiti drawings. He and I met at school and made fast friends when I moved to Alhambra. Art is Mexican, or "white" as Pa would say, but Pa lets me hang out with him anyway because Art gets good grades and studies hard. Art is a nerd, but I don't mind. We both like to draw, and hanging out with him is a lot more fun than hanging out with the goofy Asians in my neighborhood.

Art is late. He probably stayed after class to chat with his math teacher. I put my backpack down next to the *Street Fighter* machine and pop a quarter in. *Street Fighter* is a new game that's all the rage, but I've lost something for video games after what happened in Hollywood. I just play to kill time.

"I'll take anyone out with Chun Li. Watch me."

I don't even have to turn around to know whom the big mouth belongs to. His name is Quan, and he steps up beside me and drops a quarter into the machine so that we can fight. Quan is in the fifth grade and is four years younger than me, but he curses like a sailor and thinks he's the toughest thing around. He looks like every other Asian kid hanging out in the 7-Eleven. His head is shaved on the sides and the hair on top is long and slicked straight back, save a clump of his bangs that hangs down in front of his face, past his chin. The hanging strands are tinted orange from Sun-In, which Quan sprays on them daily. Quan tucks this strand of hair behind his left ear while we play. He is a

FOB—fresh off the boat—so he doesn't speak much English. He curses in Vietnamese while we play. When he starts to lose, the insults get personal.

"Fuck you!" he says, spiraling Chun Li down into my character's head like a corkscrew.

"Hey, kick back with your mouth. You better watch the way you talk to me," I tell him.

"Why? Are you going to go and cry like your stupid little sister?"

"What did you say?"

"You heard what I said about that little hooker."

I take my hand off the joystick and fasten it onto the back of Quan's neck. Before he has a chance to react, I shove his face into the store window next to the machine. The clerk hears the thud and yells at us for fighting in the store. When he sees the look on my face he doesn't approach us. Always the obedient one, I drag Quan outside and throw him off the curb. He trips on a pothole and falls on his side on the loose gravel.

"You motherfuck! Get out of here before I really beat your ass," I yell at Quan in Vietnamese. He scurries out of the parking lot toward home.

I notice Dragon Head to my right, leaning against the corner of the building, smoking a cigarette. His nickname comes from the colorful walking dragons you see in Chinese New Year parades. His shaved head is menacing and bulbous. Like the walking dragons, it's too big for his frame. Dragon Head walks toward me and flicks the last of his smoke into the parking lot. Everyone in the neighborhood knows him. He's the leader of the Street Ratz—a gang of graffiti artists and thugs. People say they're the ones invading homes in our neighborhood in ski masks. Asians in our neighborhood don't trust the banks, so they hide all of their money and valuables in their homes. The robbers have been forcing their way in with pistols and holding families hostage until they cough up the goods. I don't know if the Street

Ratz are the ones doing the stealing, but I've seen them selling drugs. And spray-painting. Their graffiti is amazing—better than any I've seen.

"Motherfuck, that little knucklehead needs a good beating. I beat his ass all the time but he doesn't learn," Dragon Head says to me in Vietnamese.

*I can't believe it; Dragon Head is actually talking to me.* He is approaching me because of the one thing I've never ever done in public—speak Vietnamese. I've always associated Vietnamese with the ugliness of my family and my embarrassment over my culture.

"He called my little sister a hooker," I say to Dragon Head, in Vietnamese.

"He talks a lot. He's only good for you when you need him to steal something from 7-Eleven," Dragon Head says with a chuckle.

I laugh at the joke, genuinely if too exuberantly.

"You got to teach these little knuckleheads to respect their elders. They're so disrespectful. Not toward me, though. I beat the shit out of them," Dragon Head continues.

He lights another cigarette. "You smoke?" he asks, offering me one.

I nod and take a cigarette, which Dragon Head lights for me by putting it against his and puffing hard until the embers glow red and a trail of smoke rises above them.

"What's your name?" I ask, trying not to cough with the cigarette dangling from my lips like Pa does.

"Dragon Head," he replies in Vietnamese. "From the Street Ratz gang," he finishes in English.

I notice he has two thick graffiti markers peaking out from the back pocket of his jeans. Dragon Head has presence. He's stalky, and his wifebeater top reveals a body that's covered in colorful tattoos. I see fanged serpents, phoenixes, Chinese deities, and, of course, the fierce dragons for which he's named. Unabashed by

his culture, he has the word *Vietnam* running down the inside of his right forearm in large letters. His left reads "Life's Dust" in Vietnamese—a metaphor for being a scoundrel.

The way his pants sag and a black bandana hangs from his pocket, Dragon Head's slanted eyes are the only thing that keeps me from mistaking him for one of the Kingsley Boys. This guy is hard. His thug demeanor reminds me of Sleepy, and it makes me anxious to get to know him.

Art finally shows up looking like a church boy in his black slacks and short-sleeved, white-collared shirt. I can't wait to show him what I've drawn this week. It's been a rough one, with Pa getting on my case even more than usual, and like always it turned my drawings up a notch. Unlike Pa, Art genuinely appreciates and respects my art.

"Show me your piece already. I bet it's fresh," he says, cutting to the chase after we shake hands.

I open my black scrapbook, flip the pages toward the middle, and show it to him.

"Ooooh . . ." Art says, exhaling into his fist as he speaks.

I revel at the look in his eyes as he examines every detail of the two-page spread. He holds my drawing with both hands and pores over it wide-eyed for a good ten minutes.

I hear the sputtering sound of cherry-bomb mufflers as a couple of Hondas pull into the parking lot. I look up to see some of Dragon Head's gang, the Street Ratz, coming out of their cars but pretend I don't see them as they walk behind Art, who is still looking at my work.

One of them catches a glimpse of my drawing and stops. "You spray?" he asks, wanting to know if I draw my graffiti on building walls.

"Just on paper," I answer.

"He's the best graffiti artist in Alhambra," Art boasts. "He's fresh as can be. He'll battle anyone."

"Oh, yeah?" the Street Rat asks me.

"Nah, man. I don't spray," I say. I give Art a look that lets him know he better not say another word.

"You should come out with us one of these days and show me what you got—on walls. Fuck paper, homie. Let's see what you got on those walls."

"So *you* spray?" I ask him.

"Yeah, man. Street Ratz gang," he confirms, flashing the Vietnam tattoo on his forearm. It's just like the one that Dragon Head has.

His offer is tempting. I long to befriend Dragon Head, and it would tickle my soul if the Street Ratz liked my art, but it isn't worth the risk of Pa finding out. I might not live to see another day if he caught me vandalizing the neighborhood—or worse.

"You should battle him, Lac," Art blurts all too loudly as the Street Rat opens the door of the 7-Eleven. He hears Art's comment and looks over his shoulder with an acidic smirk.

"Art, you gotta cut that shit out, man!" I snap. "You have to stop showing me off to other people. That's not why I draw."

"Okay, but are you going to go out with them?"

"No, man, my pops would kick my ass if I got caught vandalizing, especially with a graffiti gang."

"Well, if you change your mind and decide to go out with them, call me in."

"Okay," I say, hoping it will end the subject. I look at my watch, "Oh shit! I gotta get home. My father's going to buy me some new shoes."

"You're still coming over tonight, right?" Art asks, looking a little bit desperate.

"Ya, ya, as soon as I get my shoes." Before packing up my things, I tear the drawing out of my scrapbook and sign it for Art. I use my tagging name, Tiny.

Art rolls up the paper and places it delicately into his backpack.

"Just between you and me, Lac, you've got the dopest graffiti in Alhambra."

"Aight, Art, just between you and me."

I shove the front door open and Arnold's chubby cheeks put a smile on my face. Vinnie is watching our favorite TV show, *Diff'rent Strokes*. I put my bag down and sit on the couch next to Vinnie. On cue Arnold blurts out a gruff, "What you talkin' 'bout, Willis?" and Vinnie and I roll around on the couch in laughter.

I love the way Mr. Drummond talks to his adopted sons. I know it's just TV, but I can't help but fantasize that Mr. D is my father, too. Arnold and Willis break the rules just like I do, but Mr. D forgives them every time. Not only that, he hugs them and tells them he loves them at the end of every episode. I wonder what it would feel like to have my father tell me he loves me. My mind wanders to the days in Da Nang when Pa would hold my hand as we strolled the streets. The last time he sniffed my cheeks was years ago, when I was pretending to be asleep.

Pa enters the room and snaps me out of my reverie. "Let's go," he says.

We hop in the car, and I stare down at my beat-up Pro Wings. My right shoe is so worn out that I can stick my toes through the hole in the sole. Pa tried to fix them by gluing rubber from a car tire onto the soles. He scrubbed them with bleach, too, to make them look "new." His fix wouldn't hold, so Ma is making him take me to the store for my very first new pair of shoes. At five feet four inches, I'm a veritable giant in comparison to Pa and his friends. He doesn't know anyone with a pair of hand-me-downs that I can fit my feet into. I can't wait for my new shoes.

But I'm going to have to wait because the car won't start. Pa gets out and fiddles with the engine for a few minutes. He plops

into the driver's seat and fires up the Chevette. I blow hot air into my hands to warm them up while Pa listens to the engine. He notices that I'm cold.

"For heaven's sake, son, go put on a jacket. It's cold and you're going to get sick."

The concern in Pa's voice warms me right up. I'm afraid to leave the car to go and get my jacket.

"Don't leave without me, Pa."

"I won't. Hurry!"

I sniff the snot back into my runny nose and dash inside the house to retrieve my jacket from the closet. Pa has left me plenty of times before when he promised that he would wait. His patience is razor-thin when it comes to me getting ready. I come back outside and am relieved to see he's still there, fiddling with the carburetor. There's no rubber between my big toe and the freezing pavement. I hop into the car with my jacket half on, and Pa reaches over to zip me up tight.

As we make our way into the Kmart, I absorb the festive atmosphere. There's something about Christmas that makes me feel loved inside. The normally banal store is awash in festive energy. Alvin and the Chipmunks sing high-pitched Christmas carols over the loudspeakers. Poinsettias atop fake white blankets of snow decorate the ends of the aisles. The Salvation Army man in his crooked Santa cap clangs his bell out front. The sweet candy canes hanging in a row make my mouth water. Pa is an atheist and refuses to celebrate Christmas. He doesn't see what I see or feel what I feel.

I know exactly where the shoes are in the store. I speed-walk my way through the aisles, and Pa follows. I know I won't get a brand name, but as long as they aren't Pro Wings I'll be happy. I get teased incessantly at school for wearing my "Poor" Wings.

"Is this leather?" Pa asks, bending my chosen pair of sneakers between the heels of his palms.

"Yes, it's leather," I reply, nodding my head with a shit-eating

grin. I don't really know if it's leather. I'm awestruck by the design. The beautiful shoes have a neon-orange stripe running up each side that matches the neon-orange tongues perfectly.

"Try them on," Pa instructs, handing me a box with shoes that are way too big for my feet.

I rip out the wads of tissue paper and slip my feet in without even touching the laces. "They fit, Pa! I want these," I say anxiously.

"Are they comfortable?"

"Yes."

"Does it hurt anywhere on your feet?"

"No."

"Are you sure?"

"Yes."

"Walk around. Let me see."

I take a few strides up and down the aisle while Pa focuses intently on my feet, inspecting the shoes from all angles.

"Do they hurt your feet?"

"No."

Pa squats down onto his haunches before me and pushes onto the ends of the shoes with his thumb to feel where my toes are. There's a good two inches between my toenails and the ends of the shoes. He squeezes the sides of the shoes and sticks his index finger in the back behind my heels. Pa snorts the phlegm from his nose and swallows it.

"Let me see you run around in them," he stands and says nonchalantly.

There are a couple of kids my age in the aisle trying on shoes with their parents. I'm too embarrassed to move.

"You're *still* growing. I don't want you to grow out of these before they're used," Pa explains. "Let me see you run around in them."

I take off running, but I lean back like I have a piano tied around my waist.

"Why are you running like that?"

"That's how I run."

Pa lifts his eyebrow. "Like a girl? Now run like you normally do. I want to see how your feet bend with the shoes."

I take off running again, this time really fast to the end of the aisle and back.

"Again," Pa demands.

After a few more trips up and down the aisle, Pa is finally convinced that the shoes are worth the $24.95 the store wants for them. He pays with cash, and we make our way back to the car.

"Is this my Christmas present, Pa?" I ask while we're stopped at a red light. I hope he thinks my question is funny, but I really want to know.

*"What?"*

"Are you buying these for me for Christmas?"

"Christmas? What are you, *religious* now?"

"No. That's what my friends' parents do for Christmas . . . They buy them presents."

"That's their business; they're white. We're not. We're boat people."

"But you said I don't need shoes. Then why did you get me these?"

Pa doesn't answer. He looks away and taps a cigarette out from the end of the pack.

"Christmas, *my ass*," he says with a smirk and lights his cigarette. "There's no such thing." He inhales deeply and blows the smoke out the crack in the window. "Don't talk about those white ways to me again . . . *Christmas*. Do you even know what Christmas is about?"

*To give presents away . . . Santa Claus . . . Rudolph . . . candy canes.*

"Tell me, son, who is Jesus?"

"I don't know . . ."

"You don't know the first thing about Christmas, yet you're

ready to dive right in and celebrate it!" Pa's tone turns grave. "You're getting influenced by the whites and you don't even know it."

Pa doesn't explain any further. We ride the rest of the way home in silence. When we arrive, I sprint inside and put the shoebox in my closet. Then I head over to Pa's, find his green sweater, and put it on.

"Ma! Pa!" I yell in the direction of the kitchen, "I'm going to Art's to do some homework . . ." I skip out the front door and head toward Art's house to celebrate Christmas. *He'll* know who Jesus is. His family prays every day to God before they eat.

The aroma inside my surrogate home lifts my spirits. Art's parents are standing in the kitchen in matching green wool sweaters with colorful reindeer woven into the fabric. A roaring fire crackles in the living room, casting a warm glow onto the presents that sit beneath a Christmas tree that stretches all the way to the ceiling. I can smell cookies baking in the oven. Fresh tamales lay steaming at the center of the dinner table, along with all the Christmas fixings—beans, rice, salsa, and sour cream. Art's mother brings out a kettle of *champurrado*, the Latin version of hot chocolate, to warm our bellies. I feel festive and right at home sitting at the table in Pa's green sweater.

"Hi, *mijo*. How are you? How was your day today?" Art's father asks him while taking a seat at the table.

Art pulls a hand free from the cookie he's munching on to give his dad a big thumbs-up.

"*Hola*, Lac," Art's dad says to me with a smile. "*Có-mo es-tás?*"

"Good."

"Ohhh, *bien*? *Sí*? Say it Lac. *Bee-en.*"

"*Bien*," I say.

"*Bueno!*" Art's dad exclaims with a clap.

Art's dad gets up, walks by me, and messes up my hair playfully on his way into the kitchen. I watch him as he sneaks up behind his wife and kisses her on the cheek. "We have so much to

be thankful for. All of this food here, it looks delicious," he says before tearing off a piece of ham and popping it in his mouth.

*My God, what a perfect family. No wonder Art makes the honor roll every semester, speaks three languages, plays the sax, and is a Boy Scout—he gets the kind of love that you only see on TV.* I watch Art with envy as he polishes off another warm, gooey chocolate-chip cookie.

When we're all good and stuffed from two servings of dinner plus dessert, Art's parents lead us into the living room to sit by the fire.

"Wow, Papá!" Art squeals. "We have *so many* presents under the tree this year. Who are they for?"

"Most of them are for you, son. Santa knows just how good you've been this year."

"Can I open one?"

"Let's see . . ." Art's father rubs his chin as he surveys the mound of presents. "How about you open this one; it's from me."

Art grabs the video cassette–sized box from his father with both hands and tears the wrapping off with one smooth rip.

"Wow! What is it, Papá? Is it a game machine?"

"It's even better," Art's father replies with a grin. "It's an electronic thesaurus and dictionary." He takes it out of the box and turns it on. "See . . . you just type in a word and, *voilà!* It gives you the definition, pronunciation, and synonyms, too. Now you won't have to spend so much time looking up words in the dictionary."

*"Thank you, Papá!"* Art says, leaping up from his seat to give his father a hearty bear hug. "It's just what I needed. Now I can write my essays with fancy words. Thank you. I love you, *Papá.*"

"I love you, too, *mijo.*"

I'm transfixed by the verbal interchange between Art and his father. Phrases like "thank you" and "I love you" flow so freely from their lips. I try to grasp how these exchanges of affection work. It's as if they're programmed to know these words, just

like the Texas Instruments spell-checker. Maybe you just have to input something in order to get something out. It must be true. When Art says "I love you," his father says "I love you" right back to him. I realize that I've never told Pa that I love him. This revelation rattles about noisily in my head for the rest of the evening.

"Santa came by and gave you a gift, too," Art's father says to me. He gets up from his chair, walks over to the tree, and locates a present the same size as Art's in green wrapping paper.

"It's a special gift for you because you've been a good boy this year, too," Art's mom says to me.

*No, I haven't. Pa's beatings remind me every week just how bad I've been.* I stare at the present lying in my lap.

"Go ahead, *Lacsito*, open it," Art's mother prods.

"Yeah, open it, Lac," Art chimes in.

I pull on the golden ribbon, but the knot is stuck. I begin a tender struggle to untangle it. I don't want to ruin the nice wrapping and bow tie.

"Just rip it apart, come on!" Art blurts.

I really don't want to open this present. I feel guilty for taking it. I look up sheepishly at Art and his parents. Art's father comes over and, with one yank, rips the wrapping apart. My eyes widen when I see it's a matching Texas Instrument thesaurus machine.

"Now the both of you can do homework together," Art's mother says.

I don't know what to say, what to do, or how to react. I feel like the surprise millionth shopper at a grocery store—minus the confetti and balloons.

"You're Art's good friend, and you deserve it," his dad says to me. "Merry Christmas and we love you."

His words make my face tingle and my chest light. "I love you, too."

"Oh, *mijo*," Art's mother coos. She walks over and gives me a big, warm hug.

Art's dad is right behind her. His warm embrace is comforting and safe, like a giant pillow just out of the dryer. He pulls back slowly and looks me in the face, with a gentle hand on each of my shoulders. "Stay friends forever," he says with a smile.

On the cold walk home, the whole love thing makes perfect sense to me. It feels like I'm walking on a cloud. The crisp night air and bitter Santa Ana winds are no match for the warmth inside me. *This is how I should feel, every day—every hour—especially around my family. Why haven't I been given this by my family? Maybe, just like this Texas Instrument, I have to put something in before getting anything in return. That's how things work; if you want something in return, you have to give something.*

The warm feelings evaporate the moment I catch sight of my house. Fear and stress take their place. I unlock the front door. Unlike Art's cozy abode, my house radiates with bright fluorescent lighting, and a haze of cigarette smoke hangs in the air. I tiptoe around, looking for Pa. I find him in the backyard, with his legs sticking out from under the Chevette. He can't hear me come in over the clicking of his ratchet.

"Pa?"

He pushes hard on the frame and rolls out from underneath the car on his creeper. His face is streaked with grease. "Where have you been? It's dark outside."

"I was at Art's house. I ate dinner there."

"What the hell are you doing eating at other people's house?" Pa snarls, still lying on his back on the creeper. "We have food here. They're going to think we don't feed you. Don't eat there anymore, you hear me!"

"Art's father gave me this for Christmas . . . It's a present."

Pa sits up and takes the electronic thesaurus from my hands. "Why did you take it from him? Now we have to spend money to give *them* something. Go give it back to them." He hands the thesaurus back to me.

"But it's a present, for Christmas."

"What did I tell you about using the word Christmas? What are you, a fucking American now with all this Christmas bullshit? Give it back to them *tomorrow!*"

"It's a present. They gave it to me to help with my homework."

"You don't need a machine to do your homework for you. *You* do the homework. Now give it back to them."

"I can't. It's a present."

Pa gives me a familiar piercing look. It's the look that means, "If you say one more word, I'm going to come over there and knock you on your ass." When I don't respond, he slides back under the car.

I stand there with the thesaurus in my hand, feeling defeated. I look at Pa's legs. I want him to love me just like Art's dad does. *You're forgetting about the Texas Instrument machine, Lac. You have to put something in if you want something back. That's how love works.*

"I love you, Pa," I say proudly.

"What . . ." Pa's words are muffled by the Chevette. His ratchet clangs against the concrete, and he comes sliding out from underneath the car.

"I love you." I smile.

"What the fuck?" Pa leaps up from the creeper and kicks it back against the garage door with his heel. He gets right in my face. "*Motherfuck!* What did you just say? Who the fuck do you think you are? Who do you think *I* am? Are you trying to imitate those *white* people by telling me those fucking words? *Stop that shit!* Don't you ever say those weak words to me ever again, you hear me?"

My fantasy is shattered. My eyes swell with tears. *It shouldn't be this way. He's supposed to say "I love you" back to me. Aren't families supposed to say these words to each other? Isn't Pa my family?* A lone tear rolls down my cheek as I stare into my father's fiery eyes.

"Oh, now you're fucking crying? *Stop it!*" Pa pokes me between the eyes with his index finger as he speaks, "You are such a fucking pussy . . . *a pussy!* First you say 'I love you,' and now you stand there crying like a fucking pussy. Is this what the whites are teaching you at school? To say stupid things and stand there crying like a girl? If you love me, show me. *Show me!* Don't stand there and tell me stupid things and then start crying. *Show me* you love me . . . through actions, not with *pussy* words. Words are useless—they do nothing but piss me off. Get out of my face with your pussy cries."

Pa grabs the creeper and throws it onto the ground, stopping it with his foot. He lies down and pulls himself back underneath the car. I wallow out of the garage with the sound of Pa's ratchet clicking away behind me.

# DAWG FOOD

Pa praying to our ancestors for protection and prosperity.

reach behind the woofer that's next to my bed and pull out the suicide jar. I stare at it, cradled in my hands. I know I shouldn't drink again tonight—it's the fourth time this week— but I'm chasing too much pain these days. The suicide jar is an old Jif container that holds every kind of alcohol imaginable. Anytime Ma and Pa have company over, I pour the leftovers from their beer, cognac, and other hard drinks into the Jif jar. I told myself I would only drink from it in an emergency, but that plan was thrown out the window long ago. I unscrew the

red metal lid, which slips out of my hands and lands on the floor with a clang. A pungent odor emanates from the can. It makes my nose sting.

The last time I drank from the suicide jar, it tasted good—a bit like Lindemans Framboise. This time the potion has fermented a bit and smells like cheap cough syrup. I hold the jar up with one hand and pretend it's a fine bottle of Louis XIII cognac. I take a sip and cough violently. It tastes just like it smells. My sips graduate to gulps until I can hardly taste the foul flavor. My neck gets hot, my face goes numb, and the pressure and sense of hopelessness that dominate my existence just float away. I lie back on my pillow and smile to myself as the poison takes hold of my mind. Now I can see things like they were meant to be seen; I feel like I'm supposed to feel. Like three other nights this week, I'm at peace until I pass out.

The next morning, nothing has changed. Things are just as crappy as they were the day before. Pa is in pain again and mad as hell. After months of sipping on herbal medicine and pills to rid himself of the unexplained pain in his body, he finally decided it was time to go and see a real doctor. The doctor did just what I had hoped—he took Pa off the herbal remedy and pills that were given to him by the Chinese shaman. Pa is diagnosed with chronic rheumatoid arthritis and severe depression. The doctor gives him more pills to take, which he abruptly quits because they make him feel weak. He throws the orange bottles of Tylenol 3 and Wellbutrin under the sink next to the Ajax and Ma's bag of tampons.

Pa is getting increasingly paranoid these days about being weak. He hobbles around the house complaining that no one in the family respects his authority because of his weakness. The shaman insists he keep taking the herbal remedy and pills to fight the pain. Pa keeps popping them by the handful, to the point that his face grows puffy and bloated. He weighs more than a hundred pounds for the first time in his life, and his loose-

fitting shirts now cling so tightly to his frame that the buttons look like they are going to pop off. He's also more aggressive, agitated, and short-fused than usual. He reminds me of a little Asian Incredible Hulk (except my father doesn't fight for truth and justice). I walk around the house on pins and needles, careful not to attract his attention. Even in avoiding him, I'm reprimanded for not acknowledging him. I think the shaman is giving Pa steroids. We're learning about them in health class, and Pa's transformation fits the description to a T.

I cope with him the best way I know how—I drink and leave the house. Dragon Head's place has become my home away from home lately. The Street Ratz are almost always there, hanging out in his garage. We only ever hang out in the garage because Dragon Head isn't allowed in his parent's house. His father has tried to kick him out a bunch of times—going so far as changing the locks—but gave up after Dragon Head broke into the garage and started sleeping there. Now the garage is his own to do what he pleases with, and his parents pretend he isn't even there. It's like living in a motel where the only thing between you and your neighbors is a locked door.

Dragon Head's house gives me the best of both worlds—there's always booze, and I get to hang around with people who enjoy my company. I'll never forget the first time he invited me over. He bumped into me walking back from the 7-Eleven and asked if I wanted to hang out with him and the Ratz. Walking with Dragon Head back toward his house, I felt like I'd been granted special access to an exclusive club, but when we arrived, the Street Ratz pretended like I wasn't even there. They sat around the garage drinking and shooting the shit like I was invisible—even after Dragon Head had introduced me. When I started to get bored, a guy named Kip walked up to me with his right arm behind his back.

"Where you from?" Kip said to me, stone-faced behind his black Ray-Bans.

*Oh shit, here we go again. Everyone in this neighborhood wants to know where you're from.* "I don't bang," I said.

Dragon Head walked away from me to let me know I was on my own. I looked carefully at the arm resting behind Kip's back, thinking he was about to sock me right in the face. I hoped he was joking, but nobody was smiling. It was starting to look like I'd been set up.

"You got shit with the Street Ratz?" Kip asked.

"No. I'm here with Dragon Head," I said, looking in his direction and hoping he'd break into laughter and tell me it was all a joke. Instead, he swigged from his forty and gave me a look like he didn't give a fuck.

"Where you from, I said?" Kip asked again, stepping right up to my face. He let his arm fall to his side, revealing a black .22-caliber pistol in his hand.

I could smell the beer on Kip's breath. When Pa was buzzed and angry, playing the submissive role decreased my chances of getting my ass whipped. So, I decided to do the same with Kip. "I don't bang, man," I said again, as calmly as possible.

"Then get the *fuck* outta here," he spat in my face.

Dragon Head still wasn't saying a word. He just stood there with his arms folded across his chest, clutching his forty with one hand. I can usually read people's facial expressions to find out their motives, but the Street Ratz were all wearing dark sunglasses. I turned around slowly to walk away.

"This is Street Ratz Gang!" Kip said loudly behind me, cocking his pistol.

Then everyone started to laugh.

"Motherfuck, Lac, we're just fucking with you! Come here," Dragon Head called out to me in Vietnamese, pawing playfully at my back.

Since that day, the Street Ratz have treated me like family, even though I'm not a member of their graffiti gang. It's comforting to have peers with the same interests, which these days

are mostly art and drinking. A drink is all that I have to look forward to these days. I can always find a cold forty-ounce of King Cobra or Olde English at Dragon Head's house. I feel bad freeloading on their "drank," but no one seems to mind. Not yet, at least.

Malt liquor has the magic that lets my emotions flow into my drawings. When I'm good and drunk, it feels like I'm crying through my pencils. After the first couple of sips, I'm okay again. My problems don't feel like problems anymore. I find myself laughing them away with the Street Ratz. Most of them can relate to what I'm going through. They have Asian fathers of their own who scrutinize and beat on them.

Dragon Head and I have become good friends quickly. When I hang out with him and the Street Ratz, I get the same feeling of belonging that I enjoyed living across the street from the Kingsley Street Gang in Hollywood. But I'm not a little kid anymore, and the Street Ratz aren't going to let me have a free ride forever. The more time I spend with them, the more they put pressure on me to join their clique. I'm not privy to the full scope of their debauchery, but I know for sure that joining the Street Ratz would at least mean stealing liquor, vandalizing buildings around Alhambra with spray paint, and picking fights. To actually belong—to really be a part of something—is deeply tempting, but I have to resist. My world revolves around a tiny man, who I'm certain would kill me if he ever found out I was living the life of a street thug. When the Street Ratz leave on their missions, I resist and excuse myself by telling them I have to go home and take care of my sick father.

"Brother, come to dinner!" Vinnie yells.

I put my math book down and rush to the kitchen. I'm starving. It seems like no matter how much I eat these days I'm always hungry. I'm a little shaky tonight, too. I have midterms this

week, so I haven't had a drink in two days. My nerves are shot, and I wish I could gulp down a forty and take this edge off. High school is a lot harder than I expected, which doesn't help.

Ma sets a steaming bowl of beef tendons onto the table. They look delicious, but I know better than to reach out and serve myself before Ma has all the food served. I spy Pa watching me, waiting for me to reach out toward the bowl. He's like a frog waiting for an insect to fly within range. Ma returns with a massive pot of white jasmine rice. Pa digs into the pot with a wooden spoon to serve himself a bowl of rice and can tell on contact that it's overcooked.

"What is this?" he shrieks. "This rice is drier than a desert."

"I didn't mean to. I'm so absentminded. I lost track of time while I was cooking the beef," Ma says.

"Don't think just because I'm disabled you get to do things your way!" Pa growls. He grabs the table with both hands and thrusts upward, tipping it on its side. Our dinner goes flying across the kitchen. Food is everywhere. My younger siblings start to cry.

Ma gets on her hands and knees and begins picking up the pieces of meat and placing them back in the bowl.

"Motherfuck, woman, how hard is it for you to cook rice the way I like it?" Pa yells, stooping over her.

She cries and cowers as she picks up the meat for her children to eat. I get down next to her and help. Her tears splash on the linoleum in rhythmic succession. The sight of my mother picking the dinner—that she worked so hard to make—up off the floor like an animal makes me cry.

Pa hears me sniffle and gets right down in my face, "And you, *Big Head*, didn't I tell you to feed the dog twice already today? You are just as stupid as your mother! How hard is it to put dog food into a bowl?"

*I already fed Chen-Chen, the first time you asked me to.* But I won't say a word. I don't want to take him over the edge. I know what that's like.

Pa flips a cigarette into his mouth and speaks with it dangling from his lips. "You're all a bunch of animals, just like that dog. *Stupid animals!*" Pa's hands shake as he tries to light his cigarette. His breathing is shallow from the adrenaline that's coursing through his veins. He gets down in my face again and screeches at the top of his lungs, "Didn't you hear what I *just said*! Go feed the fucking dog . . . *now!*"

*Don't look at him, Lac. Don't say anything. You fed that damn Chihuahua already. It's done.*

Ma's eyes are puffy and red. The tears continue to stream down her cheeks. I look at her hands. These same hands that have soothed me so many times before are now dirty from picking food up off the floor like a savage. I feel a lump in my throat. It's suffocating me. It's utterly deflating to see Ma this way. *Is this what it's like for her when Pa kicks my ass?* I crawl over to her and whisper, "Ma, Ma, it's okay. I'll clean up the mess. Don't cry—"

Pa's angry hands take hold of my hair and drag me away, through the kitchen to the laundry room. The shooting pain makes me flop around like a fish. In the laundry room, he shoves my head into the giant bag of dog food that's lying on the floor.

Again, he crouches down right beside me, "Are you fucking deaf *and* stupid? Here's the dog food, now . . . scoop a handful . . . out of the bag . . . go to the backyard . . . and put it in the dog bowl. It's not that hard!" He smacks me across the back of the head to punctuate the statement.

I can hear Ma sobbing loudly in the hallway. "You're more worried about that dog than the welfare *of your children?*" she shrieks. "They are hungry . . . They need to eat!"

Pa tilts his head in her direction—his eyebrows perked and eyes widened.

"What did you say, you fucking bitch?" he says as he storms back to the other room. I know Ma has taken him over the edge with her comment. I've never heard her defy him so directly, and

I've watched him beat her badly for much less. I leap up and run to the dining area after Pa. When I reach him, I grab him by the shoulder to stop him and pull hard enough that it spins him around. It's the first time I've ever laid a hand on my father.

A strange look of pleasure washes over his face. "You want to be a big shot and protect your mother? How dare you touch me, you dead dog!"

Pa walks away from Ma and back into the kitchen and opens the drawer. He pulls out her meat cleaver and charges at me with the blade in one hand and the other extended like a running back about to straight-arm a defender. I freeze. My sense of time slows to a crawl as I watch my father raging toward me; I can see the beads of sweat working their way down his forehead and my mother's terrified expression as she watches him from the kitchen entry. My father grabs hold of my neck with his outstretched arm and pushes me up against the refrigerator. The impact sends the pots and pans stored on top crashing to the ground. He rings my T-shirt with his left hand until it chokes me, then pushes the blade of the meat cleaver against my Adam's apple.

Pa comes in real close, so close that the tip of his nose brushes up against my face while he speaks. "Don't you dare put your hands on me again. I'll cut your neck off, you little bastard." He speaks to me in an atypical, muffled tone, and his warm breath splashes against my face in rapid bursts, "Say *one more word* and I will slice your head off and butcher up the whole family. Say another word. *Say it.* Dare me to kill you right now."

I close my eyes and wait. He holds me there without speaking a word. When he finally pulls his arm back and lets go, I drop to the floor in a heap. I cough and choke and grab at my throat until I can get some air back into my burning lungs. After a while I stand up and get my bearings and walk slowly away from Pa toward my room. I close the door, close the blinds, get into bed, and sob.

As I lie there in the dark, it feels as if the whole world is cav-
ing in on top of me. I can hear my mother and siblings crying
and my father lamenting how worthless I am. I grab the suicide
juice from behind the speaker and gulp down what's left of it. It
isn't enough. I call Dragon Head and tell him that I'm coming
over.

I dig in my closet for the spray cans I stole from Pa's tool cabi-
net and throw them into my backpack. I slide my window open
and hop out. The cool night air is refreshing, like I'm stepping
out of a sauna.

When I get to Dragon Head's house, he greets me with a
forty of Mickey's. I crack the green cap, spin it off, and let it fall
to the ground. I head out of Dragon Head's garage and sit in his
side yard in the dark. The Street Ratz can sense that something
fucked-up has just happened to me, so they leave me be. I chug
the Mickey's quickly, only stopping to catch my breath. On an
empty stomach, the drink is quick to calm my nerves.

The Ratz crack the garage door and slide a second forty out
after they hear me break the empty bottle against the house.
Halfway through the second bottle, a raging heat is pulsing
through my veins. The malt liquor numbs my senses until the
incident with Pa feels like it was only a dream. But the feeling
isn't enough, so I get to working on my third bottle. I can hear
Kip's loud voice droning on about something behind the door. He
and the Ratz were chopping up lines of coke when I arrived, so
they're probably off their rockers by now. I swear to myself that
if he, or any of those fuckers, fuck with me tonight they're going
to die with me.

I run the evening's events through my head over and over
again, trying to figure out what in the hell just happened to me.
With no reasonable explanation to be found, I grow increasingly
frustrated and upset. Hopeless thoughts run in circles through my
brain until my whole life looks overwhelming and depressing.

But I know that I have to stay strong for my family. If I break,

my family will shatter. Our family is measured by who I become. To my parents a good son is educated, remains "Asian," and is reverent to his father's will. It's easier expected than done. It hurts the most when I'm doing my absolute best and it still isn't enough. Striving to meet my father's expectations is like climbing out of quicksand: the harder I try to get to the top, the more I'm sucked back down by his unrelenting criticism.

I stop to look up at the sky and thank God for the alcohol— without it, I wouldn't have the sanity to see life through.

"Ay, dawg, you aight? What the fuck's up with you? You lost your girl or something?" A voice breaks my concentration. It's Dragon Head.

"Life is fucked up, man."

"Shit. You're telling me?"

"It's fucked up . . ." I feel my eyebrows furrow and my head getting heavy. I don't even know where to begin telling Dragon Head what keeps me up at night. But I sense he understands me anyway. His pops is no Mike Brady, either.

"That's why we thugs. Nobody wants us . . . and we want nobody. We rats . . . dirty, hungry, and looking for something crazy to get into."

Dragon Head moves back into the garage to do more coke. The third forty is making my eyes heavy. I'm faded. I rest my face in the palms of my hands. I can feel the earth spinning. Images of Pa's face, the cleaver, and Ma crying on the floor flash in my head. I polish off the last bit of the forty, which tastes bitter and skunky. Now my head is really spinning. I crack the side of my melon a couple of times with a closed fist to stop the spinning. *It's all my fault that Ma cried today. Pa should've cut my throat because I'm an unworthy son. It's all my fucking fault.*

I stumble back to the side of the house, then move toward the garage. I fumble with the doorknob and fall face first onto the garage floor when I finally get it open. I look around for my backpack. The garage is filled with smoke from cigarettes

and weed. I walk past the patio table where the Ratz are sitting. Dragon Head is playing blackjack with Ken-Ken. Snooky and Kip are snorting rails. I reach over Kip to get my backpack from the weight bench. I don't say a word. I want to get the fuck out of here. The liquid courage is making me want to go and do something crazy.

"Where you going, foo?" Kip asks.

"I'm going to go hit up some walls."

"Where?"

"I don't know . . . *wherever.*"

"Wait up. We'll roll wit' you," Dragon Head says without looking up from his cards.

We stumble down the driveway and make our way down Fremont toward Valley Boulevard. Before I know it, we're approaching the 10 freeway. We know who hangs around here—it's written on the walls. The last time I was in this neighborhood, I was on my bicycle getting chased by cholos. I look into Dragon Head's eyes as we're walking. I'm no longer timid and intimidated in his presence. We turn down a smaller street to avoid running into cops. It's too obvious what we're up to— bald-headed Asians in baggy clothes roaming the streets late at night carrying backpacks.

We roll up to a brick building where the Ratz have an unfinished mural. They ask me to help them finish it up. I take a can of gold spray paint out of my bag and shake it up. I hesitate for a moment before spraying the first arc. Even piss-drunk I can appreciate how long I've held this moment at bay. I move through the mural with long, natural strokes. Time flies while I'm tagging the wall. Before I know it, I'm the only one touching it up, trying to make it perfect. The Ratz are supposed to be on the lookout for cops, but they're down the block laughing and carrying on like they're at a barbecue or something.

I scan the mural to see if there is anything more I can add, and I notice another gang has sprayed their name on top of it. I

cross it out and put the letters *SR* and my nickname, Tiny, next to it. Disrespecting another gang rouses something deep inside me. I start working my way down the block, crossing out every gang name I see. My movements are rabid and fluid. I polish off the gold can, toss it behind me, and reach for the other can in my back pocket. I hear a whistle in the distance and look up and down the block to see who it is. No one is there. I keep looking to see if I can find the Street Ratz. I can barely make them out, several blocks down.

I keep spraying until I hear the whistle again. It's louder this time. Loud enough that I can hear it over the hiss of the spray can. I hear it again; it's the same whistle Dragon Head gives me when he's out in front of my house. I stand there squinting into the darkness. I can make out a band of shadowy figures moving quickly toward me, from the opposite direction the Street Ratz are in. They get closer, about six or seven of them. I drop my backpack to the ground and move toward them. The liquid courage pushes me ahead. It walks me over to these strangers to tell them who I am and where I'm from. It makes me stand there stone-faced while they surround me, and it tells me to swing first. It also makes my aim terrible. My arm swings over someone's shoulder and I grab at the back of his T-shirt. Something hard smacks me in the back. I swing in all directions. My knuckles crack against noses, temples, and chins. I hear the popping of bone hitting bone, and realize that I'm the one receiving most of the blows.

I fall to the ground and I see them above me, stomping and punching and swinging. I try to cover my head but there's too many of them. Now I can hear the thud of knuckles hitting my face from inside my head. My arms fall to the ground and I gaze listlessly at my assailants. They all have my father's face. The pain from the blows starts to feel good, like an itch that's begging to be scratched. I hear Dragon Head's voice yelling "motherfuck" in Vietnamese, and the blows against my body stop.

The clicking of collapsible batons against pavement echoes up and down the street. The cracking sound of those batons against skulls is louder. I get up and try to make sense of what I'm seeing. My face stings and my body aches. Kip chases one of my assailants down the street with his baton. Dragon Head, with blood seeping from his nostrils, is squaring off against another guy. When the guy realizes his friends are gone, he takes off running down the street.

"Go, go, let's go!" Dragon Head orders. "They're gonna bring more guys. *Let's jet!*"

We take off running back to Fremont Avenue. If we don't hurry, we'll be hunted down by five or six cars full of Asian dudes. That's just how they roll. I throw my backpack in the trash bins next to a Chinese supermarket. The batons go with it. A minute later, a metro bus pulls up by the gas station. We all hop on. Blood is dripping from my nose and my shirt is gone. My back is a patchwork of bruises and scrapes. We hear police sirens in the distance. Someone must have called them.

"You're crazy, Tiny!" Kip says with an excited twang.

"Motherfuck, when did you grow balls?" Dragon Head asks, shaking his head in disbelief. "You hit that whole gang up by yourself."

I smile and shrug.

"Tiny crossed out every gang name on that block and wrote his next to it," Ken-Ken says.

All the Ratz smile and laugh and throw playful punches at me.

All except Dragon Head, who looks at me stoically as he speaks. "Fuck 'em. They know where to find us . . . You a Rat now, Tiny. You family."

His words melt away my pain and replace it with pride. I've never felt so content, so certain of where I belong. I feel alive.

# THUG LIFE

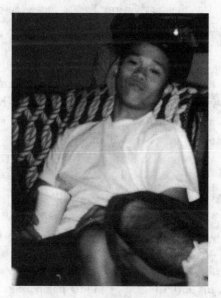

Sipping on "drank" with the Street Ratz.

**W**ho the fuck is that rolling in that Beemer?" Dragon Head asks, biting on his thumbnail. I'm sitting with the Street Ratz in our usual hangout, the patio of Lee's Donut Shop, across from the 7-Eleven. Ken-Ken is doodling on a piece of paper. Snooky has his leg up on a chair and is smoking a cigarette. Blazer is on the pay phone talking to someone who wants to buy some weed. I'm sitting next to Dragon Head drinking an iced coffee.

"I don't know. He always rolls up like he's a fucking movie star and shit," Snooky says.

"He got money, homie. Look, look! See his neck? Look at all that gold and jade he's wearing," Ken-Ken chimes in.

"Motherfuck, he must be Chinese or Taiwanese or something. Those fuckers got all the money," Dragon Head says in Vietnamese.

"Not all of them, homie. I'm half Chinese. My family doesn't have the kind of money that guy has . . . not even close," I say, watching the guy dial a call on his car phone.

"Look at those fucking rims. They're clean. They probably cost like five each," Snooky says.

Ken-Ken makes his way over to the 7-Eleven, after the driver of the BMW heads inside to buy something. Ken-Ken waits by the front door with one foot propped against the glass window.

"What the fuck is Ken-Ken doing?" I ask.

"He probably wants to know what time it is," Dragon Head answers.

"I could've told him that, it's five-thirty . . ."

"We know, Tiny. Ken-Ken wants to know the time from *that* guy," Dragon Head says, leaning his head in the direction of the 7-Eleven.

I nod but I don't understand. So, I keep my eyes on Ken-Ken, who puts on his dark sunglasses and lights up a cigarette. A moment later, the Beemer Guy comes out holding an orange Gatorade, peeling the cellophane off a pack of Marlboro Red with his teeth. Ken-Ken approaches him nonchalantly as he makes his way toward his car. Beemer Guy stops, sets his Gatorade on top of the car, and looks at his watch. Ken-Ken also takes a good look at the watch, then thanks him and walks into the 7-Eleven. A couple of minutes later, after Beemer Guy has pulled out of the parking lot, Ken-Ken walks back over to join us.

"It's a Rolie, homie. The Submariner—black on black," Ken-Ken offers before taking a seat.

"With diamonds on there?" Dragon Head asks, perking up.

"Little ones, on the numbers . . ."

"How 'bout his neck?"

"Twenty-four-karat gold," Ken-Ken replies in Vietnamese.

"Motherfuck, we want him," Dragon Head says with an air of authority. "He always comes here to buy cigarettes. He must live around here somewhere."

"I just want those rims, homie," Snooky claims.

"For what, dick? You don't even own a car," Ken-Ken teases. "You gonna put 'em on your sister's busted-ass Celica?"

"I'll keep them on the side until I get my own car," Snooky replies, undeterred.

Ken-Ken ignores Snooky and moves on. "I want that Rolie, though."

Dragon Head grows frustrated listening to their banter. "Shut the fuck up! Don't get all greedy and shit. Let's figure out how to get his shit first." He stares each Rat down to see if they have anything else to say. This puts them in their place. "Snooky, the next time that fucker rolls up, follow his ass home. Remember how to get to his house. Don't get too close to him . . . and wear a hat. Ken, you get what we need ready."

"One or two?" Ken-Ken asks.

"Two is good. One for me. One for you. Tiny, get four beanies and four bandanas. We'll need those, too."

I don't know what I'm getting into. I try to give the impression that I'm down, but I'm scared.

"You got that, Tiny?" Dragon Head seems to sense my apprehension. The other Ratz wait anxiously for my reply.

"Fuck it," I say. "Let's do it."

My face is flush from my second forty-ounce of Olde English, but I just don't feel drunk. The four of us are sitting in Dragon Head's Honda Accord, a stone's throw from Beemer Guy's house. I wish this shit would just kick in and make me numb; my anxiety is overpowering the alcohol. This is some real shit that's

about to go down, and I don't know if I'm ready. But this is what I signed up for when I joined the Ratz, so I'd better be.

It's hot and dark in the car, but we can't roll down the windows or turn the engine on and fire up the AC; Dragon Head doesn't want us drawing any attention to our presence. Dragon Head goes over the plan one last time. He's serious about making this thing go off without a hitch. It only took Snooky a week to find the guy's house and scout out a time he knew the whole family would be home. "I'm going to knock on the door to ask for a donation for a church. When he opens, I'm going to knock his ass out. Then we bum rush the house, aight?"

Ken looks pumped and Snooky is giggling. My palms are sweating. I look Dragon Head in the eyes, hoping to draw his attention away from my nervous legs, which are jittering back and forth like Pa's. Snooky tries to fire up a joint, but Dragon Head reaches into the backseat and smacks it out of his mouth. He can't have any of us doing anything stupid.

"Ken, first thing you do is show them your piece and tell everybody to shut the fuck up. Snooky and Tiny, if anybody makes a noise, you crack 'em in the face with that baton. No matter what . . . you keep them quiet. Got it?"

Nods all around. Ken-Ken checks on the guns to make sure they work. I pass out the beanies and bandanas and make sure everyone brought his sunglasses. Like bandits in an old Western flick, we tie the black bandanas around our noses and mouth. We put our sunglasses on to cover our eyes, and then pull beanies down over our foreheads. Except for Dragon Head, who's wearing a white dress shirt like a church boy.

"Okay, let's go."

We all slip out and caress the car doors shut. I look up and down the empty street, expecting a police cruiser to pull up and shine its floodlights on us. We slither down the block toward Beemer Guy's house. His black beauty is sitting in the driveway, rims shining brightly in spite of the dim streetlight. I hear dogs

barking. I can't tell if they're in this house or the neighbor's, but they sound like indoor dogs—a Pomeranian or maybe a schnauzer. We walk up to the front door. Dragon Head pulls out a notepad and pencil. Snooky and I stand on the left, in the corner out of the peephole's sight. Ken-Ken stands on the right.

Dragon Head pauses for a moment to collect himself. The image of my father's disappointed face passes through my head. I push it aside. Dragon Head raps on the door three times with his knuckles.

Nobody comes. My body itches with anticipation. *Open the fucking door already.* I reach behind my back and feel around to make sure the collapsible baton is still there. It is, and I grab hold of the handle.

Dragon Head knocks again. Nothing. He pounds on the door with his fist. No luck. He turns to Snooky. "I thought you said they'd be home?"

Snooky gives him a sheepish shrug.

The dead bolt is locked, so we walk around back to find a way in. The sliding glass door has a dowel in the track, so we can't pop it open. Dragon Head and Ken-Ken walk around the side of the house to check the windows. There's a balcony with a winding staircase, so I climb the steps to see what the windows are like up top. There's a sliding door up there, too, but it also has a dowel in the track. As I stand with my head pressed against the glass, I can make out a faint, high-pitched scraping sound below me. I walk over to the edge of the balcony and look down. Snooky is digging a loose brick from the mortar on top of a planter.

"Ay, Snooky," I call down to him with hushed tone. "What are you doin'?"

Snooky lodges the brick loose and looks up at me with manic laughter. "Snooky, *no!*" I yell and run down the staircase in time to see him hurl the brick through the sliding glass window.

The brick sends glass raining to the ground with a thunderous

crash. Dragon Head and Ken-Ken come running around the corner at the sound of the crash. I point at Snooky, who is standing there with a shit-eating grin, and shake my head.

"*Snooky,*" Dragon Head shouts through grit teeth. "What the fuck's wrong with you? The neighbors are gonna hear that shit and call the cops."

The dogs next door are barking like crazy. I peer over the fence to take a look and don't see any lights on in the neighbor's house.

"I think no one's home," I say to Dragon Head.

"You fucking knucklehead," Dragon Head says, grabbing Snooky's baton from his hand and cracking him across the neck with it.

The blow sends Snooky reeling back. He slips on the broken glass and falls to the ground. Dragon Head drops the baton on top of him. "*Come on,* let's go, *quick!*" he orders.

I follow Dragon Head and Ken-Ken into the house. Snooky dusts himself off and comes in behind us. We spread out and move through the darkness, searching for Beemer Guy's hiding places. As children of Asian immigrants, we know how mistrustful our people are of banks. If Beemer Guy is half as rich as he lets on, there will be plenty of valuables stashed inside this house.

Dragon Head and Ken-Ken run upstairs. After rummaging around the living room and office with Snooky, who throws shit everywhere and makes an incredible mess, I decide to join the boys upstairs. I find Dragon Head and Ken-Ken in the master bedroom, digging through the closet. They find a small linen bag hidden beneath layers of winter clothing. Dragon Head pulls at the sides and looks inside. He reaches in and holds up a couple of gold bands on his pinky. One is adorned with jade. Ken-Ken smiles wide as he looks into the bag. He reaches in and pulls out the black Rolex that Beemer Guy was wearing last week in the 7-Eleven parking lot. They drop the loot back into the bag, and

Dragon Head pulls the drawstring shut. The two of them start stomping on the carpet and feeling about with their feet.

"Tiny, see if you can find any lumps in the carpet," Ken-Ken says.

I drop to my hands and knees and feel my way around. The carpet is thick and shaggy and really tacky. I reach under the bed and feel where the carpet meets the wall.

"Ay, ay, there's a big-ass lump over here!" I call to Dragon Head and Ken-Ken.

The two of them bolt over and pull the bed back. They yank the carpet up to uncover three piles of crisp hundred dollar bills. My eyes grow wide. I've never seen this much cash in my life.

"Nice, Tiny!" Dragon Head swats me on the back, scoops the money up nonchalantly, and slides it into the linen satchel, which is now bulging. "Take your shank and check the light sockets."

I pull the plugs out of the nearest socket, flip my shank open, and start unscrewing the top screw. A loud crash downstairs puts a pause in our work.

"Ay, Tiny," Dragon Head says, "go downstairs and make sure Snooky doesn't do any more stupid shit. And check all those sockets."

I hop up like an obedient soldier and run downstairs. Snooky is already unscrewing a socket that was once behind the china cabinet in the living room; now the china cabinet is lying face-down on the floor.

"You find anything, Tiny?" Snooky asks.

"Yeah, I found a bunch of cash under the rug, and Dragon and Ken found some jewelry . . . and that Rolie."

"Yeah! Yeah!" Snooky yells and goes back to working on the socket.

I kneel next to an end table and push it aside to get a clear shot at the socket. As I lean down to unscrew it, a picture on the

table catches my attention. It's a portrait of Beemer Guy with his wife and daughter, who looks awfully familiar. I pick the frame up and take a closer look at the photograph. "Oh shit! This bitch is in my English class."

Now I know why no one is home—our school is having an open house tonight. I turn to Snooky, who doesn't look like he heard me. He has the plate off the wall and is feeling around inside the wall cavity with his hand. I get up to show Snooky the picture, and before I can make my way over to him his body goes erect. He begins shaking uncontrollably with his right hand and forearm inside the wall. I freeze. He writhes and twitches for a few seconds until his arm falls out of the wall cavity, clutching the purple velvet pouch from a Crown Royal bag.

"Oh, shit, homie! You aight?" I drop the frame and kneel down next to him. His eyes look sleepy and confused.

"What the fuck happened?" Snooky asks.

"You got fucking electrocuted. You all right?"

"Ay, fuck, my arm burns, dawg." He holds out the arm that was digging around in the wall cavity and there's a small burn mark below his wrist.

"Can you get up?"

"I don't know. My feet's numb."

"Your *feet*?"

"Yeah, man, they sting on the bottom."

I think Snooky might've electrocuted his brain. Why else would his feet hurt from a shock to the arm? Snooky has to get up, so I hold his arm and he pulls himself up into a seated position. He looks like he's coming to, and he realizes that he's still holding the purple bag in his hand.

"Open it up, dawg."

I take the bag out of his hand. It looks almost empty, but the bag is heavy enough that I know it's holding something dense. I pull the bag open and turn it upside down to empty its contents on the floor. A lump of rings and necklaces fall to the floor.

Snooky scoops them up and we take them over to the kitchen table, where there's more light. We scored. There are four cocktail rings, each adorned with rubies and sapphires, a large diamond pendant, and some gold necklaces, one of which supports a thick, forest-green jade Buddha. Snooky notices another ring tangled up in the bundle of necklaces. He digs it out and holds it up to the light to reveal a massive, square canary-yellow diamond. Snooky grows so excited that he looks like he's getting electrocuted again. Dragon Head and Ken-Ken come thumping down the stairs.

"You find anything?" I ask.

"Naw, dawg, there ain't shit in those sockets," Ken-Ken says.

"Look what Snooky found in the socket behind that cabinet," I say. Dragon Head and Ken-Ken pour over the stash for a moment, then slide it off the table into the linen sack holding the cash and jewelry from the bedroom. "Snooky got electrocuted."

"That's what you get, you stupid fuck," Dragon Head barks. Snooky just laughs like the village idiot. Dragon Head pulls a fat black Sharpie from his hip pocket and writes in big block letters on the counter: "WE KNOW WHERE YOU LIVE. CALL THE COPS AND WE'LL BE BACK . . ."

When he's done with the note, Dragon Head gives us marching orders: "Let's get the fuck outta here."

It's all too easy. We hustle down the empty street, hop in Dragon's car, and drive away. The next day, while I'm in school, the Ratz drive into Chinatown and sell the loot to Asian jewelry stores. The stores don't ask questions, and they don't pay anything close to market. I don't know how much the Ratz take, but there's a bunch of new crap in Dragon Head's garage when I show up after school. The Ratz are decked out in fresh clothes, bumping music from brand-new speakers and sipping from an aged bottle of Hennessy.

Dragon Head hands me my share of the loot, five one-

hundred-dollar bills, which I accept reluctantly. I was already feeling remorse for stealing from my people—no matter how wealthy they are—when I saw Beemer Guy's daughter in English class. She looked frazzled, like she'd been up all night, and it made my heart sink. Now I feel terrible about the whole thing and wish I could take it all back. But five hundred dollars is a lot of money. I don't take it back; I take it straight to Kmart and buy myself Dickies and flannel so I can dress like the Ratz. Then I head over to Foot Locker and get my first pair of Jordans. I get Vinnie some clothes, too, and give the rest of the money to Quy and Bo. I tell myself that we're just like Robin Hood, stealing from the rich and giving to the poor, but it does little to alleviate the guilt that lives inside me. I never rob another house with the Ratz.

I'm in my bedroom listening to music when the phone rings. The Ratz don't call me here, and I've alienated my other friends since joining their gang, so I don't have any interest in who is on the other end of the phone. Pa hates talking on the phone—he thinks it's a complete waste of time—so he lets it ring several times before relenting and picking it up.

I head into the kitchen to fix myself a snack when Pa's unusual conversation pricks my attention.

"Ahlo?" Pa answers the telephone in broken English. "Who yis?"

Pa listens to the person on the other line, and then he starts speaking in Vietnamese. "Lac?" Silence. "Who's talking?" He listens to the response. "Who are you?" A short break and then it's, "What school do you go to? Are you getting good grades? Who's your father? Do I know him?" In rapid succession.

The interrogation carries on for a few more minutes, so I stick around in the kitchen to eat. I flip nonchalantly through the Chinese newspaper as I munch on my food, pretending to be

uninterested in Pa's conversation. But I am gravely interested in whom he's speaking with because the only person that would call our house looking for me and speaking in Vietnamese is Dragon Head.

Finally, Pa calls me over to the phone. "Lac! Your friend is asking for you. He better not be a hoodlum!"

*If you only knew, old man. A hoodlum he is, and you've got another one right here that you're passing the call to.*

I tell Pa I'll take the call in my room and run down the hall to do so. I'm afraid that if it is Dragon Head, he's going to be in some kind of trouble. I haven't seen him since we divvied up the loot, and the crime just seems all too easy. I worry that someone must be on to us by now. I shut my door carefully and walk over to my phone. I pick up the receiver timidly and put it up to my mouth. "Uh, hello?"

"Tiny, fuck dawg, you better come over here quick. I need a favor," Dragon Head says.

"Why? What's going on? Where you at?"

"I'm at a pay phone right now, but meet me at my house in fifteen minutes . . ." He lowers his voice and then continues, "I'm being watched . . . get over *quick*."

*Click.* Dragon Head hangs up the phone without saying another word. I can tell he's in some kind of trouble. I know I'll have to prove myself through various missions now that I'm a Street Rat, but I hope today isn't anything like the home burglary. I've been feeling awful about it. I thought it would be fun being a straight-up thug and taking loot from a guy who has more than he needs and is stupid enough to go flashing it around the neighborhood. But now it just doesn't seem right—stealing from our people. I pray that I won't ever have to see or do again what I saw and did that night.

Still, I'm fiercely loyal to Dragon Head, so I grab my jacket without hesitation and rush out into the kitchen to tell Pa.

"Pa, my friend and I are supposed to study for our math test

today, but I forgot my book in my locker at school," I say, trying to appear earnest.

"What about dinner?" Pa says from behind the newspaper.

"I'll grab something near the library. I need to study more than I need good food."

Pa puts the paper in his lap and looks up at me. "You better not be lying to me. Don't be out wandering the streets and doing stupid shit. I'll give you half an hour to get your book and two hours to study with your friend."

"Okay, Pa."

I run out the door and catch the RTD bus to Dragon Head's house. When I arrive the garage is empty. *Where the fuck is he? He never goes in that house.* I walk out front to look for him and then check the side yard. Nothing. After a few more minutes of waiting, I decide to knock on the side door, which, due to some feng shui thing, is the entrance to his parent's house. No answer. The last bit of sun sinks beneath the horizon.

"Dragon!" I call out to him.

I hear footsteps in the kitchen that's behind the door. I knock some more and wait. A few more minutes go by before I catch a set of eyes peering out at me through the mini blinds. Someone unlocks the door but doesn't open it for me. I dig my fingers into my scalp. *What the fuck is going on here?* I open the door and walk in. No one is there. The door slams shut behind me. I spin around and see that it's Dragon Head, who was lurking behind the door in the darkened pantry. He looks shaken up; it's something I've never seen in him.

"What the fuck's up, homie? Where are your parents?"

"Hurry, follow me."

Dragon Head locks the door and takes a peek out the mini blinds. He leads me toward the rear of the house and into his parent's bedroom. The curtains are drawn, and the room is dark.

"Are you supposed to be in here? Where's your mother and father?" I ask in Vietnamese.

"At the Bicycle Casino." Dragon Head sits down on the bed. "Fuck, dawg. The fucking DEA has been running surveillance on my house."

"Why are they watching you?"

"Dick . . . the cocaine . . ." he snarls in Vietnamese. "They served a warrant and searched my friend Phuc's place this morning."

The Ratz infused the lion's share of the money from the heist into their drug running. Scarcely a month has passed, and they've already flipped a few kilos of cocaine. All of the Ratz sell it, except for me. Dragon Head let me be when he realized I wasn't ready to get that deep.

My heart starts racing. "Did they bust him?"

"No—not yet, at least. He wasn't holding."

"Are they out there now?"

"I don't know. Maybe."

"Why do you have it? I thought Snooky was holding it for you."

"He's holding too much already. I took some to help him out."

"Where's Snooky? Get his ass here to take that shit."

"Nah, dawg; it's too obvious. I don't want people creeping right now."

"What should we do?"

"I have a dude who will hold it until shit dies down a little."

"But how the *fuck* are we gonna take that shit out of here? What if they're out there now?"

"Easy does it. We'll hop the wall in the backyard. My car's parked over there. But we'll wait a little longer, until it gets good and dark."

Dragon Head gets up from the bed and walks over to the

window to scope out the backyard through a crack in the curtains.

"What time are your parents coming home?" I ask.

"Fuck, I don't know. They left early this morning."

Dragon Head walks away from the window and over to the closet. He gingerly slides the mirrored closet door open and looks up at the ceiling. "Come help me take this shit down." He grabs a steel folding chair, positions it over the track for the closet door, and steps up onto it. He takes a screwdriver from his back pocket and begins removing the screws from the vent that's covering the heating duct.

"Did you bring your backpack?" he asks me.

"Nah . . . I didn't," I reply nervously. *Is he going to want me to carry this shit? Fuck!*

"Mine is in the garage. Go get it . . . use the back door."

I tiptoe out the back door like a cat burglar. Unable to resist, I walk over to the driveway and take a peek out into the street to see if the A-Team van is parked out front of Dragon Head's place. I picture the DEA using the most sophisticated equipment available, which, as far as I'm concerned, is B.A. Barachus's black 1983 GMC van with a matching satellite dish on top. I'm relieved to see there's no one out there. I go into the garage, grab Dragon Head's black Jansport backpack, and hurry into the house.

When I walk back into his parent's room, I'm shocked to discover three white bricks of cocaine wrapped neatly in plastic wrap on the bed. Next to them there's a large and small scale, as well as a handful of small plastic bags that look to be holding a gram each. I've seen cocaine on tables and in little plastic baggies, but the kilos are awe-inspiring. They look just like the bricks on TV that they show when there's a big drug bust.

"Take all those fucking books out of the bag," Dragon Head

orders. He isn't one to get uptight, but given the circumstances, I can't blame him.

I unzip the bag and turn it upside down so that the books fall to the floor. Dragon Head takes it from my hands and stuffs the bricks into the bottom. He puts the scales on top of them and the baggies into the smaller pocket. He zips it up and carries it to the living room. I follow. We sit on the couch, in the darkness, and wait for the right moment to bounce. We don't talk. Dragon Head can't sit still for even a second.

A bright light shines through the window and floods the room. We rush over to the window and look out to see a car coming up the driveway. *Fuck. It's the DEA. Shit.* I start to panic. Dragon Head drops the backpack onto the floor and keeps his gazed fixed out the window.

I sneak up alongside him. "Who is it?" I whisper.

No answer.

"Let's get the fuck outta here . . . We can go through the bathroom window," I continue.

"Hold on . . . hold on," he says while tapping his hand on my shoulder. He opens the blinds a little more to get a better look, and his face turns sour. "*Shit!* It's my fucking parents."

"Let's get the fuck outta here. You shouldn't even be in here," I say.

Dragon Head looks around frantically, like a guy with explosive diarrhea at a movie theater who runs into the bathroom only to discover that all of the stalls are locked.

"How we goin' to get out?" he asks.

"Out the bathroom window, like I told you. Hurry, let's jet, dawg," I respond, still thinking it's a great idea.

"But I can't fit through there."

A car alarm chirps. The dead bolt turns. The door opens.

"Here, hold this shit," Dragon Head picks up the backpack and tosses it underhand into my stomach. "Let's just walk out."

*Just walk out?* I look at the backpack that's lying in my arms like it's a sack of elephant shit.

"Put it on . . . hurry," he implores.

I hear footsteps clip-clopping on the kitchen linoleum. There's no more time for debate; I slide my arms through the straps. The load can't be more than ten pounds, but it feels like the weight of the world on my shoulders. The kitchen light turns on, and keys clang against a metal dish.

"That blackjack table is bad luck . . ." Dragon Head's father laments to his wife. "Strange because that same table gave me money last time."

Dragon Head waves me forward. We walk into the kitchen.

"*Oh!* You scared me!" Dragon Head's father blurts. "What are you doing in my house?"

"Lac needed to take a shit," Dragon Head says.

"How did you get in here? Did you break in? What did you steal?" Dragon Head's father moves between us and the door as he rifles off questions.

"Nothing. You left the backdoor open."

"You liar. Let me see what's in the backpack."

"It's just Lac's books."

"I don't believe you. Come here and let me check."

His father reaches for my shoulder to take the backpack off. I try and talk my way out of it, but I'm in a panic. "It's my books. Hey, I gotta go . . . I'm late for my bus home." He doesn't buy it, so I wriggle free and head for the door. "It's good to see you again, Mr. Nguyen."

I'm a couple steps away from his father when I'm pulled backward by a firm tug on the backpack. I try to keep moving forward, but he doesn't let go. I end up walking in place, so I yank harder. I break free from his grip, and the extra momentum sends me straight into the wall. I regain my balance quickly and slip out the door without looking back. A flood of anxiety greets me in the side yard—if the DEA pulls up right now, I'm

done. I turn and run toward the cinder-block retaining wall in the backyard and scale it like a gymnast mounting the pommel horse.

I stand next to Dragon Head's car and wait for him. To anyone walking down the street, I'm just an Asian kid on his way home from the library, but it feels like I have a giant neon sign flashing "COCAINE" above my head. I'm convinced that someone is going to jack me, if the DEA doesn't get to me first. I'm not sure exactly how much three kilos of coke is worth, but I'm willing to bet it's more than my life.

When Dragon Head finally comes out, we throw the bag in the trunk and motor on out of there. He drives to a house near Almansor Park that looks like it belongs to an elderly couple, not a drug dealer. The one-story home is freshly painted, the lawn is lush and green, and the hedges are neatly trimmed. The house is dark except for a single lamp that shines through the shades covering the bay window.

Dragon Head goes to the back of the car to get the backpack. "You coming with me?" he asks.

"Whose house is it?"

"Don't worry about it. It's somebody that owes me a favor."

"Nah . . . I'll just wait for you here in the car. Hurry the fuck up."

Dragon Head opens the side gate and disappears behind the house. He returns fifteen minutes later, visibly relieved. He starts the car and moves slowly down the street.

"Where are we going?" I ask.

"We're going to Sylmar. I feel like racing."

"Just for fun?"

"Nah, I wanna race some fools for money."

I look at my watch. I'm supposed to be home in less than an hour. I don't say a word.

"You want a rail?" Dragon Head asks, taking a little baggie of coke from his pocket.

"Nah, I'm straight."

"I need something to chill me the fuck out. Here, roll this for me."

Dragon Head takes a dollar bill from his wallet and hands it to me. Using his right knee to steer the car, he places a small, rectangular mirror on his thigh and shakes a small mound of white powder onto it from the baggy. I roll the dollar bill into a straw while he chops the coke into two massive, elongated mounds with his ATM card. I hand him the rolled-up dollar bill. He sticks it into his right nostril, picks the mirror up off his leg with the other hand, and holds the mirror beneath his nose with his index finger plugging his left nostril. He runs the dollar bill along the line, getting progressively faster the farther he goes. He finishes with a loud snort, cocks his head to the side, and blinks his eyes uncontrollably. The car swerves and he grabs the wheel with his hand to right it. I throw my shoulders back out of reflex and smack my elbow against the passenger window. Even though we're crawling down a residential street, reckless driving gives me fits.

Dragon Head hardly notices my reaction. He's too busy positioning the mirror under his left nostril to repeat the process. After the second line disappears, he licks his finger and runs it along the mirror to pick up the remaining flakes. Then he rubs the finger on his gums like he's giving rum to a colicky baby.

"*Goddamn!* I needed that," he says, his eyes growing wide.

We turn onto the freeway on-ramp, and Dragon Head mashes the gas pedal to the floor. He hits the freeway and swerves the Accord out into the middle lanes. I grip the oh-shit handle with both hands. He bats at his nostrils with his thumb, then leans back and drives with one hand. I sit there, white-knuckled as Dragon Head darts back and forth between lanes at more than a hundred miles an hour. We come up on the ass of a car that's doing seventy in the fast lane, and my foot stomps uncontrollably for an imaginary brake pedal. At the last minute, Dragon

Head swerves between two cars in the lane on our right and out
into the middle lane. He corrects a bit too late, and we almost
touch the wheels of a semi in the next lane over. I flinch to the
left, as if there isn't a door between myself and the semi. I flinch
back and forth uncontrollably the rest of the way to Sylmar as
we whiz by cars. I've never been street racing before, but I have a
feeling it's going to feel tame in comparison to the ride over.

# THE NEW KID

Chasing pain.

It's four in the afternoon on a school day, and I'm cruising the neighborhood with the Street Ratz after a ditching party that Dragon Head hosted at a Motel 6. Our crew is running four cars deep, each one crammed full of Ratz who are drunk, high, and itching for trouble.

As usual, I'm riding shotgun with Dragon Head, and Snooky is in the backseat talking a gang of shit. I roll the window down and stick my elbow out into the breeze. I gaze out at the hazel-blue Southern California sky. *If only life could always be this good.* At least that's what the alcohol is telling me.

"Ay, dawg, San Gabriel is having a dance tonight. That bitch from the Taco Bell wants us to kick it with her friends. You down?" Snooky asks the group.

"Fuck that bitch . . . She's stupid," Dragon Head says without looking back.

Snooky doesn't argue when Dragon Head speaks.

"I asked her to get me with one of her friends . . . just to fuck around. You know what that bitch told me? She told me her friend only likes schoolboys." Dragon Head continues with a chuckle, "What the fuck is that? She don't even know me."

"That's what my bitch told me, too, but I'm *getting* with her," Snooky says.

"Schoolboy, *my ass* . . . I like to read and shit," Dragon Head says. "Maybe she wants a dude like Tiny . . . fucking quiet and nerdy and shit."

I throw him a playful smirk.

"Hook up with her, Tiny," Kip jumps in.

"Fuck that, homie. She reminds me too much of my sister. Plus, I fucking hate her voice. Why she gotta whine whenever she talks?" I look out the window and mimic her voice: *"What school do you go to? What's your favorite class?"*

The car erupts with laughter.

"No shit!" Dragon Head says. "She does sound like that, homie. That shit's fucking annoying!"

N.W.A's "Dopeman" comes on the radio, so Dragon Head turns it up until the thumping bass line makes our seats shake. The Ratz get amped on the music. Snooky and Kip spell out our gang name with their hands in time to the beat.

We stop at a traffic light next to a strip mall, and a familiar face pricks my attention out in front of the pizza parlor. I take another look before I'm totally certain it's him. "That motherfucker . . ." I say to myself.

The light turns green, and Dragon Head hits the gas.

"Whoa, whoa, whoa . . . slow down, Dragon!" I insist.

"What is it?" he asks, pushing on the brake.

"Pull into that parking lot right there. I think I just saw someone."

"Who?" Dragon Head asks in Vietnamese.

"That Cambodian kid from school who's loud in the mouth . . ."

"Where he from?"

"I don't know . . . He just moved here. He's in my English class and he talks a lot of shit."

"To who? You?"

"Yup."

"You wanna get him?"

"Throw a bitch and go into the parking lot of that pizza place."

Dragon Head switches to the left lane so that he can make a U-turn when the light changes.

"Where you going!" Mhu, another Rat who's driving behind us, screams from the window of his car.

Dragon Head sticks an arm out the window and points the way into the parking lot.

"Park in the back," I say. "I'll go in through the back door and see if it's him."

I get out of the car, just as the other Ratz pull up next to us.

"Why the fuck we here?" Mhu asks. His puffy cheeks are flush from the alcohol, making his face look like a ripe tomato.

I walk past his car without responding.

"Don't throw down without me, homie!" Snooky yells as I step through the door.

When I walk in, the scent of pizza and sound of arcade games take me back to my days at the Shakey's in Hollywood. I can see Javi's face and Pa throwing me nude out in front of the apartment. *The liquor is talking to me.* I shake off the troubling thoughts and look for Veasna. He's fat, like Javi, but not so sloppy. Veasna thinks he's the shit and dresses the part in a white Adidas track-suit and matching sneakers, but his pug face and Asian razored mullet tell the real story.

I spot him leaning against the *Rampage* arcade game. He's sipping on a soda, laughing with a group of friends whom I don't recognize, and flirting with a couple of girls. As always, he's being a loudmouth and making sure he's the center of attention. I smirk when I realize how bad we're going to hurt him.

I work my way over to the arcade games and pretend I don't notice him.

"Ay . . . there's that buster from school," Veasna tells his friends.

Veasna and his friends walk over to me and look me up and down. Veasna snorts and gargles like he's going to hawk a loogie on me. I put my head down and walk away. The time for talk has long passed.

"Fucking buster!" he teases. His friends laugh and slap hands.

The nonsense in the arcade just fuels the fire that's burning inside me. I've been in so many fights since joining the Street Ratz that I've lost count, but Veasna is the first guy I've asked them to jump. It started his first day at our school. He swaggered into English class and the teacher assigned him the seat behind me. He stared me down as he walked past and jerked his shoulders forward like he was going to throw a punch. I just put my head down and continued reading. Veasna snickered behind me as if he'd just taken me to task.

Most kids at school leave me alone because they know I roll with the Ratz. Veasna doesn't seem to care. He loves the attention he receives at my expense. He'll trip me on the way out of class or yell "Buster!" when I walk by him and his friends in the quad—all things I can easily ignore. But last week, he took it too far. I was walking down the hallway on my way to lunch when someone pushed me from behind and slammed me into some lockers. When I turned around and saw that it was Veasna who pushed me, I finally stepped to him. "Ay, man, you gotta stop doing that shit. It's not funny, homie," I said.

"What you say, buster? Wassup? You want some shit?" was his reply.

"Just stop it. That's it," I said and walked away.

Veasna was with his friends, so naturally he ran his mouth as I walked away. "I'm going to find you after school and kick your ass. Can't fuck with us . . ."

I knew Veasna wouldn't have the balls to come looking for me, and I wasn't even set on beating his ass at that point. But then, last week, he decided to spit on my shirt from a stairwell as I walked into my geometry class. I didn't say a word. I knew I'd catch him slipping soon enough.

When I come out the back door of the pizza parlor, Dragon Head is sitting on the hood of his car smoking a cigarette. He looks at me, shrugs, and holds his palms up to see what the deal is. I respond with a quick nod and a slender smile that instantly propel him off the hood and into his car to grab his collapsible baton. He twists it open, then sticks it behind his back to make it less conspicuous. When the other Ratz see him, they know just what to do. They hop out of their cars, and some go into the trunk to grab their weapons of choice—crowbars, batons, brass knuckles, and mini slugger bats. They move quickly, quietly, like they mean business. I don't wait for them.

I walk right back into the pizza parlor. Veasna is right where I left him. When I see his face, my vision turns narrow and blurry. Every bit of sound in the noisy pizza parlor fades away. Veasna looks up and sees me charging at him. I cock my right arm back and throw my clenched fist into his Adam's apple. The blow chokes him, and he grabs at his neck, gasping for air. I follow with an upper cut into his unprotected chin. He stumbles and falls.

Before his friends have a chance to take me down, the Ratz go to work on them, swinging and bashing without mercy. The melee sends chairs and tables flying, distracting me momentarily from Veasna. I find him on one knee, leaning against the

wall that separates the arcade from the rest of the restaurant. He's still holding his throat. I charge into him again and give him a left hook into the side of his face, followed by a cartilage-popping right hand that he takes square on the nose. Dragon Head joins in, and with a single blow to the head from his baton, Veasna falls to the floor.

We move in close and finish him off by stomping our heels onto his skull. Snooky joins us with a belligerent fury of blows that are each punctuated with "Motherfuck you!" in Vietnamese.

"Stop it! Stop it! No more, no more!" a deep voice calls out behind us.

We continue tromping Veasna without looking back.

"Stop! Stop!" the voice continues. Now it's right next to us.

I still don't lift my eyes from Veasna's bloodied head. A warm hand grabs my right triceps. I spin around with my arm cocked, ready to punch whoever has just grabbed me. It's a stocky white man wearing a short-sleeved collared shirt and black pants. His name is printed on a small red badge that's pinned to his shirt. It reads, "Brad, Manager."

"I'm going to call the police!" Brad yells.

Mhu runs right behind him, chasing the last of Veasna's mobile friends into the restaurant area with a crowbar.

When I turn around, Snooky and Dragon Head are squatting over Veasna like zombies with a fresh kill.

"Let's go, Snooky!" I yell.

They're too busy beating Veasna's face in to heed my call.

"Snooky! Let's get the fuck out of here!" I yell again. He doesn't respond, so I walk over and grab his arm. He pushes me away.

"The cops are coming! Cops!" I yell. Dragon Head is the first one who's up and out the back door. "Snooky, let's go, hurry!" I screech in Vietnamese.

Snooky still won't let up on Veasna. "Can't fuck with the Street Ratz, homie!" he yells in Veasna's face. "You fuck with one of us, you fuck with *all* of us! Fuck you!" He gives Veasna a last

kick in the ass and spits on him. I hawk a loogie of my own and spit it in Veasna's face.

We rush out the back door, hop in our cars, and head back to the Motel 6 to drink and talk shit. My knuckles ache. It feels like I was punching a brick wall, not Veasna's face. Snooky breaks into his own rendition of what just went down. Mhu, Kip, and some of the other Ratz shake my hand and tell me how down I am and how big my balls are. I don't say much. I just sit shirtless in a coffee chair, sipping on E&J brandy.

It's getting dark, and the thought of going home to face my father is killing my buzz. It won't be long and he'll be out in the Chevette, looking for me. But I won't leave yet. The attention and respect I'm getting here from my "family" is not something that I can just walk away from. The year I've spent running with the Ratz is the only time in my life that I've felt in control of my surroundings. They shower me in positive regard. They show me that I have a place in this world and am no longer just life's dust. Which is why it's so frustrating that I still feel a sense of urgency to get home. *What am I going home to? A cursing and a beating? What else is new?* I must obey my father. The day will come when I will win Pa over. I will chip away at his anger until it no longer shrouds him from seeing me for what I am.

I stand up and tell the Ratz I'm leaving. I walk downstairs where Dragon Head is on the pay phone taking care of some business. He hangs up the phone and suggests I take the bus, just in case the cops are out looking for our cars. I take his advice.

An hour later, I'm walking up the steps to our porch. Before I left for school this morning, I asked Pa for his permission to go to the library after school. I should stick to that story, but it's too late for that. He'll ask questions, and he's so hard to lie to once he starts the interrogation. Telling him the truth doesn't feel like much of an option, either.

I pause with my hand on the doorknob. *Fuck it. What is he going to do? Beat me?* A beating is inevitable at this point. It's just

a matter of how bad I'm going to get it. There's no sense in getting anxious or nervous. I amp myself up to prepare for what's coming to me. I imagine the blows to prepare my delicate flesh for its future. My thoughts race as I turn the knob and open the door to hell's castle. *Are you ready, Lac? It's about to go down. How tough are you? It's going to be furious, but quick—the same way you did Veasna. In minutes, it will be done. Ready? Buckle up, kid. It's on.*

Just as I suspected, Pa is sitting there at the dinner table with his shirt off, smoking and fidgeting his legs. There are four sticks lying neatly in a row in front of him. I cringe. Ma peeps her head out from the kitchen and sees me. She gives me a look that tells me I'm in trouble and there's nothing she can do to stop it. She walks back into her bedroom and shuts the door. Vinnie and Bo are in the living room, seated side by side directly in front of the TV.

"Hey, brother, did you get me that bag of chips like you promised?" Vinnie asks.

"Not now, Vinnie—not now," I say. I walk over and turn off the television.

*"Hey!"* Bo whines.

"Go and play in my room," I tell them. I don't want them around when Pa gives it to me.

"Why?" Bo asks.

"Don't ask why. Just go. *Now!*" I order.

"I don't want to . . ." Vinnie joins in.

"I said *go!*" I say with a hard smack across the back of Vinnie's head.

"Okaaaay," he whines, rubbing the back of his head. He tugs at Bo until she stands, and they leave the room.

I walk into the kitchen to tell Pa I'm home. The four beating sticks on the table are various sizes and shapes. One of them is new—a three-foot section of eucalyptus tree branch that's a good inch thick. Pa didn't trim it down nice and neat for me, either. The branch is covered in knots and smaller, leafy shoots.

"Pa, I tried to call home and . . ." I begin.

"*Shut up!* I don't want to hear it."

"But . . ."

"Shut . . . your . . . mouth!"

I did try to call home, but no one answered. What's the use?

Pa pauses for a moment and places his palms on the end of the table with his thumbs underneath. He speaks to me slowly and methodically. "I'm going to ask you one question, that's it. And I want you to tell me the truth."

"Yes, Pa."

"Where did you go all this time?"

"I was hanging out with my friends, Pa. I lied to you this morning," I admit.

When Pa hears me confess the truth, his eyes soften. He takes a hard drag from his cigarette and looks at me. He looks awkward and confused. His fidgeting legs slow their pace. It's not a reaction I'm accustomed to. If I didn't know any better, I'd say the old man is pleased with my answer.

"You're so lucky you're telling me the truth . . ." he says, pointing at me with the snub of his cigarette before stamping it out compulsively in the ashtray, "because I went to the library this afternoon to look for you. I was worried. I thought someone kidnapped you. I almost called the police."

I don't say a word. I never say a thing when he's talking.

"Because you're telling me the truth, I'm not going to use this big stick that I was looking forward to. You are very lucky—you have three other sticks to choose from. Think about your mistake, and choose the one that fits your punishment. Tell me how many whips I should give you."

*What do you think I am, a sissy? Beat me! Make me into a good son. I want to feel the pain.* I reach over the table and grab the stick he was going to use in the first place.

"I was wrong, Pa. I'm a liar. Use this one. And I want you to beat me until you feel my mistake has been taken care of." I

hand the branch to him. "Beat me until you think I've learned. Beat me. *Beat me!*" My voice grows loud and angry. Tears stream down my cheeks. I want to reach out and wrap my arms around him.

It's the first time I've raised my voice to Pa. It's also the first time I've asked him for a beating. This catches him off guard. He lights another cigarette and continues to look at me in silence. For a brief moment, he smirks. There is pride in his knowing smile—a fleeting confession that he sees himself in me. An acknowledgment of the man I am becoming. It melts my heart.

I smile back—big and wide and right through the tears.

He averts his gaze and then looks back at me. "All right. You've learned your lesson. Don't get all crazy and think you're something big and courageous. I'm going to spare you a whipping today. You knew you were wrong and a liar, and know the extent of your mistake. Now go do your homework before I kick your ass for something else."

I don't move. Pa's words are so different from what I'm used to hearing that they're difficult to process. Ma has overheard our conversation and has decided that it's safe to come out. She walks into the kitchen and chimes in, "We were so worried about you. You should have called. What are you doing roaming the streets late at night? You're so small . . . you can't defend yourself. You should have called . . ."

"Okay, okay. He knows he did wrong and he *apologized* already. Stop it. Don't talk anymore," Pa says to Ma.

*I apologized? I didn't hear myself say I was sorry.*

# FIVE AND NINE

The park near my school.

E ven though my uncles arrive in the United States on a 747, they couldn't be more fresh off the boat. The international terminal at LAX is packed with people, but my uncles are easy to spot coming out of customs. They wear tattered sandals, their clothes are patched with rags, and their luggage consists of water-stained cardboard boxes strung together with duct tape. They are happy to see us amid the packed crowd of greeters peeking over heads and shoulders and holding up name signs, flowers, and balloons. America is my uncles' new country, and they are anxious to make it their home.

Ma has nine brothers in all. When you have this many boys in Vietnam, it's customary to refer to them by their birth order.

My parents saved every extra cent for years, in the hope of providing a better life for family members left behind in Vietnam. Pa and Ma forked over the bulk of their savings to sponsor Five and Nine's emigration to the United States. For the sake of Ma's happiness, Pa was willing to bury the deep-seated grudge he'd been carrying since the day his in-laws cast him aside and kept his money for taking their daughter and grandchildren to America. I wasn't sure Pa could do it, but I guess he left so much behind in Vietnam that it wasn't much more to add his rancor to the list.

Adjusting to American culture isn't easy, but under Pa's watchful eye my uncles make respectable progress in their first week. He helps them get jobs in a furniture-assembly plant, and we teach them to avoid breaking basic American laws—no urinating in public, no jaywalking, and no littering. All things that are so commonplace in Vietnam, you wouldn't even notice if the person standing next to you were doing them. Other than the incomprehensible social norms they are forced to follow, my uncles see America as an incredible cornucopia of pleasure. The minimum wage of four dollars and twenty-five cents per hour that they make at the factory is eighty times what they were making in Vietnam.

A month or so after my uncles arrive, Ma, Pa, and I take them to the park near my school. It's dry and unbearably hot for a Sunday afternoon in November, and the Los Angeles smog hangs a thick veil over our neighborhood. My skin is tight from the lack of humidity, and a biting wind blows dry against the sweat on the back of my neck. The five of us sit chatting at a picnic table, while my younger siblings—immune to the weather—squeal with delight on the swing set.

"Hey, Brother, let's *nhau* this weekend," Uncle Five suggests to Pa.

Pa shrugs. "We can if you want to. Ask your sister to make the appetizers." Ma is sitting right next to him.

Uncles Five and Nine and I exchange excited glances over the thought of the upcoming *nhau*. I can't wait. I love to *nhau*. It is a party where my parents' refugee friends come together to share and cope. It isn't anything formal, but there is always lots of drinking, eating, and storytelling. The stories inevitably grow in depth and intensity as the night wears on, and the empty beer bottles line up like soliders in formation around the house. *Nhau* is a rare moment when these new Americans can share what they've been through with like-minded souls. Pa always says people drink to forget, but at the *nhau* I see them drink to remember. The older I've become, the more I've grown to appreciate it.

Other than the Street Ratz, most of the Vietnamese kids I know are busy distancing themselves from our culture. Most of the Ratz love being Vietnamese but hate their families. I'm trying desperately to love both. I cherish the *nhau* because it's a guaranteed night of immersion in who I am. Everything I hear and say during a *nhau* is from the heart; whether bitter or sweet, it is raw and uncut. By the end of a *nhau*—which is often three or four in the morning—you have people crying, sometimes screaming, and always laughing and banging on the table over a good joke.

I always learn new things about Pa at the *nhau*, often from people who've known him longer than I've been alive. To know the man he was when he was young helps me understand something of the confusing tyrant he is today. Understanding him is my only hope for keeping our family together.

Uncle Five and Uncle Nine decide to get up and check out the rest of the park. Before long, the tiny men are wide-eyed and manic, running back toward our table from the other side of the park. As usual, Uncle Five does the talking for them. "Whose dogs are those I see roaming all over the park?" he says. "They are all fat and meaty . . . We're going to catch a couple and bring them to the *nhau!*"

*Holy shit. I didn't know people really ate dog.* I think about our pet Chihuahua, Chen-Chen.

Pa goes from zero to ballistic in about two seconds. "Are you crazy!? You could go to jail for that. *Do not* do that."

"Are they just wild dogs roaming the land? They don't belong to anyone, do they?" Uncle Five continues sheepishly until Pa interrupts.

"Catching a stray dog and killing it is against the law. They may not belong to anyone, but those dogs are protected by the government, and if you kill them, it's like killing a person. They will put your ass in jail for a long time," Pa says.

Uncles Five and Nine exchange a look of shock and awe. I think of Bo's beloved Chihuahua, Chen-Chen, back at the house, and decide I better keep a close eye on him with the uncles around.

"But these are stray dogs?" Uncle Five asks.

"Do not!" Pa continues. "Do what the Mexicans do . . . Raise some chickens, some ducks, some quail. Eat those."

"Chickens, ducks, and quail are okay?" Uncle Five rubs his chin searching for a loophole to score some dog. "But those are animals, too."

"But they belong to you," Pa replies.

This gets Uncle Five smiling again. "So you can eat dogs if they belong to you?"

Pa goes back to berserk. "No *fucking* dogs, no *horses*, no *cats*—"

"Crazy Americans and their laws. What's the difference between eating a dog and eating a cow?" Uncle Five is insolent.

Uncle Nine even chimes in, "So it's okay to eat poultry?"

"Yes, just no dogs."

The uncles are smiling at each other again, which pisses Pa off. "Do you hear me?" Pa bellows.

"Okay," Uncle Five says. Nine just nods his head.

Friday afternoon comes, and I run home from school. When I party with the Ratz, no one checks to see if my homework is

done, but if I want to *nhau* with my uncles I have to show my
parents that my work is finished first.

When I walk into the kitchen, Ma is already working on the
appetizers. They smell delicious. All of my favorites are spread
around me in various stages of preparation—shredded papaya
with beef jerky and liver, beef tripe marinated with sugar vin-
egar, and pig's ears. Tonight, all will be dipped in a spicy fish
sauce that spikes the flavor as well as everyone's alcohol con-
sumption. My anxious stomach grumbles, and I head back to my
room to get started on my math problems.

Homework is slowly replacing drinking as my after-school
pastime these days. I've been spending less time with the Ratz
ever since Dragon Head got hauled off to juvie. He broke into
his parents' house a few weeks ago when he was high on PCP
and gave his father a savage beating. Snooky says he's going
to be locked up for a few months. The Ratz are getting sloppy
without Dragon Head's leadership. Most of them have quit going
to school, and Snooky has them stealing cars and selling crack.
Every time I'm with them, it feels like everything is going to
come crashing down. Snooky just doesn't know when to say
when.

Now that Pa thinks I'm getting too old for beatings, he is
finding new ways to teach me a lesson. His current favorite is
taking me Dumpster diving, like we did when I was a small boy.
His frugal habits make trash-picking a fruitful hobby for him,
and an embarrassing waste of time for me. Until last week.

When I brought home my progress report, he took one look
at it and told me we were going for a walk. I knew what was up,
so I grabbed a baseball cap and pulled the bill low to cover my
face. When Pa asked me to jump into a Dumpster and toss him
empty cans and bottles, I spoke up.

"Pa, why do we have to go through the trash?" I lamented.
"These cans don't even earn us much money. We would have to
collect like a thousand of these to get ten dollars at the dump."

Pa smiled, loving that I was so ashamed of digging in the trash. "At least you're smart enough to put two and two together. Now get in."

"Are we *that* poor?" I asked, hopping over the lip of the Dumpster.

"Money doesn't just fall from the sky, you know. Uncle Sam is very generous to assist us with the welfare checks and food stamps, but I don't want *you* to rely on it. You can do better than this, I hope."

"I'm not going to look through trash for my family," I said with a cocky drawl.

"What makes you so sure?"

"Because it's dirty."

"Oh yeah? What if you don't have any other choice?"

Pa crushed cans with his feet while I thought about this.

"What if you don't have any other choice, son?"

"I won't. I'm going to be the boss."

"Then tell me . . . what are you going to do to be *the boss*?"

"Excel in school."

"But a lot of people do that. There's more to it."

"Like what?"

"Do you know how many houses our landlord has?" my father asked, never reluctant to answer a question with a question.

"No. How many?"

"Guess."

"I can't guess."

"Guess."

"Um, I'd say—"

Pa grabs me by the waist and turns me to my left to face the street. He points at nine different houses on our block and counts them off. They all belong to our landlord.

"That's nine already, just on this block," Pa said. "He also has other houses in Alhambra, Rosemead, Monterey Park, Azusa . . . everywhere."

*So . . . what's your point?*

"But come the first and the third Monday of every month, who do you see mowing our lawn? The owner. When the sink leaks, he fixes it. When the pipes are clogged, he comes over with the snake and pushes our shit out with his own hands. Do you think those houses just dropped from the sky in his name?"

Where I first found contradiction in his homily, I could now see a sharp point.

"People like our owner know the value of a dollar. They work hard because being smart is not enough. Don't ever be afraid to get your hands dirty, son. Any crap you get on your hands from hard work can easily be washed away with soap."

Was he comparing me to them? Saying that I, just like them, have to work hard and rely on more than my brains? It was the closest he'd ever come to complimenting my intellect.

"I work hard," I said.

"I saw your report card, Big Head. Not with those grades you don't."

Pa was right. My best grade was a C.

"You'll never get into college with those grades. How are you going to be the boss if you don't go to college?" Pa just crushed cans while he spoke to me. He didn't get in my face like he normally would; he didn't even threaten me with bodily harm. I began to wonder who this man talking to me was, and what he had done with Pa.

"What do I have to do to get you to study hard like Duong's boy? He goes to UCLA now, you know."

"But Hieu went to the magnet school. They kick you out if you don't stay on track to go to college," I tried to explain.

"You can't stay on track for college at Alhambra High?"

"It would be a lot easier at the magnet school."

"Why? What's so different about this *magnet* school?"

"I don't really know; I don't know that much about it. But there are lots of, um, distractions for me at Alhambra—" The

Ratz may not be in class with me anymore, but the reputation of running with them makes every day at Alhambra a challenge.

"*Girls?*" Pa asked, growing irritated by the thought of it.

"No, not girls."

"Well, I don't want you going to that *magnet* school. There's a bunch of white kids over there—Duong told me. I want you staying here, with your people."

"Yes, Pa . . . but my people aren't always what you . . ."

"You don't want to be around your people?" Pa asked, looking even angrier than he was at the thought of the fairer sex giving me bad grades.

"No, no, I love my people," I said earnestly.

"It's settled, then. Get your grades up, so you can go to college, but do it here in Alhambra, surrounded by your people."

Even though Pa won't let me go to the magnet school, that conversation has lit a fire inside of me. It showed me that he believes in me, that he thinks I'm smart enough to go to college. I feel loved by my father in his own way, and I don't want to let him down. I'm trying so hard now to make his dream come true, to prove that his journey to America was not for nothing, to show that we're better off because of his sacrifice. But, sometimes, life just gets in the way.

Halfway through my math problems I hear yelling outside. I pull a gap in the blinds and peer out. My uncles are coming up the walk. Uncle Five is lugging something in each hand. I assume they are groceries in plastic bags, so I head toward the front door to help him.

"Lac, hurry, come open the door!" I can hear Uncle Five shriek from outside. "Hey, we're home! It's time to *nhau*! For heaven's sake, we're going to *nhau* tonight!"

They must have won the lottery. Every Friday night on television, we watch Asian and Latino immigrants strike it rich on

the California Lottery's Big Spin. I have often fantasized that my father is the one in front of that big wheel of fate, and after his ball lands on the million-dollar slot, I rush the stage ecstatic and translate Chuck Woolery's questions for him. Like most of my family, it seems that nobody who wins on the Big Spin speaks a word of English, so I've always figured we have a good shot. *Uncle Five must've done it! What else could he be this excited about?* I sprint down the hall, rip the front door open, and freeze when I see what Uncle Five is bringing inside our house.

Uncle Five is grinning from ear to ear as he steps over the threshold. "Look what we have! Your mother will cook them for us right now, while they're still fresh."

Uncle Nine follows, smiling submissively, yet feeling proud as punch.

"We've got something special this time," Nine whispers as he walks by me.

Ma comes in from the kitchen. "What is that?"

"They're fresh white ducks!" Uncle Five beams. Two plump, white geese dangle from his hands. Uncle Five squeezes one tightly and holds it up by the crook in its neck. The bird is so large—and Five so short—that its webbed feet nearly touch the carpet. I haven't moved, but I'm grinning with wonder, trying to figure out what's unfolding in front of me. Our family has eaten poultry fresh from the cage before, but never *this* fresh, where the feathers are still attached to the bird and it stinks up the living room like a wet dog.

"Why didn't you buy them with their feathers already taken out?" Ma asks.

"Heaven sakes, who is going to do *that* for you? It was tough enough catching them," Uncle Five says. "It took so long we thought we were going to miss the party."

"*Where* did you catch them?" Ma's posture stiffens.

"Heaven sakes, there are hundreds of them roaming around the park by Lac's school. We got two of the fattest ones there."

Uncle Five is thrilled with himself. "We're going to have a wonderful feast with them tonight, Sister!"

Ma goes ballistic, rattling off questions faster than most people can hear. "You caught them at the park? *Are you crazy?* Didn't your brother-in-law warn you not to catch the animals at the park? Did anyone see you?"

"It's okay, Brother said we just can't catch dogs, horses, or cats, but it's okay with ducks or chickens . . . Don't worry, it's okay. Hurry, let's cook them while their blood is still sweet," Uncle Five says.

"I warned him," Uncle Nine mutters. Five throws him a sour look.

"Look, I wipe my hands of this. Come with me," Ma orders. Uncle Five sullenly follows her into the kitchen, dragging the geese in tow.

"I'll cook these for you," Ma explains, "but if your brother-in-law asks you where you got them, you better not tell him you caught them at the park. He is going to *kill you* if he finds out."

"Don't worrrrry. We won't tell him," Five says triumphantly. "I'm going to take a shower, freshen up, and get ready to *nhau!*" Uncle Five hands her the geese and cruises down the hallway to the bathroom. I can hear him lighting a cigarette while he waits for the hot water. He throws his dirty T-shirt and week-old pair of Wranglers into the hallway outside the bathroom. They reek of goose shit. While he waits for his turn in the shower, Nine searches through my closet for an outfit to wear to the party. I'm glad they are going to bathe; they need it.

Ma is still in the backyard plucking goose feathers when my uncles' friends begin arriving for the *nhau*. One by one, they enter the yard, greet my mother, and then sit quietly sipping beer while they wait for Uncle Five to come out and breathe life into the party. After a good round of Ma pulling feathers and me chasing them around the yard to pick them up so Pa won't see, the geese are ready to be cooked. Their pasty, dimpled flesh

reminds me of the tourists who come to California in the middle of winter and insist on going into the freezing ocean.

The bathroom window facing the yard cracks, and Uncle Five calls out, "Make sure you drain the blood out from those ducks for me . . . I'm going to make us an appetizer. Heaven sakes, it is going to be goo-ood with that duck blood so fresh." Ma shakes her head and walks the birds into the kitchen.

Ma prepares "his" appetizer by placing a rope around the feet of each bird and hanging it upside down from the patio awning. She slits their throats, and the blood drips for about twenty minutes into plastic Tupperware containers. I am mesmerized by the blood. I watch it drip rhythmically into the containers to the beat of a Vietnamese love song blaring from a boom box.

My uncle's chubby friend Tiu sits in the corner of the yard. His doughy cheeks are already rosy with inebriation, and he sings along to the song with his eyes closed tightly: "It's the autumn season . . . the leaves fly . . . my lover has left me . . ."

Twenty minutes later, Uncle Five emerges through the sliding door, his hair wet and parted neatly to one side.

"*Motherfuck*, let's party tonight. I got two fresh ducks!" he yells, throwing his hands into the air.

"Why didn't you buy the ducks without the feathers, instead of making your sister pluck them for you?" Tiu asks.

"No one told you? Me and Nine caught these ducks."

"Caught them where?"

"At the park, of course. There are hundreds of them just running around by the pond. That place is a feast waiting to happen," Uncle Five says, looking at the rest of the crew for approval.

Uncle Five lights a cigarette, pulls hard on it, and exhales with a crooked smile. The smoke rises above his friends' blank stares. He continues with the story. "Me and Nine just waited in the distance to find the fattest ones. We were looking for white ones with big chests. You know you can get seizures from eating brown ducks, right?" Five looks around and everyone nods.

"As soon as we found the right one, we just chased it around and around until we caught it. They didn't fly away or anything. Took us an hour, though, before we could get our hands on two of those puffy white ducks."

"Did anyone see you?" asks Bao, a young man with a Vietnamese accent as thick as his glasses.

"Yes. There were people there watching, but no one said anything," Uncle Five assures us.

"You guys could go to jail for that!" Bao snaps.

"That's what you say now, but wait until you taste it," Uncle Five replies with a wink. He is tickled with himself despite the confines of reality. This loosens the boys in the yard up a bit.

"How did you kill it?" I ask sheepishly, being careful not to assert myself in an adult conversation.

Uncle Five jumps to his feet. "Easy. Just break its neck," he says and runs over to the clothesline to grab one of my father's shirts. Uncle Five rolls the shirt up, and twirls it round and round over his head like a cowboy readying to rope a calf.

"Once I get hold of a duck by the head, I just swing it around like this," Uncle Five explains matter-of-factly.

The yard erupts in laughter. Uncle Five is the life of the party, a comic relief, no matter what the situation.

"Heaven's sakes. You're so cruel," Bao says as he lights his own cigarette. "You didn't have to go to the park to kill birds for us to have a good *nhau*. Your sister made plenty of appetizers."

"But you can't get fresh blood like this," Uncle Five says as he tosses his cigarette aside and runs into the kitchen. He comes back out toting a lopsided tinfoil pan. It's filled with dark-red goose blood, sprinkled with seasoning.

Goose blood appetizer is a delicacy that few know how to make properly. It's hard to get birds that are fresh enough, and word in our family is that Uncle Four married a woman who taught our kin how to make it right. This doesn't stop Uncle Five from claiming the recipe as his own.

"It's not ready yet. It will be delicious once the blood coagulates a bit. We have mint leaves and rice-flour chips to eat it with. In a couple of hours, it will be perfect," Uncle Five explains to nods of appreciation.

Uncle Five is good and drunk by the time my father arrives. As much of a big shot Uncle Five is around his friends, he always turns it down a notch when Pa is around. Uncle Five is well acquainted with Pa's heavy hand, and the geese from the park will certainly bring it out—if Pa finds out where they came from.

I know by the rituals when the *nhau* has officially begun. Cigarettes are lit, beers are cracked, and the appetizers make their way to the table. Every bite follows a dip in my mother's hottest fish sauce, and my uncles and their friends begin most sentences with the poetic grace of "Motherfuck!" I sit back in the corner—where the table meets the wall—next to Uncle Five, studying his every move so that I can become the person everyone admires. My father demands respect, but people are always on edge around him. One false remark or gesture and Pa is in your face to challenge your views. Uncle Five is more tactful. He has a knack for manipulating words in an affable manner, for getting his opinions across without offending or scaring the shit out of you.

I absorb my uncle's words, the way he purses his lips and squints his eyes when he takes a drag from his cigarette, and the way he times his exhales to create dramatic pauses in his stories. Uncle Five scans the reactions from across the table, his head nodding ever so slightly while the smoke pours out his nose. I like the way Uncle Five takes long, loud swigs from his beer and dashes his cigarette out on the table when he is really faded. Especially endearing is the way he jumps out of his chair and yells, "Dare me!" if anyone doubts his willingness to do something crazy. Uncle Five is a straight-up thug.

Five is the loudest man at the table, but he always looks over to Pa for confirmation. "Ask my brother-in-law, he understands what I'm talking about." If my father agrees with Uncle Five's boast, Pa nods quietly. When Pa disagrees—which is often—his response to Uncle Five is deafening. "You're a youngster! What the fuck do you know?" No matter how drunk Uncle Five gets, he never answers back to Pa.

Finally, Ma comes to the table with the main course, a huge glass dish holding the roasted geese. The birds' heads are still attached, and the birds are so large that their necks hang down over the side of the tray. Their skin is now brown and puckered to their frames, and their eyes are black and squinted from the heat of the oven. As Ma struggles to balance the tray while the men clear room for it on the table, the birds' necks dangle to and fro.

Fat-face Tiu walks right over to the table, grabs a goose by the neck, and rips it from the body. He wrings the greasy flesh with both hands to tear a piece off for Pa. The grease runs down his wrist as he passes it over.

"Thuy, we're out of fish sauce, can you make some more . . . and bring some more rice chips for these gentlemen," my father tells Ma—and she's back into the kitchen.

"*That's right!* The duck blood should be done by now." Uncle Five scans the eager faces, his head remaining still so as not to grab too much of Pa's attention. In a flash, he follows after Ma into the kitchen. My mother comes back out with the rice chips and mint leaves, and Uncle Five is behind her with the pan of goose blood, now coagulated into gelatin. Pa has his nose in the tray before it even reaches the table.

"Where did you get the duck blood from?" Pa barks at Five.

Silence. My stomach churns.

"Did you go all the way to Garden Grove to get a live duck? That's the only place I know that sells birds this fresh. Who took you all the way down to Orange County?"

No reply.

"Brother, you should try how I marinated it. Brother Four's wife taught me how to marinate it," Five stammers.

Pa looks longingly toward the tray of blood gelatin. He cracks a piece off a rice chip, dips it into the wiggling tray, scoops a hunk of blood into his mouth, and chases it with a handful of mint leaves.

"It's pretty good," he moans with blood glistening along the perimeter of his mouth. "You can tell the blood is still fresh. It's so much sweeter."

"Ha! I told you!" Uncle Five erupts. He leaps from his chair to throw a hand on Pa's shoulder; he uses the other hand behind Pa's back to signal a thumbs-up to his friends. "The fresher the duck, the sweeter the blood."

My father eyes the rest of the spread and reaches over to find the fattest piece of goose. He bites into it and is chomping happily when he stops abruptly. Reaching into his mouth, Pa pulls the spine of a scorched feather from between his teeth. "This place didn't clean their duck too well. There are still feathers." Undeterred, he dips a piece of goose into the fish sauce and puts it into his mouth. "Wow, this is really fresh duck, even the meat tastes fresh . . . very sweet," Pa says. "You should tell me where you got this. It's so good."

Cornered by my father's line of questioning, Uncle Five finds salvation in a quick raise of his Corona to toast the *nhau*. "For heaven's sakes, we have duck blood to eat!" Everyone cheers and chugs their beers, including Pa. Pa loves a good toast; I can see the gleam in his eye as he holds his beer up high, basking in the glow of the family's security and freedom since fleeing Vietnam. Pa loves to chat even more, and he's soon lost in a rowdy conversation about "the old days" that takes his mind far away from the inquisition over the source of today's delicacy. Five has dodged a bullet.

Tinh, an old man sitting next to me, nudges my knee and

tilts his beer in my direction, suggesting I take a sip. I snatch the bottle, put it in my mouth with both hands, and look up at the sky, pulling it empty with a quick series of ravenous chugs.

"Hey, just a sip; you're going to get drunk," Tinh snaps.

I don't care. I hold out my tongue to catch a final drop that's bulging on the lip of the bottle and keep a wary eye toward my father while I wait for it to fall. It's been a while since I've had a drink, and the beer tastes better than I remember. I put the bottle down gently and feel my cheeks grow warm. I smile at the old man, who is shaking his head. My mouth grows dry. I grab a piece of cuttlefish jerky, dip it in the fish sauce and throw it in. Problem solved. A Pavlovian flood of saliva fills my mouth to coat the spicy piece of fish. I ask the geezer if he wants another beer.

"Of course I want another beer . . . You just finished mine . . . you little bastard."

I get up from the table and walk over to the Igloo. Behind me, I can hear Tinh selling me out; he's telling my father that his little boy is too young to *nhau*. I pretend to look through the Igloo while I wait for my father's response. He's against me drinking and smoking, especially at fifteen. I worry my *nhau* is going to end early tonight and they won't invite me back. With no response from Pa, I peer over my shoulder at him. I'm lucky; Pa is drunk and far too involved in Uncle Five's story about how he lost his virginity to show interest in the snitch.

I crack open Tinh's new beer, and as I watch the foam rise in the bottle I contemplate spitting in it to get him back. As angry as I am at Tinh for trying to sell me out, I choose the higher ground and leave him be. Uncle Five and his crew always pick on Tinh, and I don't want to be in the habit of beating on the downtrodden. It doesn't stop me from taking a good pull off his fresh beer, though.

I walk back to the table, hand Tinh his beer, and have a seat. I love to hear the old men's stories at the *nhau*. I never talk much,

as people my age aren't supposed to chime in on adult conversations, so I have plenty of time to listen and learn. I light the men's cigarettes, get them beer, and help Ma make sure the table is always filled with food. I do my rounds quickly, anxious to get back to the table next to Uncle Five.

Around midnight, a belligerent Uncle Five grabs me by the neck and tells me it's time I step up and eat some fresh duck blood. I look into what's left of the picked-over tray and see a wobbling, disgusting mass that bears a strange resemblance to grape and cherry Jell-O sprinkled with pepper. By now, the blood is losing its purple hue and turning red. A little too red. Nobody worries about getting E. coli from the blood, because they believe the alcohol in the beer and cognac are sure to kill any bacteria. I'm not so sure.

Uncle Five won't stop goading me, so I snatch a rice chip, break it in half, and take a bold stab into the throbbing blood gelatin. The blood is so dark that the chip quickly disappears beneath it, along with the tips of my fingers. I freeze for a moment at the sight of this and take a sheepish look around the room, only to be locked into Pa's intense stare. His gaze is so utterly piercing that it raises the hair on the back of my neck. I know why Pa is watching me—he's noticed that I've avoided the blood all evening and he wants to see if I'm man enough to try it. Without further hesitation, I pull the overflowing chip from the tray and shove it and its globby cargo into my mouth. As I make a frantic search for the mint leaves and discover the bowl is empty, I can feel the gelatin spreading between my teeth and oozing under my tongue. At first, the mint leaves I seek are an insurance policy—all I can taste from the blood is the seasoning, and it tastes good: a little garlic, some chili . . . shallots. But before I can turn to Ma and ask her to refill the bowl, it hits me—the overpowering taste of iron. Like the time I smashed my giggling mouth onto the steel bar of the whizzing merry-go-round, the bitter, metallic taste of blood comes like a flood

to overwhelm my senses. By the time my mother arrives with the mint leaves, the blood's pungent aroma has crept into my sinuses. I stuff the mint leaves into my mouth, one after the other, until I can no longer taste the blood. Then I wash it all down with a Coke just to be sure. Maybe goose blood is an acquired taste, like the beer.

"Big Head, do you like it?" A smack on the neck from drunk Uncle Five, whose teeth are still covered in blood.

"It is so good. It is sooo fresh," I lie with a smile.

"Motherfuck, this guy is beginning to inherit the *nhau* genes," Uncle Five suggests. "Not too many kids can eat this shit, but this guy . . . he has the *nhau* genes for sure. Don't let your father catch you *nhau*-ing with us, he'll kill you . . . Here, take a sip of beer to kill the bacteria." Uncle Five chuckles.

Pa is no longer watching, so I down the rest of Uncle Five's beer. My uncle is too drunk to notice.

A few minutes later, I slide up next to Uncle Five, and he turns to his friends with gravity in his voice. "Motherfuck, this guy . . . my nephew . . . he doesn't want to let go of his Vietnamese roots. Too many kids these days don't even know how to use chopsticks, but Lac, he likes to *nhau* with his uncle." Uncle Five then points, stammers, and falls into me in an attempt to lean in close. With his left elbow on my shoulder and his right hand pointing toward the sky, he tells me, "Wait until I take you home to Vietnam to *nhau* with dog meat, then you'll really know what this *nhau* tradition is all about."

Uncle Five grabs his right forearm with his other hand and squeezes it aggressively in front of his face. "Dog meat will make you strong and stiff," Uncle Five slurs before tugging back and forth on his forearm like he's jerking off. This sends the room into an eruption of laughter. Everyone drinks to this joke, at my expense. I can't imagine why anyone would want to eat a dog. They are my favorite pets, like our little Chihuahua, Chen-Chen, that we raised as part of our family, play with, cuddle, and bathe.

I'm glad Pa has forbidden Five to eat dogs in America because I don't know what I would do if confronted with that situation. Actually, I might do it to impress my Uncle Five, but I just don't know if I'd be able to keep the poor pooch down in my stomach long enough to earn my uncle's respect.

I'm already feeling drunk and queasy from the goose blood, so all this talk of eating dogs is too much to take. I decide to go hit the sack before I end up puking and embarrassing myself in front of the family.

The next morning greets me with a wild headache and a heavy dose of cotton mouth. I'd love to solve this problem with some of the leftover cuttlefish, but when I enter the kitchen I realize the ambience of the *nhau* ritual is missing. Cuttlefish and fish sauce only taste good at a *nhau* with beer, people, and cursing. Instead I open the fridge and get some soy milk. I don't usually eat breakfast. Food in the morning makes me feel like I'm going to vomit. I guess growing up poor taught my stomach to treat breakfast as an insult.

Ma has already been up cleaning for hours, and I can smell the leftover aroma of the roasted geese mixed with Pine-Sol. I ask Ma if Uncle Five made it through the night without Pa finding out where the geese came from, and she tells me she'll make sure Pa never finds out.

# GUN MEDDLE

Where you from?

My math teacher places my geometry test upside down on my desk. I don't even need to flip it over to know my grade. I can see the red ink from a big letter *F* bleeding through the paper. It's no wonder I've failed. I blew off studying the night before to welcome Dragon Head home and party with the Street Ratz. I could scarcely keep my eyes open during the test. A hangover from cheap brandy left me burping up a sour liquid that stung the back of my throat.

I've been trying to do right and get good grades so that I can go to college, but when things are going bad at home, I don't know where else to run but the bottle. School isn't exactly peachy, either. Veasna is back in class and looking like we dragged him behind a truck. He keeps his distance from me, but there's a rumor floating around the hallways that he's got brothers and they'll be moving to Alhambra soon. People say they're gangsters and they plan to kill me for what I did to their little brother. I don't know what to believe. Part of me is terrified, but sometimes I feel, if the rumor is true, that they'll be doing me a favor by putting an end to all this.

As soon as the final bell rings, I lumber home, hoping to bury my heavy head under a pillow. When I walk into the house, Ma and Pa are in the midst of arguing about something petty. Lately their small arguments find a way to escalate into something crazy and chaotic, like Pa dumping our dinner in the trash. I'd love to sneak out and head over to Dragon Head's house to blow off steam, but Pa's been keeping a close eye on me since my grades started slipping. He still refuses to consider the magnet school and dismisses the distractions I face at Alhambra High as figments of my imagination.

It's hot as hell in the house. Pa insists we keep the windows and curtains closed, which traps the spring heat and bakes us like an oven. He's so depressed that he finds comfort in closing himself in. Unfortunately, we have to be closed in along with him. I head to my room and close the door. I strip down to my skivvies and lay in my bed facedown. My parents' squabbling echoes through the thin walls of our home. My brain begins to pound against my skull. I take a deep breath and hold a pillow over my head to muffle the noise. I close my eyes and try to sleep away the despair.

Fifteen minutes later, while I'm on the brink of slipping away to never-never land, Vinnie and Bo come storming in from school. They slam the front door, which rattles the walls, and

turn the TV on full blast in the living room. They fight over the remote control. Vinnie wants to watch *He-Man* and Bo *Woody Woodpecker*. I contemplate getting up to handle the situation, but my body feels heavy; I've sunk too deep into the mattress to move. I close my eyes tighter, trying to block them out. Ma intervenes. She gives the remote to Bo because she's the youngest. Vinnie won't stop whining. Ma threatens to hit him. He ignores her and snatches the remote from Bo. Ma takes it back and smacks Vinnie across the face. He gets pissed and hits Bo. Bo shrieks and wails.

Pa's loud, cackling voice radiates from the kitchen, "Where's Lac? It's four o'clock already. He's probably out in the streets again doing God knows what. He's going to get it bad from me when he gets home!"

"Maybe he's in his room." I hear Ma's footsteps coming down the hallway. She opens my door and peeks in, "For heaven's sake, he's asleep!"

Pa yells back to her from the kitchen, "That *lazy* bastard! All he does is mope around the house and *sleep*!"

*Fuck me; will someone please just make it all stop?*

Ma walks back into the kitchen, and Vinnie and Bo start up again in front of the TV.

"Give me back the remote!" Bo yells.

"No, it's mine. I got it first!" Vinnie snaps back.

*"Ma!"* Bo tattles.

Ma screams, "Give that thing to your sister. *Now!*"

"She always gets what she wants . . ." Vinnie whines.

Ma goes back into the kitchen. Vinnie must have snatched back the remote because Bo keeps wailing. Her high-pitched screams grow louder and louder until I can't take it anymore.

Something snaps inside of me. I leap out of bed and rip the door open. I storm down the hallway and take a left into the kitchen. Pa doesn't even look up from his newspaper. I open up the cabinet where he keeps his whipping rods and take hold of

the one that unleashes the worst pain—the mini-blind rod. I head straight for Bo. All I can see is her mouth, open wide and bawling at the top of her lungs. I grab her by the hair, yank her to the ground and unleash a blinding windmill of blows against every part of her body. I beat her until I'm out of breath, and then I stand there, shaking. Pa looks over at me for a moment with a banal expression, then returns to his newspaper.

Something comes over me like a train in the distance that is barreling down upon me. I realize one thing—I am my father. The thrill of beating Bo turns over into guilt. I can no longer hear her cries. Now, all I can see is her helpless face, the terror in her eyes, and her tears—massive clear droplets running down her face, over her chin, and onto her neck. I drop the rod to the ground like it doesn't belong in my hand and leave the room.

The next morning when I'm getting ready for school, Bo is in front of the TV again. She's watching *Muppet Babies*. I sit down next to her and watch. Bo leans to one side with her knees tucked underneath her. Her bare calves stick out from the bottom of her nightgown. They are covered in pink and red lines, just like mine after Pa beats me.

She looks up at me warily and guards the remote.

"I'm not gonna take it. You can watch your show," I tell her.

She watches *Muppet Babies* in a state of bliss, immune to the troubling thoughts that are flooding my brain. I contemplate her youth, her innocence. I long for her to be free from the weight of the burden I bear. I go into the bathroom and get the jar of Tiger Balm. I sit back down next to Bo and unscrew the cap. I stick my index and middle fingers into the balm and rub it gently into the marks on Bo's legs.

"Does that feel better?" I ask.

"Uh-huh," Bo nods, keeping her eyes locked on the television.

I know no other way to soothe her. My eyes grow swollen and

hot. I tell myself I'll never put her in this position again. Tears bead up in my eyes and fall down my cheeks.

The program goes to commercial and Bo looks up at me. "Why are you crying?"

"I'm so sorry, Bo. I'm so sorry I hit you. I don't want to be like Pa—it was a mistake. Please don't hate me . . ." I say to her, sobbing. "I promise to never lay a hand on you again, okay?"

Bo frowns at me and nods. Her show comes back from commercial and she flops back onto her elbows, propping her chin up on her hands. The smile returns to her face, as she is once again entranced by her cartoon.

I head back to my room to finish getting ready for school. I feel good. Not relieved of the guilt of hitting Bo, but something more. My steps feel lighter. The birds chirping outside my window sound whimsical and melodic. On a normal day, I'd be plucking them off the branches with my BB gun to stop the racket. I decide against wearing my usual khaki Dickies and white tee— the Street Ratz uniform—opting instead for something I want to wear because it looks good and makes me feel good. I dig through my closet and find brown corduroy pants and a butter-yellow polo. I put them on and look in the mirror. I try tucking in the polo, but it doesn't feel right. So, I pull it back out.

I head out into the kitchen to retrieve my backpack. Pa is making himself a cup of tea.

"You're still here? Why aren't you on your way to school yet?" Pa asks.

"I still have time, Pa. Plenty of time."

"You better not be late. I don't want those people from your school calling here and saying things to me that I don't understand."

"I know, Pa. Don't worry; I'm leaving now."

I float through my day at school. The flurry of bewildered looks I receive on each trip through the hallways between classes bear no consequence. When the last bell rings, I retrieve my

books from my locker and head out the back gate of campus toward home. With the Ratz off doing God knows what, I'm free to do as I please.

I decide to take the side streets home, just in case Veasna really does have brothers who are looking for me. I contemplate paging Dragon Head for a ride home, but then I'd have to find a phone, page him, and wait around for a call back—and I might not get one. Today I'd rather just head home.

I pass the 7-Eleven and the doughnut shop. The patio is empty. The Ratz are probably partying at Dragon Head's house. I pop my Slick Rick tape into my Walkman and lose myself in "Hey Young World." I zigzag through the streets toward my neighborhood. As I move down an unfamiliar street, I notice some Asians up the block drinking tallboys and leaning over a tricked-out Mitsubishi Eclipse with its hood propped open. Others are squatting on the porch steps smoking and talking. I don't recognize any of them. Something else about them strikes me as unusual, but I don't pay them much attention as I walk past. They're much older than I am and unfamiliar, and I learned long ago to mind my own business when I'm walking the streets.

When I get to the corner a few houses down, I wait for a car to pass and walk across the street. In my peripheral vision I notice someone at the same pad pointing in my direction. I look to my left toward the other side of the intersection to see who he's after. As I'm scanning the people over there, something clicks that makes my blood run cold. It's the mullets. All those guys standing around that car are sporting finely trimmed mullets—the same mullet that Veasna charmingly adorns. I don't want to turn around, but I have to know. I act like I'm looking at the ground but peer to my right and there he is. Running over to his brothers from the porch and pointing at me. One of them reaches for something inside the car, and the other five take off running in my direction. I slip my backpack off my shoulders, drop it to the ground, and run for dear life in the opposite direction.

I run right across the intersection and weave my way through an onslaught of traffic. Horns wail and tires screech behind me as I hop the curb on the other side and run between two apartment buildings. I don't look back and I don't stop running. I turn right down a long street and search for a quick exit. I pump my arms high and gasp for air as I run. I can hear stomping feet behind me. I need a way to evade these fuckers. I dart to the left and head through an open gate into the backyard of an old one-story house. My perception of time slows down as I move into this obstacle-filled environment. I jump over a plastic Big Wheel as I storm through the yard, then hop a chain-link fence into the alley below.

The six of them are right behind me, darting through the yard toward the fence. Without taking a good look around, I flee down the alley in the direction of home. They gain on me as I sprint down the alley. I can now hear the cadenced swishing of their polyester tracksuits. Chain-link fence gives way to a cinder-block retaining wall separating the alley on both sides from the adjacent yards. My pursuers are so close behind me that I can feel them there. I turn my head to the side to take a look. The wind whips saliva from my bouncing, flaccid lips. The sight of their hands reaching out for me increases the pace of my whirring legs. All hope of outrunning them is lost. Out of instinct I cut to the right like a receiver running an out. I leap onto the wall and get my right arm, up to the elbow, over the lip. I claw and clamor my way to the top like a crazed animal.

I can taste freedom as I scrape my belly across the jagged crest of the cinder-block wall, until a firm hand reaches up behind me and grips my trailing calf like a vice. I straddle the wall on my stomach, clutching it dearly with my arms and legs. The hand on my calf gives a violent jerk, which sends me flipping over on my back to the concrete below. I land hard. A circle of mullet-framed faces stare down upon me.

"This is the guy that jumped you, Veas?"

"It's him. He's with the Street Ratz. He's the one . . ."

"Ay, dawg, you sure? *This* little motherfucker right here?" Veasna's brother taps his foot against the side of my face as he speaks.

*"Hell yeah, that's him."*

Veasna's brother reaches down and picks me up by the collar of my shirt. I take some of the weight off my neck on the way up by sticking my arms and legs back like a crab. The alley is deserted and silent. A thin puddle of water runs down the middle. The cinder-block walls on either side keep us out of sight from the surrounding homes.

Veasna's brother pushes me up against the wall and squeezes my collar tightly inside his left fist to keep me there. His hand smells like engine grease. He's much older than Veasna, probably in his mid-twenties. His skin is tanned dark from the sun and thin. Wiry hair protrudes above his lips. It's hardly a mustache. His parka is open in the front, revealing a stained wifebeater. He cocks his right arm back like he's going to slug me, then looks to his left and his right. I squint my eyes and flinch my chin up slightly, expecting the blow. Instead, he reaches around his back and pulls a matte-black Beretta pistol from underneath his jacket. The gun looks stubby and clean. He brings the top of the Beretta up to his other hand and racks a bullet into the chamber.

He takes a tighter grip on my shirt and brings the gun up in front of my face. The safety is off. His friends begin ambling about, looking up and down the alley to see if anyone is coming. He pushes the barrel hard into my left temple. The gun metal feels cold and heavy against the side of my skull. I've seen, held, and fired plenty of guns, but this is utterly shocking. My limbs go limp and useless. I slide down to the ground with my back against the wall. Veasna's brother bends over with me and holds his position. His finger rests firmly on the trigger.

Veasna is wild-eyed and manic. He looks like he's on speed, bouncing around his brother, cursing and spitting in my face.

His brother bucks the barrel back and forth, shoving it deeper and deeper into my temple.

The other guys move about nervously, ordering him to do the deed.

"Shoot his ass!"

"Fuck him up!"

"Come on . . . pop his ass! Look what he did to Veas, homie."

He comes in close. His eyes are vacant and bloodshot, and I can smell the alcohol on his breath. I want to cry and plead and beg, but something Pa told me takes hold. He has prepared me for situations like these—for silence when you're controlled by someone in the throes of anger. Words only add fuel to the fire. I stay frozen. I say nothing. I close my eyes and await my fate. Strange thoughts and images flood my mind in the ensuing moments behind the barrel. I hear Vinnie's voice calling out to me. I see Pa's look of disappointment. I see Bo looking up at me and crying. I see Ma stroking my hair and sniffing me. I see my dead brother Zeal. I see Vu crashing through the railing in Da Nang.

Laughter snaps me back to reality. I open my eyes. Veasna and his entourage are standing around me, cackling. His brother is stuffing the gun behind his parka. "Get up!" Veasna's brother orders.

I stumble to my feet, and Veasna's brother turns around to walk away. I'm addled by the chain of events. I relax a little, thinking I've been given a pass. My shoulders slouch. He spins around and clocks me straight in the nose. My knees buckle and I fall back to the ground. Then I feel the pain that Veasna endured. Heels stomp my face, my ribs, my legs. Feet and fists fly into my stomach and back. My body jerks and convulses, wrapping into the fetal position only to be pulled open again by my assailants. My arms can no longer shield me. I gasp for air. I struggle to remain conscious. It's the worst I've ever been beaten.

I hear them laughing and hawking loogies, but I cannot feel the phlegm as it splashes against swollen face. I hear footsteps

stomping down the alley, away from where I lie. I wonder if they've finally left. A foot mashes down hard onto the back of my head, sending a sharp pain down my spine.

Veasna's brother whispers in my ear, "The next time you fuck with my little brother, you get a bullet in your head. Go tell your homeboys who we are . . . You know where we live. Come see us. We'll be waiting for you . . ."

I remain sprawled out on the concrete waiting for the strength to return to my limbs. My vision is blurry. My face swollen and throbbing. My back wet and cold. I discover that I'm lying in the putrid water that runs the length of the alley. I roll onto my left side to get myself out of it. Every inch of my body aches. My corduroys are ripped and stained. My shirt that was bright yellow this morning is now covered in blood and footprints. One of my shoes is missing.

My hope for the future, like me, has been thrown into the gutter. I am unable to escape the environment that surrounds me. It's a place I've been thrust into, and yet a place I've helped create. I feel stupid for not seeing this coming. Stupid for trying to be anything other than a Street Rat, if only for a day.

I pick myself up off the ground and hobble down the alley toward the road. A woman passes me on the street and stares with horror, pulling her purse tight against her stomach. I move slowly down the block, putting one foot in front of the other. The struggle to move forward stirs my anger. I think about the Glock pistol in the grocery bag I have stored beneath our house. I think about the Street Ratz who are ready to die for me . . . at least if Dragon Head is there to tell them to. I don't get very far and a blue Ford station wagon pulls up alongside me. A white man with glasses and neatly combed blond hair steps out of the car and walks over to me. He looks like he's on his way home from work.

"Are you all right?" he asks in a nasal voice.

I don't respond.

"Of course you're not all right . . . Look at you. Can I give you a ride to the hospital?"

"I just want to go home," I tell him.

"Come on. Get in. I'll take you." He opens the passenger side door for me and helps me into the car.

"What street do you live on?"

*I should just tell him to go to Dragon Head's house. When he and the Ratz see me like this, it's on. Shit'll go down quick. I want to blast those motherfuckers. I want to continue this beef, and release all this hate they've given to me.*

"I'm sorry, are you okay?"

"Um, yeah, just take me to Olive Street."

"Well, that's not too far at all. We'll have you home in a jiffy."

The man drives methodically toward my house, careful to switch his turn signal on before every lane change.

"Say, if you don't mind me asking, what happened—I mean, um, who did this to you?"

"Oh, this? I got jumped by some crackheads who were trying to steal my lunch money."

"Steal your *lunch money*? Why would they try and do that? Weren't you on your way *home* from school?"

"That's crackheads for ya."

"Ow, that's terrible! I imagine they took your backpack and your shoe?"

I nod.

"What is this world coming to? With all these drugs and *the AIDS* . . . a man can hardly walk the streets anymore."

I haven't been around white people much, but if the rest of them are anything like this guy, I think I'll pass. He pulls up to my driveway.

"Well, you better run along inside. I'll bet your parents are worried *sick*. Do you need any help getting out of the car?"

"I'm aight. Thanks for the ride."

I walk up to the side of the house. I look in the hole where my gun is hidden and I can see the top of the grocery bag, right where I left it. Mr. Rogers is still sitting in my driveway, idling his car. So, I make my way up the front steps and wave. Standing there, with my hand on the doorknob, I start to feel shaken up. Like the little kid who falls and scrapes his knee and doesn't cry until his parents notice. I tell myself that I'm just going inside to put my Dickies on and get some shoes, so that I can make my way over to Dragon Head's house.

I open the door and walk inside. Pa is sitting there in the living room waiting for me.

"You better have a good explan—" Pa says from behind his paper, stopping himself when he sees me. "What happened to *you*?" he says, throwing his paper down and getting up from the couch.

"I . . ."

"Sit your ass down on the couch," Pa orders and disappears from the room.

I do as I'm told and wonder if I'm about to get a beating for ruining my best clothes. Pa comes out with the Tiger Balm and a hot rag.

"Lie down," he says.

I lie down on my back and Pa rubs the moist cloth gently against my skin. He cleans my wounds, one at a time, dries them, and then rubs them with Tiger Balm. His tenderness erases the pain, and it snuffs out the fire inside of me that longs for revenge.

"Who did this to you?"

"I got jumped by some Mexicans. They took my backpack and tried to take my shoes."

"You still have one shoe . . . You kept them from getting your other shoe?"

I nod my head. Pa doesn't smile, but he looks proud.

"Where did this happen?"

"A few blocks from school."

"For heaven's sake. I'm going to put a stop to this."

"You are? I'm okay, Pa. It's just a random thing."

"Yes. I can't have my firstborn son getting killed on his way home from school. I'm going to talk to Duong and enroll you and Quy in that new school."

"You are?"

"Yes. I guess you'll have to be with your people *after* school. The whites can have you during the day. It will all be worth it once you become a doctor."

"*Yes*, Pa."

"I didn't ask you." Pa moves over to his chair and lights a cigarette. He's thinking about who knows what.

I watch him sitting there, fidgeting his legs while he ponders. As clever as Pa thinks he is in hiding his love from me, I'm learning to read between the lines. *I love you, too, Pa.*

"Now, go and get some rest," he says. "Those wounds aren't going to heal if you're up moving about. I don't want you looking beat up when you start the new school."

I don't know if busing an hour and a half each way to attend a magnet school in East Los Angeles is going to solve my problems, but I'm eager to find out. I'm ready for a fresh start.

I float on over to my room to lie down.

. . . Like a feather in the wind, here I go again.

# DAWG EAT DOG

Da Nang, during my first visit back to my beloved Vietnam.

These are the stories of my childhood. I knew early on that I didn't want to suffer these experiences in vain. I expressed my frustration with my pen, drawing and writing to release the pain inside of me and maintain some order in the world. Anything that I could not tell my father, I told him on paper.

Like my very best pieces of art, only the most defining journal entries survived. The rest were tossed away. What I kept lay dormant in a cardboard box that was meant to hold cans of condensed Carnation milk. I kept them there, beneath the piles of boxes in my parents' garage, so that they would never be seen

again. But never came too soon. In college, while I was looking for boyhood pictures to show my girlfriend, I stumbled upon the faded Carnation box. It was tucked away under another box Pa had curiously labeled "Lac's Toys—1985. Do Not Open."

I had to lift the flap and take a look inside. The first piece of writing I pulled out had sprawling, cursive letters across the top: *"My father kicked me out."* It was the story that became "The Naked Truth." I read several paragraphs from the brittle paper. Old feelings rushed to the surface, suffocating me in shallow breaths. I threw the piece of paper right back into the box and left it there, where it remained for twelve years, until I decided to dig it up again and write this book. I've found that when I try hard enough to face painful memories past, I also dig up the people and events that shaped the positive in the person I have become.

My father always told me that there is no such thing as God, and the "heaven" a man seeks is here on earth. He may be right, as I've come across a couple of angels in my days here on earth. The first was a girl I met when I transferred to the magnet high school. Her friendship poured unconditional positive regard upon me—something I had never experienced in life. Friendship blossomed into love, and she became my wife. The second angel is our bright-eyed daughter, an apparition that made our life complete a little over two years ago.

My father's dream was for me to become a physician, but it shattered during my first elective class as a premed student at UC Irvine. The Introduction to Psychology course convinced me to change my major, and psychology changed my life. Everything I learned in psychology helped me to understand my father and, more importantly, myself. Things began to make sense.

Now I'm in graduate school, months away from finishing my Ph.D. in industrial-organizational psychology. Helping people to understand themselves and be more effective at work is as positive as psychology gets. I like that about my work. It makes

me feel good. I work at a company called TalentSmart, helping people to increase their emotional intelligence. I suppose I'm as experienced as any in the dark side of emotion that erupts unchecked.

I'm taking a couple weeks off from work to head out on a school-sponsored tour of Southeast Asia. We'll witness the inner workings of the industrial complex in Thailand, Laos, Cambodia, and Vietnam, which is my idea of a good time these days. I enrolled in the course the moment I saw Vietnam on the list. It will be my first visit to my homeland since fleeing the Communists with my family.

I plan on making this trip without my father's knowledge, and so far I've succeeded in making sure he doesn't know. Probably not something the average guy in his thirties would be proud of—hiding his activities from his father—but I'm not your average guy. My world still revolves around a tiny man, and he has a way of bringing me back into orbit when I stray too far. Pa would throw a fit if he found out I'm returning to Vietnam. So, he'll have to wait till I get home to find out.

I stuff my toothbrush and some mouthwash into the side pocket of my suitcase. I walk into the office to find my headphones and throw them into my backpack along with copies of *XXL*, *The Source*, and *Psychology Today* for the flight. My cell phone buzzes loudly against the surface of the dresser. There are still too many things I need to do before my flight, so I don't answer. I wander about the house, searching for my passport and worrying about the trip. My thoughts race. *Will Vietnam recognize me? Will I remember her?*

The phone rings again. I look at the screen. It says "Pa-Home." I'm not in the mood to hear my father's voice. I don't pick up. Instead, I walk out the door and head to a convenience store to pick up a tiny tube of toothpaste for the trip.

When I get back from the store, the light on my phone is flashing. I pick it up off the dresser and see there are eight

missed calls—all from "Pa-Home." When he can't reach me, Pa will usually give up after a couple of tries. I can't imagine what he's thinking trying me eight times. *Maybe it was an emergency. Maybe he fell and broke his leg. Maybe he wanted to let me know that he was about to down a bottle of pills because he wanted to die. Maybe he wanted to tell me he loves me. That would make my life.* The phone buzzing in my hand stops my train of thought. I have a voice mail.

I hold the number-one key down until I can hear ringing. My voice mail message comes on, "Hello, this is Lac. I'm sorry I'm unable to take your call right now, but if you'll please leave me your name and number, I'll get back to you just as soon as I can. Have a good—."

I press the pound key and enter my password to access voice mail.

The computerized voice of a woman on the other end instructs, "You have one unheard message. To listen to your message, press one."

My heart pounds and my palms grow moist. I press the number one.

"First unheard message."

"Haf a goo day, my dick!" Pa shrieks in broken English. He switches to Vietnamese and rattles off words like a machine gun. "Whenever I fucking call you, you never answer! Motherfuck! Why don't you fucking answer the phone when I call you! Motherfuck! You fucking bastard!"

Click.

Blood boils straight to my head. I chuck the phone against the wall and it shatters into pieces. I'm about to embark on an important trip to revisit my beloved Vietnam—as a prerequisite for my Ph.D., no less—and all he can say is, "Motherfuck." My hard work feels as though it is for nothing.

I don't call Pa back. Instead, I crack open a bottle of Jack Daniels and fix myself a stiff drink before heading to the airport.

---

It's another sultry night in downtown Saigon. I can't believe I'm in Vietnam. July is the warmest month of the year, and the muggy heat is enough to make every crevice in my body sweat. Having grown up in the arid climate of Southern California, I'm not accustomed to humidity; it feels like I'm stepping into a steam room every time I exit my air-conditioned high-rise hotel.

I'm still in awe of the country that birthed me. Ma insisted that I never return to Vietnam, but so much has changed—the government, the country's promise for her people and me. I owe it to myself to come back here, and I'm ready to take full advantage of this beautiful night.

My journey to this moment was paved with obstacles from start to finish. The psychological turmoil created by my father ensured my young life was a constant struggle and often a comedy of errors. There are still things I'll never be able to shake. Such is the reality of having a harsh and unforgiving father who rejects the very culture that I've fought so hard to be accepted into.

I wander the streets of Saigon at dusk. The smog is overwhelming. Los Angeles's dirty haze is a breath of fresh mountain air by comparison. People-watching is a favorite pastime. I see young lovers strolling the waterfront, street vendors hustling a buck selling knockoffs to tourists, and men in coffee shops arguing about U.S. President George W. Bush. The way the men yell, smoke their cigarettes, and squeeze "motherfuck" into every sentence reminds me of my uncles at the *nhau*.

After walking for a couple of hours to build an appetite, I decide to give my host, Tien, a call from a pay phone. He's a business professor at the local university who makes a habit of befriending American tourists so that he can hone his English. We connected right away.

"Tien, what are you doing?" I ask in Vietnamese.

"I'm still at my office working on some things," he replies. There's an echo when he speaks like he's in the bathroom. This must be his cell phone.

"Are you taking a shit?" I bluntly ask in English.

"Taking a what?"

"A shit."

"What's that?"

"Are you taking a shit?" I ask again in Vietnamese.

Tien laughs. "No, I'm in my office. *Shit*," he says to himself, "I need to remember that word . . . *shit*."

"It's a beautiful night in Saigon . . . Are you too busy to go out?" I ask.

"It's Ho Chi Minh City, not Saigon anymore," he corrects me.

"It's still Saigon to me, professor."

"I'm almost done grading papers. What do you want to do?"

"I don't know . . . something crazy and fun. I'm in that kind of mood."

"You Americans, impulsivity somehow equates to fun for you guys."

"Come on, now! I'm on vacation . . . I want to experience something new."

"All right. I'll go home and take a quick shower and then I'll pick you up. Where should we meet?"

"I'm at the hotel you dropped me off at yesterday after my haircut."

"Okay. Meet me in the lobby in an hour."

I hang up with Tien and walk back to the hotel. I sit at the lobby bar and order a beer, which the bartender serves on ice. I drink it fast, so it doesn't get watered down, and contemplate ordering another. I don't want to get too crazy—yet.

I walk over to the front entrance of the hotel feeling anxious and impatient and looking for someone to talk to. The two bellboys are standing around talking and flirting with a female

concierge. I walk up to them and join their conversation. The shorter bellboy is happy to see me. His name tag reads "Duc."

"You have plans tonight?" he asks me in Vietnamese.

"No. I'm bored. What is there to do around here?" I reply in Vietnamese. Duc is quite amused by my accent.

"You want girls?" he asks.

"What do you mean?" I reply.

"*This guy,*" Duc says, turning to the other bellboy. "What do you think I mean?"

"I don't know what you mean," I say. Duc smirks at the other bellboy, who mimics my accent. This makes me feel like a sell-out, like I'm not Vietnamese enough for them.

"Stink box, dried tuna, sewer hole . . ." Duc mumbles.

"*Oh* . . . no, not for me. I want to go dancing. Maybe a club or a bar?"

"Is that right? There's plenty of that around here, but the best one is Club Magnolia, around the corner."

"Really? What time do they open?"

"You could go now, but people don't get there until after eleven."

"What else is there to do in the meantime?"

"Come with me."

Duc walks me out to the street in front of the hotel. He puts his fingers in his mouth and whistles twice—the first one shorter than the second—without looking up.

"What's that?" I ask.

"You'll see . . ."

A minute later, a teenager rides up to us on a bicycle. He carries a homemade wooden rattle that he shakes back and forth. It sounds like he's playing the maraca. He wobbles and swerves on the approach, steering the bike with one hand and shaking the rattle loudly with the other.

"You want girl?" the boy speaks to me in English. These people can tell from a mile away that I'm a Viet Kieu. Kieu translates literally to expatriate, and the Vietnamese harbor great

disdain for their former countrymen, many of whom flaunt their wealth upon their return.

I can tell Duc is having fun with me by bringing me out here, so I don't respond to the boy's question. He continues, "Cocaine, meth, weed, heroin?"

Duc jumps in, in Vietnamese, "This guy doesn't believe you have the youngest and most beautiful girls in the city."

"How old you want? Fourteen, fifteen?" the pimp asks in Vietnamese.

I smile and tell him I'm not interested. This turns his expression from friendly tour guide to hostile hustler.

"What the fuck you wasting my time for if you don't want nothing?"

"I'm trying to get him a girl, but he doesn't believe me," Duc says.

"You want it or not, Viet Kieu?" the pimp asks.

"No. That's okay."

The pimp points his index finger at the bellboy and mumbles something under his breath. Then he turns to me as he hops back on his bicycle to leave. "Don't let me catch you walking down these streets tonight. I have my eye on you, Viet Kieu." He rides off on his bike, shaking the rattle back and forth.

"You better watch out. He's a little crazy in the head," Duc warns me.

"*You* asked him to come over; not me."

"Are you scared he's going to cut your dick off and feed it to the pigs?" Duc taunts.

I believe there's a chance that might happen. So, I don't answer him. The chaotic start to my evening gets me thinking about something my uncle Five told me way back when. A crazy idea pops into my head: *I'm going to eat dog meat.* The thought of doing something that outrageous excites me. Pa and my uncles claim it's really good if you go to the right place. *I should try it. When in Rome, right?*

"Ahh . . . hey, Duc. You know where I can go to eat dog meat around here?"

"What? *Dog meat?*"

"Yeah, but good dog meat. My father suggested I try it when I'm here."

"For heaven's sake. There's plenty of other meat here in Vietnam, why would you want to eat *dog*?"

"Because . . . I just want to try it."

"You're not scared?"

"No, not if it's cooked right. Have you tried it?"

"No, but Phuong has . . . and he likes it," Duc says, pointing toward the other bellboy, who is helping a tourist with a bag.

"Let's go ask him, then," I say.

"Crazy Viet Kieu," Duc mumbles under his breath. "Of all the things he could do in Vietnam with his money, he wants to eat dog."

When we get back inside, Duc yells across the lobby, "Hey Phuong! This guy wants to eat dog meat!"

I cringe. A young couple at the check-in counter turns to me and snickers.

"When? I'll take you when I get off work," Phuong says.

"What time do you get off?" I ask.

"Midnight."

"My heavens, that's too late. My friend is coming soon to pick me up. Just tell me where to go."

"There's one place by the airport, an hour from here on moped. It's on a quiet street, so if you don't know your way around there, you'll miss it. People call it Dog Meat Avenue. There's a bunch of little restaurants, but you want to go to the one called Thit Cho Ba Bac."

"Thit Cho Ba Bac," I repeat to help me remember. It means Ms. North Vietnam's Dog Meat.

"It is *the best* dog meat in all of Vietnam. For heaven's sake, her marinades are to die for! You will be mesmerized, hypno-

tized, tranquilized . . ." Phuong says, looking up at the ceiling and closing his eyes.

"Is it *that* good?" I ask.

"For heaven's sake, go eat it and then come back tomorrow and tell me how good it was."

"Okay, I'll ask my friend to take me. I'll see you guys later," I say and make my way toward the exit.

I can hear them talking behind my back. "Maybe he can't get his little soldier to stand up straight," Duc says. The two of them burst out in laughter and it tickles me. *These are my people. I love my people. This is my homeland, and if I want to try dog meat tonight, I sure as hell can, and will.* I think about something my Uncle Five once told me: "You're not a real Vietnamese until you *nhau* with dog meat with the locals." Indeed.

Excited by the idea that I'm going to eat dog tonight, I grow anxious waiting for Tien. I think about how desperate for dog meat Uncles Five and Nine were when they first came to America. I know that Uncle Five loves to *nhau,* and if he loves dog meat that much, it can't be so bad. After a couple of beers and some time chitchatting with Tien, dog could well be pork. A dog can't be any dirtier than swine, can it?

Tien pulls up on his moped, and the bellboys come over to us.

"Have you heard of Thit Cho Ba Bac, down by the airport?" Duc asks.

Tien is caught off guard by the question. "What, dog meat? What are you talking about?"

"Your friend here wants to go eat dog meat. Do you know where Thit Cho Ba Bac is? It's the best place to take him."

Tien looks at me and smiles. "You really want to go and eat dog meat?"

"Yeah. Have you tried it?"

"It's quite tasty. The weather is too hot for it right now, though. It's best to eat dog when the weather is cold. It keeps *you* warm."

Duc and Phuong laugh out loud at the joke. Tien looks over at me, expecting the same.

"Ohhh, I get it now. It keeps me . . . *warm*," I say. "Is it true that it's an aphrodisiac?"

"It could be . . ." Tien replies.

I'm confused again.

". . . if you believe in it."

Phuong interjects, "When does it get cold here in Ho Chi Minh? Never. If this Viet Kieu wants to try dog, then for heaven's sake take him."

"Let's go, then," Tien says.

I hop on the back of Tien's moped and off we go, racing through downtown Saigon. At first, it's a bit awkward holding onto another guy on the back of a moped, but once I see everybody else doing it, it helps me to relax. Tien takes about a million wrong turns on the way over. The streets are dark and desolate on the approach, but when we turn the corner onto Dog Meat Avenue, there's no mistaking that we've reached our destination. Bright neon signs line the boulevard. Thit Cho Thanh (Thanh's Dog Meat), Thit Cho Cuong (Cuong's Dog Meat), Thit Cho Chien Bo (Fried Dog Meat in Butter), Thit Cho Nhuong (Barbecued Dog Meat), and, of course, Thit Cho That (Real Dog Meat).

Where do you want to eat?" Tien asks.

"Um . . . how about Thit Cho . . . Ba Bac," I say, struggling to remember the bellboy's recommendation.

"That's my favorite!" Tien says.

He parks the scooter in an open spot a few restaurants down from our destination. I hop off like a cocky cowboy and walk in a circle to get the blood flowing back into my legs. *I'm going to make Pa and Uncle Five proud. I'll show them I'm real Vietnamese, not just some second-rate Viet Kieu.* And then I hear it. It comes from behind the restaurants, a sound that's muffled by the row of concrete buildings between us.

They're squeals: the kind of shrill, sad noises a dog makes when he's had his foot stepped on or been bitten into submission by a larger foe. *Oh my God! This is getting out of hand.* I start to feel queasy, American, even white. Those poor dogs! Wait a minute . . . forget the dogs. What about me? What if they don't cook it right and the meat releases some bizarre karma-induced chemical or virus into my body? Imagine explaining that to the doctor at Cedars-Sinai. "Um, I was eating some dog, doctor. I think it was a black flat-coated retriever. No wait, it was definitely a chocolate lab."

Tien and I walk into the restaurant suggested by the bellboy and ask for a table. The owner, hostess, and chef goes by the name Ba Bac. She recognizes Tien and asks how his family is doing. She gives me a strange look and asks us to sit down. I don't take offense, but I do look nervously around me to see what's on the other tables. To my surprise, the dishes look normal, like beef or pork. But I know these people are actually eating dog, and the thought raises my blood pressure. *They are eating dog, for Christ sakes!* A dog is an animal to pamper, speak to, snuggle, and play with—not stir-fry.

The men at the table next to us are chuckling and throwing pieces of greasy meat into their mouths like popcorn. My stomach turns and I take a hard pull off the thirty-ounce bottle of 333 beer Ba Bac just placed on our table. You don't make reservations on Dog Meat Avenue. Nor will you find a pretty Vietnamese girl at the front in a fitted gown waiting with menus in hand to seat you. The restaurants on this street are situated like front porches. They are set up with six or seven little plastic tables with short chairs around them. When you sit down, it feels as if you are squatting. Men, mostly in their late thirties and early forties, crowd around these tiny tables drinking beer, chain-smoking, cursing, and eating. The pooches are served like Spanish tapas—a variety of small dishes that everyone at the table shares.

"What do you want to eat?" Tien asks.

"I don't know, man. It's my first time eating dog. I'll eat whatever you think is good."

We sit in silence drinking the beer, and I take a moment to soak in the beautiful night around me. I feel strangely "at home" in Vietnam. I'm in awe of the fact that everyone in this big country speaks my native tongue, even if they think I'm a lowly Viet Kieu. It's so different from the U.S., where you have to go to a particular part of a city to speak and hear your language used so freely. At the same time, it's strange for me because I'm so accustomed to using the English language. Here, I'm forced to speak my broken Vietnamese, and it's bittersweet. Bitter because I'm no longer fluent in it, and sweet because it brings back a lot of memories and makes me feel connected to people who are just like me.

The first dog-meat dish comes to our table. It's "barbecued yellow dog," and it looks like pork marinated generously in lemongrass and ginger. The strips of dog meat are piled on top of one another with eight wooden skewers. I pick one up, bring it to my nose, and smell it. It doesn't smell strange. Just lemon, ginger, and a hint of grease. I would never have guessed it was a dog if no one had told me.

"It smells pretty good. A lot of lemongrass," I tell Tien.

"This is their best dish. If you don't like it, you're probably not going to like the others I ordered."

I take another big swig of beer and look at the skewer that's dangling in front of me. I can't get the image out of my head of a beautiful golden retriever running through the park after a Frisbee, its hair flowing in the wind.

"Go on, Lac, try it," Tien says.

I bite into a piece of the meat and tear it away from the skewer. It doesn't taste like much—salty and heavy on the ginger. I chew, swallow, and pause, amazed that my body isn't breaking into convulsions. This calms me down. So, I take another bite.

After about fifteen minutes, lots more alcohol, and some chitchatting with Tien, my mind drifts away from what I'm eating. Dog turns into something of a delicacy—a new, exciting taste that I'm working to acquire. Out comes the dog stew, which is quite delicious.

"You like the stew?" Tien asks.

"Um, huh," I mumble, sipping the steaming liquid off my spoon.

"They put the head in the pot while the stew simmers," Tien explains. "It adds flavor."

The image conjured by Tien's comment gives me pause as I stare at the bowl of silt-colored liquid in front of me. I shrug it off and dive back in. I figure if I'm eating Rover, they might as well make good use of all the parts.

When the plate of dog intestines arrives at our table, my journey down the back alleys of fine cuisine takes an abrupt turn toward reality. We Vietnamese are no stranger to animal intestines. They have an intense flavor that, like your typical sausage, is quite delicious. But something about the dog intestines isn't quite right. I look at them skeptically, all neatly coiled in front of me on the serving plate. I can't put a finger on it, so I pick one up and take a bite. The texture is strange. Instead of the meat being dense and flavorful, like most sausage, the dog intestines are bland and crunchy. The crunch really throws me sideways on my second bite. The flavor that ensues fails to correct the experience. I look over at Tien, who seems to be enjoying the intestines more than the previous courses, and I smile politely.

I'm not interested in taking another bite, but since it doesn't taste like much, I figure I'll be polite. And then it hits me. As I sit there chewing a mouthful of dog intestine, I realize where the crunch is coming from. It's dog food—salty, throat-closing dog food. I pick up the beer and chug it until my skin turns rosy, which is a good thing, because without it, Tien would've seen my skin turn green. Spitting out food, or even showing that you

don't like it—the Vietnamese consider this incredibly rude. So, I smile and watch Tien munch away on the salty, crunchy dog intestines.

There's no dog dessert served on Dog Meat Avenue, so the main course is our last. It's boiled black dog, which looks something like traditional corned beef with large chunks of under-cooked bacon resting neatly on top of it. It looks good and smells only slightly questionable, so I dig in without hesitation. My first bite of boiled black dog is, without question, the most repulsive thing I've ever placed in my mouth. To my chagrin, the "bacon" is actually large pustules of fat that burst in my mouth as I chew. The grease has an acerbic flavor that numbs my lips as it spills out over them. The taste of the grease is simply awful, but it isn't nearly as bad as the smell. Like the intestines, I force more down to be polite and fail to habituate to the flavor.

After about eight beers and way too much dog meat, Tien and I decide to call it a night. I can't wait to go home and tell Pa and Uncle Five. The ride back to my hotel seems shorter, less riddled with traffic. I smile as we dart through the streets, savoring the smell of the humid, smoggy air in my beloved Vietnam.

## FEELING BLUE

My wife and I decided to start a family right around the time I began penning chapters for this book. She and I were creating our future at the same time that I was digging deep into my past. I was forced to relive the experiences that became this book, and fear took over. I wondered if the cycle would repeat and my father's heavy hands would be reborn in mine. If my child was a boy, what would that do to me? How would I be? Would the ass-whippings become a part of my children's upbringing?

In becoming a father, I wanted to raise a better me, but I wasn't ready to see myself in a little boy. I was writing about my

boyhood throughout my wife's pregnancy, and I decided that our first child had to be a girl. I got what I asked for, and we named her Sky.

While I was writing "The Wrong Way Home," I had dreams of the boat ride in which I would look into the ocean and all I could see was the color blue. There were also dreams of me and Vu running in the tomato garden catching dragonflies. When I looked up to the sky, it was a beautiful hue of aqua-blue. I felt like a child again, and I wanted this beauty and tranquility to be reflected in my daughter's name. I still want it to be reflected in her experiences growing up.

As a father, I want my children's eyes to sparkle with happiness. I want them to feel content. When Sky looks at me, she sees eyes full of acceptance, love, and trust. Everyone says that Sky has my eyes. I never want them to see the fear, terror, and desperation that mine witnessed.

I love my father. I realize now that I always have and always will. I understand what he was trying to teach me all those years. My father always talked to me like I was already a man. It was all he knew. In a sense, I had to grow into the wisdom that my father bestowed upon me so bluntly at such an early age. I see now that he was building a bridge for me to cross—from boyhood to manhood. Pa was always working on this bridge, and it was in sight while I was growing up, though it was too far from being finished for me to appreciate. When I finally reached the bridge, it was there for me to cross with ease. I realize now that Pa lived in fear. He invested so much neurotic energy in making sure I'd get to the bridge because he was terrified that he would never see its completion.

The painful trek to reach his bridge crippled me. Somewhere deep inside the pain will always remain.

# ACKNOWLEDGMENTS

In memory: Zeal, Vu, Maternal Grandpa and Grandma (Ne), Fraternal Grandpa and Grandma.

To Pa and Ma: I know what I want to say to you, but my feelings of gratitude and love travel from my heart and then freeze at my finger tips before I can write them down. I realize there's no need for words. Please allow me to say two things: Thank you, and I love you.

To my siblings, Quy, Vinnie, and Bo: Thank you for granting me permission to include you in this book. You guys played a huge part in my life and continue to do so. Without you, there wouldn't be us. I owe you my deepest gratitude for this heirloom.

To my wife: Thank you for loving me unconditionally since day one, and especially for the past three years when I painstakingly relived the memories needed to create this book. I realize there were times when you questioned who I was—yet you still stood by my side because you knew how important this book was, and is, to me. You are my angel.

To my children and godchildren: I wrote this book especially for you. When you are old enough to understand the things written in this book, let's carve out some time to talk about them. Papi's/Nino's wish is for you to pass these stories down to your children and their children. I'm doing my best to love you the way I wanted to be loved.

To my confidant Travis Bradberry: It was on that day, three years ago, on a golf course that you convinced me to jump-start. You've been a bright source of inspiration and encouragement,

and I couldn't have written this book without you by my side. Thank you for believing in the worth of my story guiding me along to its fruition.

To my agent, Gillian Mackenzie: You had me at "hello." Seriously, it was your enthusiasm for my story that gave me an inkling that it was worth sharing. Thank you for being in my corner throughout the process and beyond. Let's get this thing on screen.

To my editor, Rakesh Satyal: Thank you for signing me on! It was a pleasure to work with you in shaping this book into what it is, and also for allowing me to keep my voice, while suggesting things that I might have overlooked. It was a joy to work with you and I hope we can do it again some day. Thanks to the rest of the team at Harper Perennial, including Rob Crawford and Mary Beth Constant.

To my parents-in-law, Deacon Arturo and Marilu: (Yes, I would love some tea now, please). Thank you for accepting me into your family and for loving me as one of your own. Dad, you have been such a wonderful advocate and supporter while I was writing this book. I learn so much from you, and I look forward to discussing my life stories further with you. I love you, Mom.

To my circle on whom I most rely: Uncle Five, Uncle Nine, Mike & Adriana Viera, Ken McKay, Arlene Barragan, Erika Gallo, Ryan & Reshma Thomas, Shivani Patel, Andrew (A.J.) Jones, Rajeev Arhi, Mario Laza, Franco & Ericka Heguy, Christian Felix and the Pico Rivera Family, Daniel Salcido, Jean Greaves, and Melissa Monday.

To Fran Cooper and Dr. Patricia Venn-Watson: Thank you for helping me manage the demons in my head while I was writing this book. I hope the madness is all temporary.

To EM123: Thank you for your interest and feedback in the initial phase of this book. It helped me tremendously.

To my virtual friends on MySpace and Facebook: Thank you for all your support and kind words of encouragement. A special

gratitude to: Kimberley Allard, Larry Safley, Kim Brittingham, Wanda Foust, Davina Wan, Steve Nguyen, Neil Cotter, Dyana Quênh Chi Bùi, Caritta Lee, the Memoirists Collective, all the Vietnamese Student Associations nationally and internationally, Asian American Associations, Susan Henderson, Harper Perennial, Lisa Mae, Lit Park, Trish Luu, AnhToan-AnhTuan, Kim-Duyên Nguyen, Bobby Liu, Big Doh, Mag Flux, Pac 10, Brian L. Tan, FPS UCLA, and Dirty Cookie Productions.

To Augusten Burroughs: You are my memoir idol. You have inspired me in so many ways. As a kid, the sellevision made me want to be like the white people. But the wolf at my dinner table told me otherwise. It was like running with scissors the way I balanced between the cultures inside and outside of my household. In my search for love, I was on my own and left to dry. But my magical thinking has guided me through life and eventually took me out of my misery. From what I've experienced, there might be some possible side effects. Thank you, Augusten.

## About the author

## About the book

Insights,
Interviews
& More . . .

## Read on

# A Conversation with Lac Su

### What do you fear most?

There's something about the unexpected that scares me. For example, I don't like to be the deer in headlights at surprise parties. When that has happened, I've tried my best to look like I'm not pissed off, but inside I'm fuming. I don't understand the reason for a party to be a surprise. I guess I'm a person who likes to be in the know. In general, I like to plan how things will turn out for me. I envision events beforehand to prepare myself for the unexpected. When things take a turn in reality, I get nervous and try to plan how I will get out of that. This fear of the unexpected also applies to roller-coasters and suspenseful movies. The idea of not knowing when the roller-coaster drops one hundred

feet or when the Texas Chainsaw murderer pops out from behind a tree gives me the creeps. And I hate balloons. The bigger and shinier they are, the antsier I am around them. My heart feels like it stops and my face goes white the moment a balloon pops unexpectedly near me. When I see them at birthday parties, I pop them purposefully with a needle to keep myself at ease. I don't mind the pop that it gives—just when it pops without my knowledge.

*Name the top ten things you have to do before you say "see you in the next lifetime."*

### Spend a year in a Buddhist monastery in Sri Lanka

I don't know . . . the idea of escaping to a place where nobody knows who I am and what I'm about really entices me. I think it started when I was a kid watching kung-fu flicks—the ones depicting the life of the Shaolin monks. It seems as though they live a simple life. They only need to think about two things: perfecting a craft—martial arts—and learning to be a good human being. It's a consistent daily routine that those monks have come to expect. They wake up really early, read and chant, eat vegetables, do chores, practice martial arts, and then sleep. Every day! They live a lifestyle without drama. No MTV. No cell phone. No Sirius radio. No *Cosmopolitan*. No pressure. Their main objective in life is to learn how to reduce suffering by understanding one's self. I want that. I wish for peace of mind and peace around me.

### Have a son

I often wonder how, as a child, my father could look at me after what he did to me. ▶

> **And I hate balloons. The bigger and shinier they are, the antsier I am around them.**

**A Conversation with Lac Su** *(continued)*

I want to be able to put myself in his shoes and look at my son and try to feel what my father felt under certain circumstances. How things could have put him there—emotionally, spiritually, and humanly. I will never lay a hand on my children—this I am sure. I'm just curious to know how someone can be *that* angry. I'll need to have a son of my own to know. I don't think I will be able to comprehend the "how" part.

**Find the perfect tattoo to ink my body**
I admire tattoo art, especially the Japanese tradition. The really good ones are masterpieces on human canvases. The colors created by the needle—on human flesh—look different than those of any other tools used in any medium. It's beautiful. I'm talking about the work of trained and seasoned artists, not Joe down the street who uses a sewing needle and India ink in his garage. I'm looking around for the best tattoo artist that does Japanese art. I talked to one from San José, and he told me he does his work with a special needle that's attached to a bamboo stick. I asked him, "Don't you have a machine?" And he told me, "You want machine? Go to American tattoo parlor. I do Suiboku style." Supposedly the ink he uses changes colors in the sun.

**Learn to speak Spanish fluently**
To me, Spanish is a very romantic language, yet it can also be an aggressive language. It all depends on the way you say things. I like that kind of control when I speak. Vietnamese, on the other hand, is not a sexy language. It's

> ❝ I will never lay a hand on my children—this I am sure. I'm just curious to know how someone can be *that* angry. ❞

throaty. Words are controlled in your sinuses and throat. My wife, Maria, speaks Spanish to our daughter, Sky, and what I know in Vietnamese I say to Sky also. Since Spanish is the stronger language of the two, it's dominant in our household. Sky is now saying words to me in Spanish that I don't understand. Maria tries her darnedest to speak Spanish to me, but she's so advanced that I don't understand half of the things she says. This frustrates me. And it's not like she slows it down for me, either. I'm getting Rosetta Stone–Spanish for Christmas. This way I can tell Maria how frustrated I am when I don't understand her—*en Español como chingón*.

> " I'm getting Rosetta Stone–Spanish for Christmas. This way I can tell Maria how frustrated I am when I don't understand her—*en Español como chingón*. "

**Learn to play the piano fluently**
I want to be sexy like Jamie Foxx.

**Get a Ph.D. in something**
No, not the "Player Hating Degree" but the "Poor, Hungry, and Determined" degree. I took my father's advice to advance myself to the highest educational degree possible, and psychology was my calling. I can just about check this one off of my list.

**Showcase my own art exhibit**
In my spare time, I paint gestalt abstract in acrylic. I also dabble a little bit in photography. I take pictures of regular people on the streets that I find interesting. I'd like to showcase my work in an art gallery one day.

**Write a memoir**
Done. ▶

### Donate a ton of cash to the libraries

I want to be able to give back for all the books
I stole from the library when I didn't have the
money to buy the ones I loved. I'm working
on the "ton of cash" part, but I make a
contribution whenever I can.

### Tell my father I love him (again)

I recently told my father over the phone that
I love him. He replied with a much calmer
tone this time, "What does that mean? I don't
understand." Then I said, "I'll tell you in
person when I come home." More to come.

### *What are you currently reading?*

Honestly, I don't have much time to read
these days. If I am reading, it's usually skim-
reading magazines and how-to books.
I'm currently skimming *Reading People:
How to Understand People and Predict Their
Behavior—Anytime, Anyplace* by Jo-Ellan
Dimitrius. When I had more time to read,
I'd get into autobiographies. I've read
Bill Clinton's *My Life; Che Guevara:
A Revolutionary Life,* by Jon Lee Anderson;
*Gandhi: An Autobiography: The Story of
My Experiments With Truth,* by Mohandas
Karamchand Gandhi; *The Autobiography
of Malcolm X,* by Alex Haley; and *Mother
Teresa: A Complete Authorized Biography,*
by Kathryn Spink. Stories about people
who've changed the world and what led
them to do it fascinate me.

### *And what, if anything, are you writing?*

I suppose you could say that I'm still writing
this memoir. When I finished the manuscript,

> I suppose
you could say that
I'm still writing
this memoir.
When I finished
the manuscript,
I didn't put my
pen down.

I didn't put my pen down. Memories of my last couple of years in high school and my experiences in college came flooding back to me as I wrapped up *I Love Yous Are for White People*. It's amazing how my perspective of these events has changed as a result of writing this book. I can see how things connect—how the stories are all interrelated—and I have a sense of humor about them. For example, I just completed a story about how I joined the water polo team before I moved to the magnet school. I didn't even know how to swim! I didn't care a lick at the time; I was looking for anything that would keep me away from my father and the negative influence of the Street Ratz. As it turned out, the only way to conquer my fear of water—like everything else in my life—was to dive into the fear headfirst. I'm anxious to document the next chapter of my life.

### Which passage in your memoir was the most difficult to write?

The "Crazy" passage was brutal. I had repressed most of my memories of those incidents and writing that chapter brought them all back to me. It was harsh to dig that deep and see what bubbled to the surface. Reliving those moments through the story was, at times, too much for me to bear. It drove me to drink.

### Where and when do you prefer to write?

I approach writing the same way I do painting—when I get a spark of inspiration, I run with it. There were memories that ▶

**A Conversation with Lac Su** *(continued)*

inspired me more than others. "A is for Boy, B is for Cat" is one of them. "Five and Nine" was also a joy to write. For the tougher chapters, I knew I had to go back to uglier times. I remember these events clearly but dreaded sitting down to put myself back there to record the events play-by-play. The only way I could do this was at night in my home office when it's quiet. Ample amounts of Diet Mountain Dew and sips of Jack Daniels kept me awake and kept me from running away on the more painful chapters. There were many times when seeing, feeling, hearing, smelling, and tasting things again upset me and made me sad and lonely— just like I felt the first time around. ⌒

66 Ample amounts of Diet Mountain Dew and sips of Jack Daniels kept me awake and kept me from running away on the more painful chapters. 99

## "At Last"

IT FINALLY HIT ME. A few sentimental words from soul singer Etta James were all it took for me to bring this book to a close. By the time my publisher asked me to pen this P.S. section, I had already, quite literally, closed the book on my childhood. The manuscript was delivered and edited months prior to their request. The agonizing, yet cathartic, exercise of putting my early experiences to the page no longer swayed me. I was gripped by the most intense bout of writer's block I've ever endured. Like millions of others killing time, I found myself on an aimless YouTube mission, rotting my brain with videos of Argentinean kids doing Iron Maiden covers. And that's when I stumbled upon footage of Etta James singing her classic, "At Last." I'd heard the song a million times before; maybe that's why it struck me so deeply. The Kingsley Boyz used to bump it on their porch. The Mexicans in my neighborhood played it during barbeques and while they washed and buffed their cars to a perfect shine. Etta's voice thrust me back to the days in East Los Angeles when dudes would cruise the boulevards in their Impalas with their girls in their arms.

As Etta belted "My lonely days . . . they are over," her words found their way straight into my heart. They beckoned me to let it go. I thought of my daughter, Sky, and realized it's just not about me anymore.

My darkest days are sprawled across the pages of this book. Things that I've managed to hide from people my entire life are now out in the open. People exposed to the ▶

> 66 Like millions of others killing time, I found myself on an aimless YouTube mission, rotting my brain with videos of Argentinean kids doing Iron Maiden covers. 99

## "At Last" *(continued)*

manuscript thus far often ask, "What will your father feel about the things you said about him?" Unless my words are translated into Vietnamese or Chinese, my father will never know. If such a translation ever comes to pass, I'll have to sit down with my father and talk about these things—for the very first time. I fear this possibility, and I welcome it.

Even though this book was painful to write, it helped me to heal. I learned important things about myself along the way. I grew up believing that I was worthless, and it's been hard to convince me otherwise. I'm learning now to love myself and to trust that everything I've experienced played an important part in molding me into the person I am today. I often try to imagine what my life would be like if my father had given me the version of love that I desired. It's impossible to picture Pa that way, just as it's unimaginable that I would pass his version of love on to my children. Some things will never happen.

My father named me Lac because it means happiness in Chinese. But happiness was something that I rarely felt growing up. Pa once told me that to become happy, I must endure and understand sadness. As strange as it may sound, I thank him for this. Understanding sadness has made me into a more sympathetic and caring man. I know what it's like to yearn for love. I know what it's like to be hungry, to be left out, to hurt, and to lack hope. I am humbled by my father's lesson. Now I face the great challenge of teaching my children happiness—without hurting them.

As it went, I couldn't afford the luxury of quitting my day job and living a writer's life.

Bills needed to be paid. People at TalentSmart needed to see my face in the office. My daughter needed a father, and my wife needed a husband. My family needed their son and older brother. My doctoral dissertation needed to be completed. I poured the remaining time and energy into this book. What kept me up late at night and often into the wee hours of the morning was the thought of you, the reader. And case after case of Diet Mountain Dew. I'm picturing you reading this right now as I complete this sentence. The stories in this book aren't any more drastic or dramatic than any other memoir, but they're mine. I really want you to know me.

And I have so much more to tell. This book ends when I was in the eleventh grade, right before I transferred to the magnet school in East Los Angeles. I planned on telling my whole life's story in this book. The more I wrote, the more I realized that sharing my past was going to be a lot like tipping over a Coke machine: I can't just do it in one fell swoop; it'll need to be rocked back and forth a few times first. My road through high school, college, and beyond has been a bumpy one. Adversity, I've found, is not easily eluded.

Every once in a while the little boy inside me shows his face. I grew up too fast, and I've learned to cherish these moments as precious gifts from my past—they're opportunities to be a kid that slipped away while I was one. And if I'm ever given the chance to meet you in person, don't be surprised if I tell you that I love you. I can't seem to say it enough these days. ∾

> **❝** What kept me up late at night and often into the wee hours of the morning was the thought of you, the reader. **❞**

# And the Beat Goes On: Songs That Spoke to Me

*"Music is what my feelings sound like."*

*I gravitate towards music that depicts what I'm feeling inside. I'm awed by the way one old song can take me back to the day when I first heard it and it spoke to me. As I listen to my favorites, I realize why I connected with them. It was more than the melodies—the lyrics in these songs kept me whole. There are far too many songs to mention, and I feel the deepest connection to those you see below. They are my heart songs; their lyrics touch me.*

### "Hey Young World," Slick Rick

I specifically remember listening to this song a few days after Veasna's brother pointed his gun to my head and asking myself, "What the fuck are you doing, Lac?" Listening to Slick Rick's words forced me to take a look at my life. He told me to get my shit together and "get ahead and accomplish things." At a time when things around me were spinning out of control, this song motivated me to try and make things right.

### "To Live and Die in L.A.," Tupac Shakur

This song reminds me of everything that I love about Los Angeles. The happenings Tupac raps about go down everyday in L.A. Though I'm at another place in my life now, Tupac's description of the City of Angels stirs fond memories of my days on Sunset Boulevard. Even as a grown man, I sometimes can't help but swagger in my walk because

"everybody [from] L.A. has a little thug in him."

## "Please Please Please Let Me Get What I Want," The Smiths

Morrissey, the lead singer of the Smiths, sings some lonely-ass songs, and for this reason I love him. There's something about his melancholic voice and hopeless perspective that connects me to his music. I spend a lot of time sitting in my backyard, sipping on wine, and vibing to his songs. When I listen to his music, it feels as though he and I are the only ones in the world who know what it's like to be lonely.

## "Coward of the County," Kenny Rogers

I became a fan of Kenny Rogers the first time I heard his ballad "Lady." It's the first song I choose when singing karaoke. "Coward of the County" is another one of my favorites from Kenny. It tells the story of a boy named Tommy who tries to take his father's advice and avoid trouble at all cost by simply walking away from it. Until one day, when Tommy finds out that a few county boys raped his girlfriend. He breaks his promise to his father and beats their asses. In the last verse, Tommy says to his father, "Sometimes you gotta fight when you're a man." To me, when he says "fight," it is more than a brawl: it's about fighting for what you think is right.

## "Que Será, Será," Pink Martini

The hook to this song is pretty simple. It has helped me to see things as they are. "Que será, será" means "Whatever will be, will be." I trust that things in my life will turn out as they should. If they don't, that's okay too.

**And the Beat Goes On: Songs That
Spoke to Me** *(continued)*

### "How Do You Mend a Broken Heart,"
### The Bee Gees

I'm a huge fan of the Bee Gees. The Gibb
brothers, especially Andy and Barry, both
have a great set of pipes. The first time I saw
Andy sing by himself was on *Solid Gold* in
the early 1980s. I was like, "Where's the rest
of the Bee Gees?" Anyway, I often ask myself
what the title of this song really means: "How
do you mend a broken heart?" so that I can
carry on. I've found that therapy mends and
whiskey tears.

### "Yo," José Alfredo Jiménez

José Alfredo Jiménez, like Morrissey, sings
with so much passion and heartache.
Someone told me he recorded most of his
songs drunk. His songs are great descriptions
of what it feels like to yearn and hurt. In "Yo,"
it's not what José says that brings me to tears
every time, but how in pain he sounds when
describing his yearning.

### "Love Is," Common

I'd like to meet Common. I think he and
I would have a lot to talk about. He's one of
the very first rappers to talk about love. His
lyrics have power—they say something deep
without being corny. He talks about real shit.
Like in this song, when he says, "In the hood,
love we was told to run from . . . from lack of
love many hide some run . . ."

### "These Three Words," Stevie Wonder

I wish to believe that Stevie sang this song
specifically for this book. It asks the question
I often ask people, "When was the last time

that you told your mother, father, daughter or son, 'I love you?' "

When was it, for you?

**"甜蜜蜜 (Sweet Honey)," Teresa Teng**
My father used to sing this song to me when we first came to America.

**"Mùa Thu Lá Bay (Autumn Season, Leaves Fly)," Nhu Quynh**
My mother often cries when she sings this song.

**"Yellow," Coldplay**
The color yellow in this song describes the love that now exists in my life. Since my daughter, Sky, came along, everything turned yellow. It would be so easy to follow in my father's footsteps . . . raising her the way I was raised. But I drew the line. I drew the line for Sky. It's a tough thing to do. But for Sky, I'd bleed myself dry.

**"Boyz-n-the-Hood," N.W.A.**
If you weren't a gang-banger when this song came out, it made you want to become one.

**"Freak-a-Zoid," Midnight Star**
I used to break-dance to this song in Hollywood.

**"Greatest Love of All," Whitney Houston**
This song stirs bittersweet memories of my days in elementary school, especially the day of my sixth-grade graduation. This story didn't make it into the book, but I remember this song playing in the auditorium when I

walked up to the stage to receive my diploma
and an award for being the "Most Talented
Artist" at school. Pa didn't think an
elementary school diploma warranted his
presence at the ceremony, so he didn't
come—neither did any of my other family
members, except for Quy. I still looked out
into the audience for him while I was on
stage, expecting him to be there proudly
waving his hand with the other parents and
holding my congratulatory balloons. Whitney
was singing her heart out through the blaring
speakers. I knew the lyrics. I even sang along,
"I never found anyone to fulfill my needs—
a lonely place to be. So I learned to depend
on me."